Freedom is for Such a Time as Now

By Vicki Smith White

with Forward by Dr. Henry Malone

All Scripture quotations are from the Authorized King James Version.

Special thanks to Teresa G. Reynolds, whose inspired doodlings grace these pages, and to all who contributed to the publication of this book through your ministry donations, hours of proof-reading, valued input, and graphics talent. You know who you are!

Freedom is for Such a Time as Now
ISBN 978-1-889668-31-4

Freedom's Way Ministries, Inc.
P.O. Box 8097
Jacksonville, FL 32239

www.freedomswayministries.com

Printed in the United States of America. All rights reserved. Contents and/or cover may not be reproduced in whole or in part in any form whatsoever without written consent of the publisher. Permission will be granted by written consent of the publisher to copy and use the materials in this book for study and teaching to advance the Kingdom of God. To obtain written consent, please contact the publisher:

Smith & Daniel Marketing
P.O. Box 8097
Jacksonville, FL 32239
904-757-2501

Note to the Reader

As we began to go through the Bible, reading the fourteenth verse of the fourth chapter of every book that has a fourth chapter and fourteenth verse, what we saw was an amazing view of God's heart of deliverance for His creation. Our belief is that you should be able to open the Bible to any page and preach Jesus, and this work proves that belief. In HIM is our freedom. Amen.

You need to know...
    Numbers in the Bible are significant symbolic representations and God weaves His numbering system throughout Scripture as yet another proof of His divine inspiration of these Holy Words. The meaning of different numbers holds true from Genesis to Revelation, and the Lord often speaks His mysteries through numbers. As stewards of God's mysteries, we realize they are laid up for us and not from us. We are to search them out, for they can assuredly be discovered!

    It is not our intent to teach what each number means in the language of the Kingdom of God, for there are many books already written which impart the essence of this truth. In the introduction is an explanation of the numbers four and 14, to help you grasp the wonder of God's awesome revelations as you read through this book. You may find other numbers mentioned, also, and for each we've given the primary symbolic meaning to aid in clarity and understanding.

You need to know…
　　The artwork interspersed throughout this book is a series of "prophetic doodling" by Teresa Reynolds, an associate minister with Freedom's Way Ministries. She listened with pencil in hand to the messages which make up the main text of this book; and as the Lord spoke to her, she drew the impressions she received.
　　Because of formatting considerations, some of the art is not placed directly before or after the passages it represents. Do not allow this to bring you confusion! As you encounter these pictures, ask the Lord to give you vision and revelation of His Word, as well as understanding of the visions depicted. When you do, you will find them to be a valuable addition to the overall publication, and a blessing to you personally.

You need to know…
　　This book is a key to unlocking the heart of God to give you greater understanding; and it is a key to unlocking many of the prisons we have built in their own lives which prevent us from enjoying total freedom from the things which limit us. Remove the limiters from your life by praying the many prayers included in these pages. Speak your declarations out loud, so that all the host of heaven and hell will know that you have decided to agree with the Father God and His Son Jesus Christ and to walk into the freedom He has for you NOW!

Foreword

Freedom is what my life is all about. I had never put much thought into how much the Bible has to say about freedom in each of its books. It is in every book of the Old and New Testaments! This is one of the themes of Scripture from Genesis to Revelation. God is into freedom for all people. He wants us to have individual freedom from the lies of the dark side so we can walk out all Jesus died to give us.

Vicki White has done a great job in showing the evidence of God's theme of freedom in every book of the Bible. <u>Freedom is for Such a Time as Now</u> is a beautiful presentation that freedom is for everyone, and that freedom is now, not just for the future. The clock is running out for some who need to read this book and take to heart the truths that are taught on every page.

I recommend you read this book and find your own pathway to freedom for the first time, or a new pathway to greater freedom. You will be blessed if you choose this book. It will prove itself to be a great book for you and your friends.

Dr. Henry Malone
Vision Life Ministries
Lewisville, Texas

Introduction

Not so long ago, something began to happen in my life that those who don't know God would call very strange, or coincidental. But as I've gotten closer to the Lord and realized the many ways He interrupts our lives, the word "coincidence" is one I rarely use, if at all. I've come to know "God-incidences" instead. Let me explain what I mean, and how this book came about.

I was driving along, lost in thought about who knows what, when I glanced down at the dashboard clock and noticed the numbers "4:14." Big deal, you say. In a way, it was. It was a big deal first because I seldom look at clocks and second, my birthday is April 14... the fourth month, the fourteenth day. How about that!

The incident passed into the place of forgetfullness in my mind; but soon after, the numbers in their birthday sequence seemed to reappear, and not infrequently. The next few times I saw 4:14 was in the predawn hours, and always on a clock, as if God was saying, "It's time. It's time." On several occasions I was awakened – not for any reason I could determine, other than to look at the clock. Each time, it was exactly the same... 4:14. Each time, I was too sleepy to think it through and realize, "Hey, there must be a message in this." Each time, I drifted back into sleep, ignoring God's "it's time" message.

As the days went by, my husband, Jerry, began to notice the frequency the number 414 was occuring. Knowing that numbers have a Biblical significance, we searched out the meaning. In Scripture, four is the number of creation, with a secondary implication of trial or testing. Fourteen is the Biblical number for deliverance. Now the recurring "414"s took on a deeper meaning. Certainly it was true that we had been going through a time of trial and testing, and ours is a deliverance ministry. Hmmm.

The number kept appearing. One afternoon on the way home, Jerry and I stopped by the produce market for a few items. Jerry went in, bought three tomatoes, a bell pepper and an onion. Back in the car, he handed me the receipt. Four dollars and fourteen cents was the total. I could not remember ever having a receipt total $4.14, and I would have remembered, since that sequential combination represented my birthday!

A day or two later, the mail brought a sweepstakes offer. The prize? Four million fourteen thousand dollars, a very unusual number for a grand prize. (No, I didn't enter the sweepstakes, though I admit it was tempting.) At the home repair store, we bought light bulbs. Once again, the bill totaled $4.14 - the price of the bulbs, less an at-register discount, plus tax. It was a complicated way to end up with a receipt that read 414, and it shed some light on the subject (pun intended). Walking out of the store, we asked, "Okay, God, what is it that you want us to see?"

Once in the car, I opened the Bible (yes, we carry a Bible everywhere, even when we're not on the way to church) and began to read aloud from book to book every verse numbered 4:14. By Deuteronomy, we both were in awe of the message God was laying before us. "This is your next book," Jerry said.

"I think you're right," I replied. Then the numbers stopped coming in their now-familiar 414 pattern; and I did nothing. God had finally gotten His message across, and I essentially acknowledged it and then ignored it. I'm sure none of you have ever done that!

Two or three weeks went by and 414 had all but faded from memory. Then we attended a prophetic conference which was very well organized, with workbooks outlining the materials being taught. "Let's get started," said the moderator; and he read the opening scripture, which was I Timothy 4:14. WHAT? I'm sure those who saw our jaws drop open and our heads snap toward each other must have wondered what was up my husband and me. I heard God say, "Write it."

That same night, we were on our way home and stopped at the grocery store for a few things. Passing a deli case, my attention was captured by a carrot-raisin salad, and for some reason, I wanted it. I picked it up. I commented, "Doesn't this look good?"

"You don't want that," Jerry said. "You don't even like that stuff." He was right. I don't eat carrot-raisin salad. I put it back in the case and walked away. Two aisles later, I stopped and turned to my loving and unsurprised husband.

"No. I don't know why, but I really want it." He knew exactly what I was talking about. I trekked back to the deli case, picked up the carrot-raisin salad and returned at a brisk clip to the ever-moving cart, steered by my "time's-a-wasting-let's-go" husband. As I dropped the product into the buggy, I again stopped in my tracks as I saw the price for the first time. $4.14. Again I heard in my spirit, "Write it."

Jerry just stared in amazement at the price sticker - another complicated combination - price per pound per weight for the total to equal the now-expected 414. "You're going to have to do this, you know," was all he said.

I pondered, and procrastinated, through several other gentle reminders. Three of my favorites were a large price sign on a display at a wholesale buying club, and two especially meaningful Scripture references. The first scripture (Song of Solomon 4:14) was found on the back of a gift box of perfumes from Israel. A friend had ordered them especially for me - Frankincense, Myrrh and Spikenard. "Now you can smell like the Bible!" she said, having no idea of the impact her gift carried.

The other scripture jumped off the page in a book I was reading. It spoke of how our lives are purposed by God for certain works and those works affect many, many - we don't know how many - others. Basically, the author asked, "Who knows but that you were born for such a time as this?" and then in parenthesis was the reference (Esther 4:14). It jumped off the page into my spirit, and I was once again convicted.

As for the price sign, it was really the topper. The sale price of $4.14, which I had never seen as a price for anything, seemed almost to jump off the display. "Let's take a look," Jerry said, "and see what it is." The sale item was a very large box of seasoned croutons. Jerry touched his chin in that thoughtful pose he has. "Umm. Bread, sliced and diced. Tried in the fire. Salted and flavorful. Enough said." The significance was astounding.

"Write it," I heard.

"Yes, Lord," I answered.

Thank God He is merciful. Thank God He keeps after us to fulfill our purposes in Him and doesn't abandon us to our laziness and rebellion! For over two years, I had been ever-busy, too busy to "write it" as I had clearly been commissioned. Then recently, the Lord spoke to me as I was waking up one morning on one of our many ministry trips; and He told me to teach the material He gives me for this book on the teleconference line. For those who may not know, Jerry and I conduct a twice-weekly telconference meeting to teach the word of God and to pray for people. I knew that by teaching this material on the teleconference line I would be under pressure each week to get the lesson done, and the book would be written as a result.

Isn't God wonderful! His perfect plan of presenting this material live would also allow our wonderful participants to provide input and insight along the way. In so many ways, this resulting book is a product of the Holy Spirit speaking through many of His children, not just me. The Word says let those who are taught share with the teacher. And of all the important attributes of a teacher, being teachable himself is perhaps at the top of the list!

Gal 6:6 Let him that is taught in the word communicate unto him that teacheth in all good things.

Of course, I have repented for procrastinating, and allowing the urgent to get in the way of the important. Repentance is a wonderful gift. When I decided to put aside my own wants and busy-ness and repented for placing God's assignment low on my priority list, I was immediately refreshed. God knows I work best under pressure and so He put the perfect method into practice that I might accomplish the assignment He put before me.

"For Such a time as Now" is the manifest fruit of obedience, albeit reluctant, and a testimony to God's faithfulness to us, even when we're not. Without that kind of grace, where would we be?

As we began to go through the Bible, reading the fourteenth verse of the fourth chapter of every book that has a fourth chapter and fourteenth verse, what we saw was an amazing view of God's heart of deliverance for His creation. Our belief is that you should be able to open the Bible to any page and preach Jesus, and this work proves that belief. In HIM is our freedom. Amen.

Genesis

"Behold, you have driven me out this day from the face of the earth; and from your face I shall be hid; and I shall be a fugitive and a vagabond in the earth; and it shall come to pass, that every one that finds me shall slay me." – Genesis 4:14

In the fourth chapter of the Book of Genesis, we see the story of Cain and Abel, and in this verse, Cain is lamenting his fate. It's important to note that Cain was cursed from the earth, not God, as stated in earlier verses.

Gen 4:10 And he said, What hast thou done? the voice of thy brother's blood crieth unto me from the ground.

Gen 4:11 And now art thou cursed from the earth, which hath opened her mouth to receive thy brother's blood from thy hand;

Gen 4:12 When thou tillest the ground, it shall not henceforth yield unto thee her strength; a fugitive and a vagabond shalt thou be in the earth.

We need to look at what transpired and how it came about that Cain was made subject to such a curse. But even more, we need to see God's delivering hand in the midst of Cain's painful recognition of the consequence of his own transgression.

As it is recorded, when these brothers came to make a sacrifice to the Lord, Abel's offering was accepted and Cain's was not. Abel brought a firstling of his flock, and

Cain brought of the fruit of the ground. To our thinking, that seems to be okay, since Abel apparently was a shepherd and Cain a farmer. But the fruit of the ground was not a blood sacrifice. Cain's offering represented the work of his own hands. We can never be acceptable to the Lord by our own good works!

So many times, we think, "Well, if I just do more for God, He'll love me more. He'll accept me and elevate me to a higher position. I just need to do more for Him and everything in my life will be better." Consider Mary and Martha. There is a correlation of sorts in Cain's bringing the work of his own hands to the Lord, and Martha slaving over a hot stove, so to speak.

Luk 10:38 Now it came to pass, as they went, that he entered into a certain village: and a certain woman named Martha received him into her house.

Luk 10:39 And she had a sister called Mary, which also sat at Jesus' feet, and heard his word.

Luk 10:40 But Martha was encumbered about much serving, and came to him, and said, Lord, dost thou not care that my sister hath left me to serve alone? bid her therefore that she help me.

Luk 10:41 And Jesus answered and said unto her, Martha, Martha, thou art careful and troubled about many things:

Luk 10:42 But one thing is needful: and Mary hath chosen that good part, which shall not be taken away from her.

The difference between friendship and servitude is the same as the difference between relationship and religion. Servitude, because of its religious mindset that we have to do more to be accepted, is envious of the face to face relationship that defines friendship. This face to face relationship is what God intended to have with mankind – with us. Cain confirmed the break in his relationship with God when he said, "from Your face I shall be hid."

This verse is a perfect example of Psalm 116:10
Psa 116:10 I believed, therefore have I spoken: I was greatly afflicted:

Cain believed God drove him out from the earth. Consequently, he was subject to live what he believed. Had he believed God's love was toward him, perhaps he wouldn't have been so angry when the Lord brought correction into his life. We can take a word of correction from someone who loves us, because we know it's good for us. We know the person who loves us has our best interest in his heart and would never hurt us. God never said to Cain, "If you don't do well, I won't love you." He never said, "I will love you more if you do well."

The truth is, we can never earn the love and grace and mercy of God... He already loves us with a love everlasting and unconditional. When we bring Him what we've done on our own, it is a dead work. God is not pleased with dead works. Our sacrifice becomes a stench in His nostrils rather than a sweet smelling savor. We are accepted only by blood, the blood of our Savior Jesus Christ.

God spoke to Cain and told him this: "When you are operating in your own strength, sin is waiting to pounce on you. Sin lies at the door like an animal crouched on all fours, looking for an opportunity to leap into your heart when you open the door. But you can take rule over that evil thing through Me."

Cain made a choice not to listen to God, and sin came in as a spirit of bitterness. Cain was resentful and he became angry. God interrupted and spoke to Cain – "Why are you angry?" God began to reason with Cain. Again, Cain chose not to obey God. He refused to be reasonable and the progression of bitterness continued - resentment, retaliation, anger, hatred, violence and finally murder. A spirit of murder manifested. Cain killed his brother. As a result, he was cursed from the earth, which received his brother's blood.

Whatever Cain was entitled to receive from the earth, was cut off from him - by the earth. The earth would no longer cooperate with him. No longer would the land yield sustenance for Cain. His farming days were over and he would have to wander from place to place seeking a handout. All because he closed his ears to God's warning about sin. He yielded himself to the spirit of murder because he was doing things his own way instead of God's way. He didn't trust God and he didn't know God's love.

Still, the Lord was merciful to Cain, as He is to all His children. When Cain cried out in despair, here in verse 4:14, the Lord answered in mercy. The mark the Lord put on Cain was for his protection, so that none would kill him. It was a seal of safety. Even though Cain subjected himself to a life of trouble, the Lord protected him. God's love for us is never ending, everlasting and eternal! Through the mark he put on Cain, the Lord delivered Cain from violence.

We should learn from Cain that the works of our own hands will never bring us into an intimate relationship with the Living God. It is only by the blood of Jesus, and our acceptance of His sacrifice on our behalf, that we can fellowship with God. The works of our own hands will not save us, but will instead open us to a life of misery. It is the love of God, shown in His seal on us that delivers us from harm. Praise God!

The first lesson in our 4:14 study is the simple truth of God's deliverance through His love.

Exodus

"And the anger of the Lord was kindled against Moses, and he said, Is not Aaron the Levite your brother? I know that he can speak well. And also, behold, he comes forth to meet you: and when he sees you, he will be glad in his heart." – Exodus 4:14

This fourth chapter of Exodus gives us a picture of the deliverer Moses, and our reference verse gives us another aspect of the Lord's character that brings deliverance into our lives. To get the full understanding of God's response of "anger," we need to read from verse 10.

Exo 4:10 And Moses said unto the LORD, O my Lord, I am not eloquent, neither heretofore, nor since thou hast spoken unto thy servant: but I am slow of speech, and of a slow tongue.

Exo 4:11 And the LORD said unto him, Who hath made man's mouth? or who maketh the dumb, or deaf, or the seeing, or the blind? have not I the LORD?

Exo 4:12 Now therefore go, and I will be with thy mouth, and teach thee what thou shalt say.

Exo 4:13 And he said, O my Lord, send, I pray thee, by the hand of him whom thou wilt send.

Exo 4:14 And the anger of the LORD was kindled against Moses, and he said, Is not Aaron the Levite thy brother? I know that he can speak well. And also, behold, he cometh forth to meet thee: and when he seeth thee, he will be glad in his heart.

God tells Moses he is to go back to Egypt and free the Israelites from their bondage to Pharaoh; and Moses begins a protest, recorded in verse 10. "I'm not the one. I can't speak well. I think you've got the wrong guy. Can't you pick somebody else?"

God reminds Moses of who He is in verse 11 ("I'm the one that made your mouth, Moses, don't you think I know what to put in it?!"). Then the Lord answers that Moses' excuses are invalid, and assures him in verse 12 that he need not be concerned about his inabilities, for it will be the Lord Himself who gives Moses utterance. In verse 13, it seems that Moses has certainly yielded to God. He says, "Send, I pray thee, by the hand of him whom thou wilt send." This poses the question "Why would God be angry with Moses now?"

The answer lies in this insight – God had told Moses He would give Him speech, the word of the Lord; and Moses did not understand what that meant. When Moses beseeched God "by the hand" he was saying, "Okay, I'll go, but open your hand and give me power, means and direction."

Moses did not understand that power, means and direction are all contained in the Word of His power, the voice of the Word of God.

> Heb 1:3 Who being the brightness of his glory, and the express image of his person, and upholding all things by the word of his power, when he had by himself purged our sins, sat down on the right hand of the Majesty on high;

Moses was raised as a man of war, a man who had a carnal understanding of power. The Lord had elevated and trained him in Egypt for a specific leadership role, the role of deliverer. Moses was 40 years in Egypt before fleeing to the wilderness and tending someone else's sheep. He had now been 40 years in this wilderness experience of tending his father-in-law's sheep. From a place of honor and power, Moses was taken to a place of humility and submission. God needed Moses to have the leadership abilities he would learn in Egypt and the qualities of humility he would learn in the wilderness. Moses spent 40 years working in Egypt, and God spent 40 years working Egypt out of Moses.

But now Moses once more turned back to a carnal understanding of power. He wanted something more in assurance than the simple fact God would put words in his mouth. He failed to recognize it's the Word of God that saves, delivers, and sets free. Aren't we the same? How many times do we seek something more, something tangible, something demonstrative, when all we need is His Word in us? It's the Word of His power!

The Lord in His wisdom set up a team to show us we need each other and must work together. Aaron and Moses would work together to accomplish the purpose God set forth before them. Neither would act on his own in speaking forth God's Word and showing forth God's power.

We should learn from Moses it is the Word of God spoken out of the mouth of His saints that carries the power of God, and that we are never to look at our own inabilities when He chooses to send us on special assignment. No matter how great the task may appear, the Word of God carries within it the ability to succeed. Religion will tell us we're not ready – it's not time. We're not old enough, or maybe we're too old. We're not educated enough. We don't have the necessary degree in theology. We haven't been in church long enough – we're not "seasoned." Consider Jesus and the parable of the fig tree.

Mar 11:11 And Jesus entered into Jerusalem, and into the temple: and when he had looked round about upon all things, and now the eventide was come, he went out unto Bethany with the twelve.

Mar 11:12 And on the morrow, when they were come from Bethany, he was hungry:

Mar 11:13 And seeing a fig tree afar off having leaves, he came, if haply he might find anything thereon: and when he came to it, he found nothing but leaves; for the time of figs was not yet.

Mar 11:14 And Jesus answered and said unto it, No man eat fruit of thee hereafter forever. And his disciples heard it.

More than once in the Bible, the fig tree is used to represent religion. Adam and Eve took leaves from a fig tree to cover themselves. Religion and our religious associations and beliefs are what we use to justify ourselves – we hide behind the leaves, we try to use religion to cover our nakedness. But here in Mark, we see Jesus coming along, and He's hungry, and He sees this fig tree. Let me tell you, Jesus is coming, He's hungry and He's looking for fruit. The Word clearly says "the time for figs was not yet." It was not the season that the fig tree should produce. So it would appear very unfair of the Lord to curse that tree. But there was a reason, and it was valid.

In the presence of the Creator is the ability to produce. We cannot use excuses for not bringing forth fruit when Jesus is with us. Religion will say, "it's not time. You're not ready." And truly, that it absolutely true. We can produce nothing of value on our own. But in the presence of the Creator is the ability to produce. The Word of God carries within it the ability to succeed. We need only to yield ourselves to Him and respond to His ability. There is never a necessity to ask for more, because our God provides whatever is required to meet His purpose and the intent of His heart.

There is also comfort in knowing great things can be accomplished by those who feel inadequate, because it is never our strength that delivers. It is His.

Father God, I thank You for Your awesome, unending, everlasting love that delivers and sustains me. Forgive me, Lord, for thinking I somehow have to earn Your love, when it is so freely given. Forgive me for my disobedience and my unbelief, for doing things my own way and not Your way. Thank You for sealing me with Your seal of protection, Lord, as I learn to receive Your great love for me. Thank You for the Word of Your power, for putting Your words in my mouth, for providing everything I need for every task You assign to me. Help me realize that IN YOU is all I need, and that I am Your voice in the earth. Bring me into the knowledge and power of Your Word… to change my life, and to effect change in the world around me. Here I am, Lord. Send me.

Leviticus

"When the sin, which they have sinned against it, is known, then the whole congregation shall offer a young bullock for the sin, and bring him before the tabernacle of the congregation."
– Leviticus 4:14

Leviticus is the book of the law of Moses, that outlines without question the "do's and don'ts" of the old covenant. As most Bible scholars know, there is always a spiritual as well as a natural or literal meaning to Scripture; and it has been well said that the Old Testament is the New Testament concealed, and the New Testament is the Old Testament revealed. For every type of sin, God prescribed a specific atonement in the written law of Moses. But what is the law of Moses… and does it have significance in our lives today? Yes, but not as a religious set of rules that lead us into works or a works mentality.

The law of Moses was meant to be a schoolmaster to teach us of Christ, to keep us in the way of Christ, to bring us to Christ. Atonement by blood sacrifice was always God's path to freedom. The law could never make us free. Blood sacrifice under the old covenant was God's way of delivering His creation from the evil that beset them and manifested in their lives as sin. And that picture of blood sacrifice was, of course, a type and shadow of the perfect sacrifice of our Redeemer, our Messiah, our Risen Lord, Jesus Christ.

When we go back to get the context of this verse in Leviticus, we find that the sin spoken of is a sin "through ignorance." Another interesting observation is this sin through ignorance is of the "whole congregation."

Lev 4:13 And if the whole congregation of Israel sin through ignorance, and the thing be hid from the eyes of the assembly, and they have done somewhat against any of the commandments of the LORD concerning things which should not be done, and are guilty;

Lev 4:14 When the sin, which they have sinned against it, is known, then the congregation shall offer a young bullock for the sin, and bring him before the tabernacle of the congregation.

    Each of the words translated as "congregation" in these two verses are different. The first one is a word meaning "family," which would indicate a generational curse or familiar spirit at the root of the sin. It says the entire family sinned through ignorance – they just didn't know what they were dealing with. A propensity to anger or alcohol or adultery or arthritis or a thousand other things that "run in the family" is the focus here. We are perishing in ignorance UNTIL the root cause of the sin issue – the generational familiar spirit - is known.

    In Leviticus 4:14, what happened when that root cause became known? The congregation (this is a different word and means "assembly") made an offering of atonement. God says we are to bear each other's burdens, work together to cleanse ourselves and our families of unclean spirits, pray for each other and stand in the gap for each other. In this picture, which is a shadow of deliverance from generational and familiar spirits, the Lord gives us charge to come together in unity against sin.

    Are we our brother's keeper? Yes. This does not mean we are here to judge another person's sin. It means we are to come alongside that brother and restore him. And we don't restore such a one in a spirit of arrogance and criticism! We restore such a one in a spirit of humility. As we take the attitude of humility, knowing we have the position of strength in Christ Jesus, not in ourselves, we can approach every situation in meekness. This is the attitude and approach that brings victory into our own lives and into the lives of others.

Gal 6:1 Brethren, if a man be overtaken in a fault, ye which are spiritual, restore such a one in the spirit of meekness; considering thyself, lest thou also be tempted.

Gal 6:2 Bear ye one another's burdens, and so fulfill the law of Christ.

These verse in Galatians are the new covenant revelation of the old covenant law. Now let's look at how this atonement was carried out in the law. A young bullock was brought "before the tabernacle of the congregation." Tabernacle is a tent. Spiritually, it speaks about a covering of authority; and the root meaning of the word denotes a shining clarity. Coming "before" is a face to face encounter, which we've already seen is God's heart on the matter. He wants a face to face relationship with His children, and He wants us to have that same heart of fellowship one with another. Interestingly enough, the word translated as "congregation" means an appointment or fixed meeting. The young bullock represented a wild strength.

We can now conclude that once the sin is identified, it is appointed that it be brought face to face with the clear authority of our Lord. The elders put their hands on the head of the animal, and it was afterward killed. This old covenant description is a type and shadow of deliverance from evil spirits that create sin in our lives. Those who are mature in the Lord, standing in His character, take the headship (authority) of the spirit causing the problem and then destroy the wild strength of sin.

Our God is a delivering God, who made atonement in Himself for all manner of transgressions. We can learn from this verse that the clear shining authority and covering of the Lord exposes and overcomes the enemy. When we bring it to Him, He works through us to destroy sin at its root. The other vital lesson here is one of transparency. Sin likes the dark, and as long as we're hiding our actions, or the attitudes of our hearts, there is no freedom. We must bring it out. As Uncle Arthur Burt teaches, "you've got to own it before you can disown it." Denial will keep us in bondage.

Please let me add here that you don't have to confess your sins before the entire congregation of your local church. But it is a good idea – and it is God's way - to allow those mature in the Lord to pray with you. We need each other. I can't make it without you, and you can't make it without me. If you're struggling with something, and aren't sure who to consult, ask the Lord. The Holy Spirit in you will guide you to a safe place. We've learned that deliverance comes from God only, it is His love and strength, and the Word of His power. And we clearly see a corporate application. We are not meant to be alone, but to aid and assist each other. Amen.

Numbers

"And they shall put upon it all the vessels thereof, where with they minister about it, even the censers, the flesh hooks, and the shovels, and the basins, all the vessels of the altar; and they shall spread upon it a covering of badgers' skins, and put to the staves of it."
- Numbers 4:14

Here in this verse we have a picture of preparation for transition after sacrifice is made – preparation for moving forward with the Lord. We must be positioned for transition! In this old covenant picture, the vessels used in making sacrifice are packed up to be carried along with the Israelites as the cloud, the very presence of the Lord, began to move.

In the wilderness journey, the Israelites were led by the Lord, who was manifested in a cloud by day and a pillar of fire by night. The cloud gave cover and comfort from the heat of the desert day, the fire gave light and warmth against the dark and cold of night. When the cloud moved, everyone knew it was time to go! I don't know about you, But I want to be moving with the presence of God. I want to be going where He's going and doing what He's doing. We've been too long following our own ways and plans and asking Him to bless us in what we're doing. We have to begin to join Him in what He's doing!

As it was with God's people in the days of the exodus from Egypt, so it is today with God's people. We make the sacrifice of our own lives before the Lord by accepting the sacrifice of His life for ours. That is an amazing exchange!

Isaiah 61:3 tells us He gives us beauty for ashes. It's HIS beauty for OUR ashes – we don't get His beauty until He gets our ashes.

I gave up my life for His when I believed God the Father accepted the perfect sacrifice of His Son Jesus Christ on my behalf. He died for me, so I don't have to! Once we've accepted Jesus' finished work of the cross, we must prepare to move forward as He moves. We take the instruments of sacrifice with us as we follow Him because we "die daily." Our walk with the Lord is a continual death-to-self experience.

Psa 116:12 What shall I render unto the LORD for all his benefits toward me?

Psa 116:13 I will take the cup of salvation, and call upon the name of the LORD.

Psa 116:14 I will pay my vows unto the LORD now in the presence of all his people.

Psa 116:15 Precious in the sight of the LORD is the death of his saints.

Let's go back and look at the verse in Numbers again: "And they shall put upon it all the vessels thereof, where with they minister about it, even the censers, the flesh hooks, and the shovels, and the basins, all the vessels of the altar; and they shall spread upon it a covering of badgers' skins, and put to the staves of it." - Numbers 4:14

Looking at this verse in light of deliverance, we see several interesting insights. First of all, the word "vessel" in its spiritual application generally refers to the soul, and there are four instruments named as being used in sacrifice – the censers, the flesh hooks, the shovels and the basins. These rightfully may be considered reflections of the four strengths of the soul of man… our mind, will, emotions and desires.

The censer was the pan which held the coals of fire for the altar, and comes from a root word meaning to "pick up fire." Other meanings indicated are dissolution, removal, and destruction. If we correlate this instrument for sacrifice to the mind, we can see that as we pick up the Word of the Living God, the consuming fire of God contained in His Word will begin to burn away the mindsets and programming of worldly experiences and remove them from our thinking.

When we make the decision to lay our will on the altar and follow the will of the Father, we are using the flesh hooks. Our will doesn't change, we simply (but with much difficulty) submit it to His will. We may never really want to do what we know the Lord has spoken to us to do, but we make the decision to yield to His will over what we will. This may come as a shock to you, but Jesus Himself did not want to die for us – initially it was not His will to do that. He knew the pain He was facing, the degradation, the sorrow His death would cause His friends, the reproach He would suffer and the rejection He would experience as His Father turned away and could not look on Him. No, He did not want to go through the experience of the cross. In the garden, Jesus prayed to the Father, "If there is any way I don't have to do this, take this cup from me. I don't want to drink it. Nevertheless, not MY will, but YOUR will be done. I will do it. I submit My will to Your will, Father." We must do the same thing. We make the same sacrifice; and the flesh hooks are representative of our decision to put our will on the altar.

Emotions are another strength of the soul we have to bring under submission to the Lord in daily sacrifice, and the shovel speaks to our emotions. Negative emotions, more often than not, are manifestations of evil spirits God wants us to shovel out of our lives. The shovel is indicative of sweeping something away, removing the residue of uncleanness from the altar. As we recognize and repent for ungodly anger, depression, resentment, bitterness, unforgiveness, envy, jealousy, attitudes of pride and self-righteousness and all sorts of other ungodly emotions, we are taking the shovel as an instrument of sacrifice and removing those things from our lives.

Finally, we see the basin that holds our desires. As we slaughter the beast of <u>self</u>, the blood – representative of life – is captured in this instrument of the sacrifice. The ungodly desires of our individual lives are poured out around the altar, while our godly desires are sprinkled on the mercy seat and placed on our own ears, thumbs and toes. This sprinkling represents our desires being given over to the Lord so that He can then give them back to us sanctified and pure in His purpose. Religion and the church have taught us that desires are bad, but we need to realize God gave us desires, just as He gave us emotions, a mind and a will. When we give over to Him our wordly, self-focused desires, then the desires He placed in us from before the foundation of the world can come forth to lead us into our destiny. As the worldly desires we learned and acquired are poured out before Him, the Lord replaces them with desires that are both pure and purposeful.

This is the divine exchange of God in sacrifice. When we give over to Him our thought life, our minds, and yield to the Holy Spirit, then our thoughts come alive – they're fired up and become sweet to His nostrils. When we give over our will to the will of God, He can move us into our purpose in Him because we are no longer living for our own purposes. When we let Him have our emotions, He can remove the negative, demonic influences and expand the godly emotions of compassion, love, joy and mercy He's put in us. And as we let go of what we think we want, when we give up our selfish desires, the godly desires that begin to manifest through us will lead us into our destiny in God.

The instruments of daily sacrifice are placed on the altar, which was covered over in purple cloth. This represents the majesty of the Lord and the royal authority these instruments carry. They are bundled in badgers' skins dyed red, showing the safety and covering blood of our Lord Jesus Christ. Our God has made provision for the deliverance of not only our spirits, but our souls and our bodies.

1Th 5:23 And the very God of peace sanctify you wholly; and I pray God your whole spirit and soul and body be preserved blameless unto the coming of our Lord Jesus Christ.

The four instruments used at the altar are symbolic of the tools we use as we work out our own salvation (soul-salvation of our mind, will, emotion and desires) with fear and trembling!

Phi 2:12 Wherefore, my beloved, as ye have always obeyed, not as in my presence only, but now much more in my absence, work out your own salvation with fear and trembling.

Don't be confused by this verse! Read the next one…

Phi 2:13 For it is God which worketh in you both to will and to do of his good pleasure.

We cannot work our way to glory or earn our place in heaven. We are eternally saved only by the blood of the Lord Jesus Christ. As we allow the Lord's presence in us to manifest more and more – from glory to glory and strength to strength, we become increasingly able to cooperate with what the Lord is doing and working in us. He's given us the tools, we just have to be willing to co-labor. The working out of our salvation refers to the daily sacrifice of the strengths of our souls, then packing up and moving on with the Lord. Hallelujah!

We can see a progression in what God is revealing in this look at deliverance of His creation. The very first verse revealed deliverance through love. The next one, deliverance through the Word (which is also love). Next we noticed the corporate coming together and the family aspect of deliverance. And then God gave us the tools and showed us that the covenant of sacrifice is two-fold – His for us, and ours to Him. Every verse and the context of them, reveals God's heart of love.

Deuteronomy

"And the Lord commanded me at that time to teach you statutes and judgments, that you might do them in the land whither you go over to possess it." – Deuteronomy 4:14

In this chapter of Deuteronomy, Moses makes an impassioned plea to the nation of Israel not to forget the word of the Lord which they both heard and received at Mount Horeb at the giving of the Ten Commandments. He tells the people their victory in life depends on them. As does all God's Word, this remains true. The chapter begins by clearly revealing that the blessings of long life and fulfilled promises lie in our obedience to God.

Deu 4:1 Now therefore hearken, O Israel, unto the statutes and unto the judgments, which I teach you, for to do them, that ye may live, and go in and possess the land which the LORD God of your fathers giveth you.

It is evident throughout Scripture that God's love for us is unconditional, but His promises are not. Moses declares (in our 4:14 verse) he was commanded by the Lord to "teach" God's statutes and judgments. The word teach means "goad" and implies a harsh kind of instruction – to teach by the incentive of a rod of punishment. In other words, we better get it, or else we're going to get it! We get to choose whether or not we make it easy on ourselves, or whether we make it hard. We can DO these things, or suffer the consequences.

Hos 6:1 Come, and let us return unto the LORD: for he hath torn, and he will heal us; he hath smitten, and he will bind us up.

Hos 6:2 After two days will he revive us: in the third day he will raise us up, and we shall live in his sight.

Hos 6:3 Then shall we know, if we follow on to know the LORD: his going forth is prepared as the morning; and he shall come unto us as the rain, as the latter and former rain unto the earth.

As a child walking along and holding your father's hand, when you thought you'd go a different way (into the candy store), he held you a little tighter and led you on, didn't he? Maybe he said, "No, not now." If you dug in your heels and resisted his directive, what followed?

We should be reminded that the only time we feel the pressure is when we resist!

When we convert the promises of God into benefits in our lives by following on to know the Lord in our actions and not merely our words, we can enjoy long life and truly possess and live in the promised land. What is the land of promise? All five elements of salvation are our promised land – preservation, healing, soundness, prosperity and deliverance from temporal evil. Are we living in the fullness of our salvation? If not, why not?

The answer to the why not may very well lie in this chapter of Deuteronomy, in verse 24, which states, "For the Lord your God is a consuming fire, even a jealous God." Moses tells us God alone is God and to bow to no other. When we put man's opinion over God's opinion of us, we are into idolatry. When we believe a special diet or exercise regimen keeps us alive, we are into idolatry. When we exalt our children or grandchildren over God, we are into idolatry. When we trust in our job as our provision, we are into idolatry. Anything we allow to come between us and the living God becomes occultic. Let me explain: "occult" is a term used in astronomy to describe one heavenly body passing in front of another and obscuring the one behind. When we allow ourselves to trust in anything other than God, the thing we trust in comes to the forefront and obscures the truth. It is easy for us to then slide off the path, stepping out of light and into darkness, opening a wide door for the devil to run (and ruin) our lives.

The good news is that God never leaves or forsakes us, and He is ever merciful to forgive us when we turn back to Him. When we return to a recognition of His covenant and once again follow on to know the Lord, He restores us into fellowship and delivers us from the evil one.

Deu 4:29 But if from thence thou shalt seek the LORD thy God, thou shalt find him, if thou seek him with all thy heart and with all thy soul.

Deu 4:30 When thou art in tribulation, and all these things are come upon thee, even in the latter days, if thou turn to the LORD thy God, and shalt be obedient unto his voice;

Deu 4:31 (For the LORD thy God is a merciful God;) he will not forsake thee, neither destroy thee, nor forget the covenant of thy fathers which he swore unto them.

In the Deuteronomy 4:14 reference and its context, we learn that freedom from evil (deliverance) is in our salvation package – this freedom is inherent in the faithfulness of God. When we love God, we obey Him. All covenants have terms. The church seems to have adopted the attitude that we can make the terms! God loves me, He'll understand and do it my way. Yes, God loves us. Yes, He is faithful to us. Can we say the same?

Joh 14:21 He that hath my commandments, and keepeth them, he it is that loveth me: and he that loveth me shall be loved of my Father, and I will love him, and will manifest myself to him.

Father, thank You for the awesome insights You're giving me as I study to show myself approved. Thank You for helping me realize how I am to come before You transparently, and how in Your heart is the desire for me to help others and love others as You love me. Thank You for the pictures You paint for me in Your word through the times of the old covenant that lead me to a greater understanding of the Lord Jesus Christ and His sacrifice on my behalf. Lord, I ask You to forgive me for crawling off the altar, for blaming You for my troubles, for not understanding Your great love for me. I need Your help, Lord. I have to have YOU and Your mind, Your will, Your emotions and Your desires. Teach me to use the instruments of the altar in my own life and to die daily to selfish motives and a self-focused life. Lord, I know there has to be a death for there to be a resurrection, and I need to be resurrected daily in the newness of life in Christ Jesus as I work out the salvation of my soul. Change my perspective, Father, from inward and backward to upward and outward. I ask that You keep me ever mindful of Your covenant, that I uphold my responsibility to respond to Your ability and not look to the things of the world to sustain or protect me. I declare I do not want to fall into the deception of the world. I do not want to begin to put another god before You. I declare that You alone are God and I ask Your guidance as I follow on to know You, Lord Jesus, so that I can fully possess the promised land You have appointed for me. Deliver me, oh Lord, from the snare of the fowler. Amen

Joshua

"On that day the LORD magnified Joshua in the sight of all Israel; and they feared him, as they feared Moses, all the days of his life."
– Joshua 4:14

Praise God! Here we begin to clearly see the result of the process of God's great deliverance in our lives. We need to take note of God's wonderful plan as it is revealed by our 4:14 verses. Let's have a quick review of the progression so we can get this plan of God into our spirits…

First, we see in Genesis God's seal of love over us, which begins the process of deliverance. In Exodus we learn it is not by our strength, but His; and in Leviticus the authority and covering of the Lord is revealed. Coming to Numbers, we see submission and sacrifice as we give up our way of doing things for His. In Deuteronomy, obedience and repentance are added to our walk, bringing us to this Scripture in Joshua, where we are promoted.

Looking at the context of this verse, we see the crossing of the Jordan, as Joshua is leading the people (in Moses' stead) into the promised land. In his obedience to the Lord, Joshua has taken up the mantle of deliverer left to him by Moses at the Lord's command; and the people followed the word of the Lord as conveyed to them by Joshua. Let's look at the context for greater understanding.

Jos 4:1 And it came to pass, when all the people were clean passed over Jordan, that the LORD spoke unto Joshua, saying,

Jos 4:2 Take you twelve men out of the people, out of every tribe a man,

Jos 4:3 And command ye them, saying, Take you hence out of the midst of Jordan, out of the place where the priests' feet stood firm, twelve stones, and ye shall carry them over with you, and leave them in the lodging place, where ye shall lodge this night.

Jos 4:4 Then Joshua called the twelve men, whom he had prepared of the children of Israel, out of every tribe a man:

Jos 4:5 And Joshua said unto them, Pass over before the ark of the LORD your God into the midst of Jordan, and take ye up every man of you a stone upon his shoulder, according unto the number of the tribes of the children of Israel:

Jos 4:6 That this may be a sign among you, that when your children ask their fathers in time to come, saying, What mean ye by these stones?

Jos 4:7 Then ye shall answer them, That the waters of Jordan were cut off before the ark of the covenant of the LORD; when it passed over Jordan, the waters of Jordan were cut off: and these stones shall be for a memorial unto the children of Israel forever.

Jos 4:8 And the children of Israel did so as Joshua commanded, and took up twelve stones out of the midst of Jordan, as the LORD spoke unto Joshua, according to the number of the tribes of the children of Israel, and carried them over with them unto the place where they lodged, and laid them down there.

Jos 4:9 And Joshua set up twelve stones in the midst of Jordan, in the place where the feet of the priests which bore the ark of the covenant stood: and they are there unto this day.

Jos 4:10 For the priests which bore the ark stood in the midst of Jordan, until every thing was finished that the LORD commanded Joshua to speak unto the people, according to all that Moses commanded Joshua: and the people hasted and passed over.

Jos 4:11 And it came to pass, when all the people were clean passed over, that the ark of the LORD passed over, and the priests, in the presence of the people.

Jos 4:12 And the children of Reuben, and the children of Gad, and half the tribe of Manasseh, passed over armed before the children of Israel, as Moses spoke unto them:

Jos 4:13 About forty thousand prepared for war passed over before the LORD unto battle, to the plains of Jericho.

Jos 4:14 On that day the LORD magnified Joshua in the sight of all Israel; and they feared him, as they feared Moses, all the days of his life.

    The people had passed over the Jordan and the Lord gave another command — that Joshua have a man of each tribe remove a stone from the midst of the river and carry it over as a memorial to the generations to come. One interesting thing about this account is that Joshua himself also set up a memorial in the midst of the Jordan, 12 stones, where the priests stood. The text does not read that these are the same 12 stones. Apparently, two memorials were set up to commenmorate the great delivering power of God. In Biblical symbolism, two is the number that speaks of witness. We have in the setting up of these memorials a witness to God's goodness. They speak of both what we have been taken out of, and what we are taken in to.
    Even though Joshua led the people across and into the promised land, it is evident in the fourteenth verse that although the people obeyed Joshua, their hearts were not fully knit with his. If they were, God would not have had to "magnify" Joshua in their sight. The word "magnify" does not mean making something bigger, it actually indicates seeing something as it is. Magnification doesn't make the thing itself bigger than it is, you just see more of it. This verse indicates that the people didn't see Joshua as he had been appointed by God – they failed to recognize him as their leader – and God had to show them.

I believe there must have been some sorrow in the hearts of these people at having lost their leader Moses, along with thoughts that no one else could be as great, or as greatly respected. Even Joshua himself may have harbored doubt, because in chapter one of the Book of Joshua God spoke words of encouragement to him. God instructed him not to fear, and to be of "good courage" and "very courageous." God told Joshua He would never leave him or forsake him, and that all God purposed for him would be accomplished. That is a word for us today. God will accomplish in us all He has purposed for us.

Phi 2:13 For it is God which worketh in you both to will and to do of his good pleasure.

    As Joshua obeyed the word of the Lord, as he moved in step with God's plan and purpose, the Lord began to raise him up in the sight and understanding of the people. This verse states Joshua was magnified by the Lord. Again, realize when a thing is magnified it isn't made bigger, as we like to think. If you put an object under a microscope, it doesn't grow, you simply see more of it. The Hebrew word for "magnified" here comes from a root word meaning "twist." In other words, God turned Joshua and allowed the people to see him fully, from all sides perhaps, or so all aspects of his character were revealed. There were aspects of Joshua's nature the people had not recognized, and now God was revealing these qualities to the people.

    It was at that time the people began to come into alignment in their hearts with their leader. They no longer longed for Moses, but instead looked to Joshua with the same respect for, and reverence of, his relationship with God as they had toward their former leader. They saw that Joshua and God had a face-to-face relationship, that Joshua, like Moses, was favored of God and clearly God spoke to him. Joshua was promoted by God in the eyes and hearts of the people because of God's seal of love, strength, authority and covering, and Joshua's response of submission, self-sacrifice, and obedience.

In this 4:14 verse we learn of promotion. As we accept God's love for us, step into His strength, submit to His authority and covering, give up what we think and what we want and what we think we want, and yield to His way, God raises us up in the sight of others. There is a caution when that happens. We need never forget that to GOD be the glory for the levels of elevation we enjoy in our natural lives. Promotion is a part of our freedom in God. It is a portion we receive by God's delivering hand! Hallelujah!

Psa 75:5 Lift not up your horn on high: speak not with a stiff neck.

Psa 75:6 For promotion cometh neither from the east, nor from the west, nor from the south.

Psa 75:7 But God is the judge: he putteth down one, and setteth up another.

JOSHUA = PROMOTION

♥ is KEY

JORDAN RIVER

VICTORY IS ASSURED

4 GENERATIONS 2 COME

Deborah the Judge

GET UP!!!

Ruth and BOAZ

ELI = Reap what you Sow?

Judges

"And Deborah said to Barak, Up, for this is the day in which the LORD hath delivered Sisera into thine hand: is not the LORD gone out before thee? So Barak went down from Mount Tabor, and ten thousand men after him." – Judges 4:14

This verse is a beautiful picture of how we need to be reminded and encouraged in our Kingdom appointments. Deliverance is ours, victory is ours, but we must appropriate what the Lord has done! Remember when Joshua was taking the people into the promised land, the Jordan didn't part until the priests carrying the ark put their foot into the water. And the waters came together again when the priests were fully across. We see the same principle here. The victory is assured, but we can't enjoy it unless we go after it!

Deborah was a judge in Israel, and a prophetess. This woman was set up by God, promoted to a position of power, even over kings. There were kings over the nations and kings over cities. Deborah was appointed to speak God's word and to impart God's heart in matters of decision, both for individuals who were at odds with each other and for the nation of Israel. Here in this account, she is reproving Barak, who had charge over an entire city and was considered king of it. Deborah spoke a word of knowledge, saying she knew that God had already instructed Barak to go forth into battle, and that it was a battle of certain victory because the Lord had already accomplished it!

Even though he had the Word of the Lord, Barak remained in his city until the judge called for him. We are prone to the same inaction, aren't we? Sometimes we need godly people to speak into our lives to remind us of our destiny, and to confirm in us what we already know God has spoken. Even after Deborah encouraged him in the Lord, Barak still carried a seed of doubt, shown by his refusal to go into the battle without Deborah. He said, "I'll go, but only if you come with me!"

Perhaps he was testing Deborah to see if she really believed God, or perhaps he thought he would need a strong spiritual person along in case the Lord said something else he needed to hear, or maybe he thought she wouldn't go, and so he'd be off the hook. The "why" of it makes no difference to the outcome.

Deborah went along with Barak; and in this verse of deliverance, she is exhorting Barak to arise to the battle. "This is the day!" she says. "This is the day the LORD has already delivered your enemy into your hand. Now go out there and take him!"

Yes, this is the day! The Lord has already gone before and defeated our enemy.

Heb 1:1 God who at sundry times and in divers manners spake in time past unto the fathers by the prophets,

Heb 1:2 Hath in these last days spoken unto us by his Son, whom he hath appointed heir of all things, by whom also he made the worlds;

Heb 1:3 Who being the brightness of his glory, and the express image of his person, and upholding all things by the word of his power, when he had by himself purged our sins, sat down on the right hand of the Majesty on high;

Col 2:15 And having spoiled principalities and powers, he made a show of them openly, triumphing over them in it.

The enemy has been defeated. God has not called a rematch. Now WE have a work to do, and that work is to claim the victory. Is there a battle? Yes. Have we won it?

Yes, through our Lord Jesus Christ who has gone before!

I say to every one of you – and myself included - Get up, Child of God, engage the enemy and claim your victory. This is the day of victory! Is it yours? The Lord has gone before, will you follow after?

The theme of deliverance is continued in this verse, where Deborah declares the Lord has already gone before us, and victory is certain. Praise God!

STEP INTO THE JORDAN... BY FAITH

PALMYRA = VICTORY

OH, MAGNIFY THE LORD!

MEMORIAL

IN THE MIDST OF THE JORDAN

!WANTED! KINSMAN REDEEMER

BRIDGE THE CHASM

CHILDREN'S BREAD

DELIVERANCE COMES THROUGH RELATIONSHIP

Ruth

"And the women said unto Naomi, Blessed be the LORD, which has not left you this day without a kinsman, that his name may be famous in Israel." – Ruth 4:14

Here we see the picture, in Boaz, of our Lord Jesus Christ as kinsman redeemer. He is the one who has paid the price to deliver us from a position of loneliness and isolation and He places us in a family.

Psa 68:6 God setteth the solitary in families: he bringeth out those which are bound with chains: but the rebellious dwell in a dry land.

Psalm 68 tells us God takes those of us who have been cast off and who feel alone and abandoned, picks us up and puts us into a family. And it will be a family that prays for each other, and cares for each other. It may be a best friend, or a pastor or a local church that thinks of you as part of the family. Whatever it is, God provides that connection for us. He doesn't want us to be alone. He wants us to depend on each other and to enjoy face-to-face relationship, not only with Him but with other people as well. In this example, and in the example of our own lives as we learn to appropriate His goodness, God also takes us out of poverty and elevates us to prosperity!

Psa 118:5 I called upon the LORD in distress: the LORD answered me, and set me in a large place.

Psa 66:12 Thou hast caused men to ride over our heads; we went through fire and through water: but thou broughtest us out into a wealthy place.

Let's examine the historical and natural aspect of what's happening in the 4:14 verse in Ruth. According to the law and customs of the day at this time, widows were utterly without means, except a "near kinsman" (a close relative of the dead husband) took them in. In her state of destitution, Naomi would likely have had to surrender the parcel of land that once was her husband's. Boaz sat at the gates of the city and called the closest relative of Elimelech – that was Naomi's husband who had died - and a counsel of elders together.

The gates were the place of the city where decisions were made. It was here that the men came together, and Boaz charged the relative to purchase from Naomi what she had. The man said he would redeem the land; but then Boaz pointed out the man would also be required to redeem Naomi's daughter-in-law Ruth as well.

Rth 4:5 Then said Boaz, What day thou buyest the field of the hand of Naomi, thou must buy it also of Ruth the Moabitess, the wife of the dead, to raise up the name of the dead upon his inheritance.

Elimelech's nearest kinsman refused "to raise up the name of the dead upon his inheritance." He would not agree to take Ruth as his wife. And so Boaz stepped up to redeem Naomi and Ruth.

It was from this act of redemption, under the law, that the righteous line of King David was continued! Although Ruth was not an Israelite by birth, she was "adopted" into the family because of her faithfulness and dedicated declarations of trust in the Lord through her actions and attitudes. She made a decree as she claimed the Lord as her God and vowed her allegiance to Naomi.

Rth 1:16 And Ruth said, Entreat me not to leave thee, or to return from following after thee: for whither thou goest, I will go; and where thou lodgest, I will lodge: thy people shall be my people, and thy God my God:

As we read more in the Book of Ruth, Boaz makes note of how Ruth left her own family and homeland in a decision to follow her mother-in-law and trust in the Lord. He blesses her in verse 2:12 "The LORD recompense thy work, and a full reward be given thee of the LORD God of Israel, under whose wings thou art come to trust." Then in verse 3:11, he makes her a promise: "And now, my daughter, fear not; I will do to thee all that thou requirest: for all the city of my people doth know that thou art a virtuous woman."

When we look at the translation from the Hebrew of the phrase "virtuous woman" we see this: "war worthy, an army, a force to be reckoned with."

Knowing that Boaz is a type or pattern of Jesus, and Ruth is symbolic of the Bride, we can recognize some of the characteristics the Lord seeks in His bride. He is looking for a bride who is unafraid to do battle in the heavenlies to enforce the victory He bought for us with His blood, a war worthy force that will occupy until He comes. This bride will also consist of those who can be the completion of Himself so that He may display her at His side! That is the meaning in Ephesians where Paul makes the comparison of marriage to Christ and the church. The Bride is meant to be a completion of the Bridegroom, that He displays Himself in her when He comes alongside her.

Eph 5:27 That he might present it to himself a glorious church, not having spot, or wrinkle, or any such thing; but that it should be holy and without blemish.

Ruth demonstrated trust in the Lord, faithfulness, dedication, courage, willingness to work, and kindness. It is this one whom the Lord takes as His bride. Do we fit this picture? Are we willing to relinquish all that is comfortable and familiar to us to follow after the true and living God, as Ruth did? Are we willing to listen to godly wisdom and counsel, as Ruth did?

Living life in its fullest requires something of us. It is a work, but not a dead work. It is not done in our own strength, but in His. To enjoy redemption from worldly circumstances takes a walk in faith, an appropriation of His kinship to us, a realization that He is our closest relative and He alone can redeem us and bring us to the marriage bed where our destiny and purpose in Him are conceived. This verse of redemption (deliverance) in Ruth 4:14 takes us toward an understanding of the intimacy God desires to have with us. The progression of our freedom continues.

I Samuel

"And when Eli heard the noise of the crying, he said, What meaneth the noise of this tumult? And the man came in hastily, and told Eli." – I Samuel 4:14

I have to say, when I got to this verse, it certainly seemed to be a bump in the road of our deliverance theme, or maybe a chasm over which there is no bridge. To understand "what means this?" we need to fully grasp the reality that God is known by His judgment.

Psalm 9:6 tells us: "The LORD is known by the judgment which he executes: the wicked is snared in the work of his own hands…(pause and contemplate this)." We also need to have the understanding of the context of this verse. So let's begin there.

Eli is the high priest, the one Samuel grew up with. Eli had two sons who were worthless unbelievers operating in the priestly office and doing wicked deeds. As their father, Eli had not exercised the authority he had over them and "restrained" them; and the Lord was displeased.

1Sa 3:13 For I have told him that I will judge his house forever for the iniquity which he knoweth; because his sons made themselves vile, and he restrained them not.

Here is a good example of how associational sin can ensnare us and cause us to be subject to the same consequence as the one we cover for. Essentially, Eli had called evil good for the sake of love, allowing his sons to continue in the office of priest in spite of their evil actions.

Samuel was an established prophet of God, and he had previously given Eli the word of the Lord concerning his house – that God would make an utter end of it because Eli knew of the iniquity and did nothing about it. Here we see the balance between God's sovereignty and man's responsibility. Although we can do nothing without God, we are expected to respond to His ability and allow Him to work through us to maintain His righteousness in our lives. When we know to do good and don't, it is a sin to us. When we know we must restrain wickedness and do not, the wickedness becomes ours.

This is Eli's spiritual position when Israel is smitten in war with the Philistines. When the nation of Israel decided their defeat was due to the absence of the Ark of the Covenant, Eli's two worthless sons, Hophni and Phinehas get the ark and bring it into the battle. When they hear this, the Philistines - at first - are in fear; but then they rally and defeat the Israelites soundly and take the Ark as spoil.

What can we glean from this? The simple truth that we can't "use" God. The name of Jesus is useless to any person who is not standing in the person of Jesus – exhibiting His character, acting on His word, following His lead. Hophni and Phinehas had no personal relationship with God and were merely attempting to call Him like a dog to work on their behalf.

That brings us back to Eli and this verse where the high priest is sitting and watching expectantly for news of the battle. From the previous verse, we know Eli is disturbed in his spirit because the word tells us his "heart trembled" for the Ark of God. It seems Eli may have had an idea that his sons were operating once again out of their own strength and bringing the Ark may not have been such a great idea. In any case, this is the verse where we see Eli inquiring as to what's going on, and being told the bad news.

It must have been at that moment Eli knew God's

judgment had fallen. As high priest of Israel, he had failed to step up to his responsibility as priest and as a father; he had failed to discipline his sons; and the word of the Lord spoken previously by Samuel had begun to come to fruition. Eli fell over backward, broke his neck and died.

What does this event and this verse teach us?

Deliverance is not automatic, and we can't expect God to show up on our behalf when we have no relationship with Him! Deliverance comes through relationship. Here again, freedom results from our face-to-face love of God. His love for us, our response of love to Him.

To operate in the idea that God was created for us, rather than our being created for Him will always bring disastrous results.

Isa 57:16 For I will not contend forever, neither will I be always wroth: for the spirit should fail before me, and the souls which I have made.

There is a point at which God will not strive with us any longer, even though we are now living after the cross, where mercy and judgment were married in the crucifixion of Jesus Christ. God's judgment is always tempered with His mercy. His judgments cut away evil from our lives and bring us justice.

We can also be assured that the Word of the Lord will always come to pass. Is it possible that Eli could have been spared? I believe if he had repented and removed his sons from their positions, the answer is yes. He had authority over them, and refused to discipline them. But I also believe the prophecy Samuel spoke would have come to pass eventually – if not in Eli's lifetime, then in generations following. Too often we forget that God is a generational God; and that our actions and attitudes have eternal consequences and rewards both in this life and the next. And so the theme of deliverance continues in this verse, if even as a bad example. Eli could have avoided the consequence and enjoyed deliverance had he properly fulfilled the position of priest to which God appointed him. Had he not put his children above God.

As we go farther along in our study, we see that God gives us grace for a season, but He will not always wink at our foolishness. And as we grow in the knowledge of the things of the Spirit, we have greater responsibility to uphold them. When we know to do good and don't do it, there is a consequence. God is just and He will never hold us responsible for something we don't know. On the other hand, He will always hold us responsible for what we <u>do</u> know!

Father, I thank you for Your word and for the gentle reminders of Your sovereignty. Thank You for helping me realize that promotion comes from You alone, and when I follow Your direction, You will turn me so that all can see Your favor on me and Your great love for me. Thank You for showing me once more how I must step into the victories You have wrought for me, and forgive me, Lord, for those times when I hold back from going after what You have told me is already mine. Lord, I believe, help my unbelief! Lord, thank You that You are my near kinsman, that You alone are my Redeemer, my Messiah, My Risen Lord, and that You are ever-ready to save. Thank You that I can call on You in my distress because You are my hope. Father, forgive me for those times when I have put others ahead of You, when I have neglected my responsibilities to discipline my children, or covered the transgressions of others because I wanted to be liked and accepted by them. Forgive me for fear of man and for idolatry, Lord. I break all agreement with those evil things now, and ask to be delivered of them. With Your help, Lord, I will not fall back, but instead, I will advance Your kingdom and restore others. I love You, Lord, and I need You. AMEN

I Kings

"Ahinadab the son of Iddo had Mahanaim:" – I Kings 4:14

What a verse! Can we possibly get a picture of deliverance from these names and the context in which they are presented? Yes!

In this fourth chapter of the first Book of Kings, the Lord gives us the picture of the vastness of King Solomon's kingdom and the requirements of its maintenance. He names the princes who attend to various functions and duties, and who, as governors or stewards, have been given authority to oversee some segment of kingdom business.

The first to be named are those in closest proximity to the king, who likely were stationed on the palace grounds. They were called princes and had rulership over certain areas of kingdom operation and the affairs of the king. Next, the 12 men who were appointed overseers of all Israel are listed. The primary duty of these men was to provide the needs of Solomon's household one month out of the year, and that was no small task.

Ahinadab was the seventh of these princes of the outlying countryside to be named. Because seven is God's number for spiritual perfection, and 14 is the number representing deliverance, we should heed the meanings of the names mentioned in this verse. (A fascinating study can be undertaken by examining all the princes mentioned in this chapter and spiritually correlating each in his position and function in the Kingdom of God. But this is not the purpose of this book. I encourage you, dear reader, to undertake that study; and I remind you it is the glory of kings to search out a matter!)

Let's look at the names in this 4:14 verse to discover God's heart of deliverance for His people. The first name mentioned, Ahinadab, means "brother of liberality," and it is derived from two other Hebrew words. One translates "like unto" and the other "to impel, a volunteer soldier, to present spontaneously, offer freely, give willingly." Ahinadab is named as a son of Iddo. The word "son" means "builder of the family name" and Iddo means "timely." Included in the derivative meanings of Ahinadab's father's name are "praised and appointed." The deeper meaning of the name "Iddo" (root words) is "using the hand to praise, worshipping in reverence with extended hands, meeting at an appointed time, to summon to trial, direct, or gather together."

By combining the meanings of these names, we can conclude: Ahinadab is impelled as a volunteer in the army of God to freely and willingly give generously to the king from an attitude of reverential worship, and in a timely manner. And what did Ahinadab oversee as a servant to the king? From what is he to draw so liberally? Ahinidab had Mahanaim, which means "double camp." Its root meanings include "incline" and specifically "pitch a tent, to encamp for abode or siege, camp, dwell, grow to an end, rest in tent."

As the seventh officer to minister to the needs of the king, Ahinadab looks very much like a spiritual picture of the overcomers… those Kingdom-minded saints who follow on to know the Lord and to advance His Kingdom NOW. Ahinadab (think overcomer) draws from a position of rest in the tent, inclining under the covering of the Lord Himself.

Out of the double camp, we can liberally praise and worship the King. Praise is the sacrifice of ourselves. It is a sacrifice we can always give, and one that moves God's heart and His hand.

Psa 107:22 And let them sacrifice the sacrifices of thanksgiving, and declare his works with rejoicing.

As overcomers, free in the Lord, we have a place of rest in Him that allows us to grow to His end purpose, and prepares us to lay siege to the enemy. In the progression of deliverance of creation, we can see in this verse a preparation of the Body of Christ. It is a letting-go of striving and pushing and pressing to accomplish in ourselves what only the Lord can accomplish in us. It is a place of praise and rest in knowing and trusting God. The needs of the Kingdom are met in the King! Spiritual perfection in deliverance can only be achieved by allowing the Deliverer to have His way in us, to work through us and to purge us of uncleanness. The names in our 4:14 verse tell us we must be willing givers, brothers of liberality, abiding under cover of the Almighty and living in praise and reverential worship of Him!

What we learn of deliverance in this verse is simply this – the Lord wants us to live in peace, not a continual state of warfare where we wake up each morning punching demons in the air. Some Christians are so involved in warfare they've lost sight of their Captain - Jesus Christ the Deliverer! It is only IN HIM (resting in the tent) we find our freedom. We have to rest in Him and grow in Him in order to lay siege to the enemy. Praise God!

Another important point about this verse is this: God has appointed officers to serve in His Kingdom in specific tasks and in a specific COURSE. Not every officer was to provide everything, nor was every officer expected to provide everything all the time – there was a time appointed to each one. Each one of us has a course. Each one of us has an assignment in the Kingdom. Nobody is expected to do it all, nobody is expected to have all the answers, or to serve all the people. We are a part of a BODY. King Solomon divided up the Kingdom chores. King Jesus does the same. Then He points out to us that we need only to be in our course and dependent on Him, resting in Him, praising Him. It is in our sacrifice of thanksgiving and praise that we find freedom.

CHANGE

The Truth will set you free!

Shining clarity

JAVA

THERE IS NO "I" IN TEAM

GO TEAM

Faithful & True

ENTER IN SAINT

2008 YEAR OF GATES

Clean up clean out!

sweet fragrance

Precious and Few...

II Kings

"And he said, What then is to be done for her? And Gehazi answered, Verily she hath no child, and her husband is old."
- 2 Kings 4:14

Let's go back to get the context of what's happening here. This is one of the stories about Elisha the prophet. In the city of Shunem lived what the Bible tells us was a "great woman." The root word for great tells us she was "made large in body or mind or honor or estate." So let's just say this Shunammite woman was important in the community, she was respected. And every time Elisha came through Shunem, she invited him over for dinner. Then one day she persuaded her husband to build Elisha a room so he could stay over in his journeys.

2Ki 4:9 *And she said unto her husband, Behold now, I perceive that this is an holy man of God, which passeth by us continually.*

2Ki 4:10 *Let us make a little chamber, I pray thee, on the wall; and let us set for him there a bed, and a table, and a stool, and a candlestick: and it shall be, when he cometh to us, that he shall turn in thither.*

So Elisha had his own place in Shunem; and he was apparently beginning to wonder why this woman was doing so much for him. So he called his servant Gehazi and told him to go get the woman. When she came before him, Elisha basically asked her what she wanted. He thought maybe she wanted to be given a position, that she was doing all this to gain favor with the king or the people in charge. This is a very important point. Many times, we work for the man of God or do things we think will please him, but we have a wrong motive. We're not doing things to advance the Kingdom of God, we're attempting to advance our own kingdom. Let me tell you, God is not obligated to uphold any kingdom we build for ourselves.

Elisha wanted to know her heart. He searched out her motivation – what was the motivating factor that caused her to cater to Elisha and his servant, to provide food and lodging for them? What do you want, woman? But he found out this Shunammite woman was happy in her place; she was not seeking to be elevated, she was simply serving because she "perceived" he was a man of God. She could discern that Elisha was a prophet of God and she simply wanted to come alongside him and provide for his needs as he went about doing the business of the Kingdom. That's a lesson in itself. We need to discern the needs of the Body and of our ministers, and then of our own volition come alongside and help them accomplish the purposes of God.

When we do that, even though we are not actively seeking reward, we are rewarded. The woman did not name a need, she did not make a request of Elisha. After she left the room, Elisha asked Gehazi, what can be done for this woman? He answered that the woman had no son, and her husband was an old man – implying that the reproductive season was essentially over, to put it nicely.

This is our 4:14 verse. As we serve the purposes of God, we don't have to be big name preachers, we don't have to be the front line ministers or the great prophets. When we are faithful to discern the needs of others, and offer our service and support to them without expecting something from them, the Lord searches for something special he can do for us! Hallelujah!

In this case, Elisha prophesies that this barren woman

would have a son. For women in that day and culture, there could be no better gift. She was so overwhelmed at the word, she didn't even believe it.

> 2Ki 4:16 And he said, About this season, according to the time of life, thou shalt embrace a son. And she said, Nay, my lord, thou man of God, do not lie unto thine handmaid.

Here is yet another picture of our unbelief, and God's faithfulness. He tells us something wonderful is coming into our lives, and we say "I don't know. I don't think so. It sure doesn't look like a possibility."

> 2Ki 4:17 And the woman conceived, and bare a son at that season that Elisha had said unto her, according to the time of life.

There you have it. God's word came to pass. Because the woman was faithful in serving God's purpose by giving her support and substance into His purposes, the Lord searched her heart and gave her the most precious gift imaginable… one she would never even have thought to ask for because she didn't see it as possible. I think sometimes we judge what God can do by what we know can be done in the natural. We say "all things are possible," but then we don't ask for the impossible because we don't believe it will happen for us. One of the best things I ever heard was from a teaching by Bill Johnson: "You'll know you have the mind of Christ when the impossible is logical to you."

What we learn from this 4:14 reference is God is a rewarder of those who love Him, and align themselves to His purpose. He delivered this Shunammite woman from barrenness just because she worshipped Him with her giving heart. But the story doesn't stop there, and I want to go on with it because there is more to understand. Let's just read it.

> 2Ki 4:18 And when the child was grown, it fell on a day, that he went out to his father to the reapers.

2Ki 4:19 And he said unto his father, My head, my head. And he said to a lad, Carry him to his mother.

2Ki 4:20 And when he had taken him, and brought him to his mother, he sat on her knees till noon, and then died.

2Ki 4:21 And she went up, and laid him on the bed of the man of God, and shut the door upon him, and went out.

2Ki 4:22 And she called unto her husband, and said, Send me, I pray thee, one of the young men, and one of the asses, that I may run to the man of God, and come again.

2Ki 4:23 And he said, Wherefore wilt thou go to him to day? it is neither new moon, nor sabbath. And she said, It shall be well.

2Ki 4:24 Then she saddled an ass, and said to her servant, Drive, and go forward; slack not thy riding for me, except I bid thee.

2Ki 4:25 So she went and came unto the man of God to mount Carmel. And it came to pass, when the man of God saw her afar off, that he said to Gehazi his servant, Behold, yonder is that Shunammite:

2Ki 4:26 Run now, I pray thee, to meet her, and say unto her, Is it well with thee? is it well with thy husband? is it well with the child? And she answered, It is well.

2Ki 4:27 And when she came to the man of God to the hill, she caught him by the feet: but Gehazi came near to thrust her away. And the man of God said, Let her alone; for her soul is vexed within her: and the LORD hath hid it from me, and hath not told me.

2Ki 4:28 Then she said, Did I desire a son of my lord? did I not say, Do not deceive me?

2Ki 4:29 Then he said to Gehazi, Gird up thy loins, and take my staff in thine hand, and go thy way: if thou meet any man, salute him not; and if any salute thee, answer him not again: and lay my staff upon the face of the child.

2Ki 4:30 And the mother of the child said, As the LORD liveth, and as thy soul liveth, I will not leave thee. And he arose, and followed her.

2Ki 4:31 And Gehazi passed on before them, and laid the staff upon the face of the child; but there was neither voice, nor hearing. Wherefore he went again to meet him, and told him, saying, The child is not awaked.

2Ki 4:32 And when Elisha was come into the house, behold, the child was dead, and laid upon his bed.

2Ki 4:33 He went in therefore, and shut the door upon them twain, and prayed unto the LORD.

2Ki 4:34 And he went up, and lay upon the child, and put his mouth upon his mouth, and his eyes upon his eyes, and his hands upon his hands: and he stretched himself upon the child; and the flesh of the child waxed warm.

2Ki 4:35 Then he returned, and walked in the house to and fro; and went up, and stretched himself upon him: and the child sneezed seven times, and the child opened his eyes.

2Ki 4:36 And he called Gehazi, and said, Call this Shunammite. So he called her. And when she was come in unto him, he said, Take up thy son.

2Ki 4:37 Then she went in, and fell at his feet, and bowed herself to the ground, and took up her son, and went out.

  This is a fabulous conclusion to this example of God's delivering hand. The boy dies. The mother puts him on the prophet's bed, gets on a fast donkey and goes out to find Elisha. Notice this… all the while, she never confirms her son in death. Her words were "it is well." She could have fallen apart and wept and wailed and accepted the death of her only son. But I believe that once she saw the power of God to bring this impossible son into her life, she had faith to believe God could keep him with her. She knew God's power to create life, and had come to trust Him in everything about her life – "it is well." The Shunnamite woman knew the Word of God is true and the blessings of God do not cause heartache and pain.

Pro 10:22 The blessing of the LORD, it maketh rich, and he addeth no sorrow with it.

The way the boy came to life also speaks of deliverance from evil. He sneezed seven times. The devil did not want the respected woman of Shunem to continue to follow God, because she had influence and was most likely leading others to the true God. The testimony of this boy's birth and his life was a testimony to God and His greatness. Satan was probably thinking that if he took the boy's life, then the mother would turn against God. And even if she didn't, the people of the community would have thought God was cruel.

The plan of the devil was thwarted first by the response of the mother. She had authority over her son, and she was strong in the Lord. She knew what to do. Even though she was vexed in her spirit, she sought the man of God. Then even in his presence, she would not pronounce what was – that her son had died – but rather spoke of all being "well." Elisha perceived the vexation of her grief, and was compelled to help.

She clung to the prophet – the word of God in the earth – and they went back to her house where the boy was lying dead in Elisha's bed. Elisha shut himself in the room with the boy and prayed to the Lord. He was asking, "What do I do now, Lord?" At least that's what I think he was doing. And he apparently got an answer, because he systematically began to do some strange things. It would be unwise for us, I think, to take the physical actions of Elisha as a formula for raising the dead!

There's a lot of spiritual significance in this account,

but what we want to focus on is the sneezing in verse 35. One of the manifestations of an evil spirit leaving a person is sneezing. It is quite common for a person being loosed from a demon to sneeze.

The word "sneeze" in Hebrew means to diffuse, to turn aside, as a foreigner, and the implication is something strange or profane. Another implication is to commit adultery. Demons are foreigners who don't belong to us, or in us. They are strange and profane, and they cause us to commit spiritual adultery – which is idolatry. Satan doesn't really care what or whom we worship, as long as it isn't God. The devil wants us to turn our worship toward something - anything - but God.

Elisha demonstrated the love of God through his compassion for the woman and her son, and his obedience to following the direction of the Lord. The result was that whatever demonic forces were holding the boy in death were loosed from him. He literally sneezed out the devils that had been assigned to destroy him.

We can easily see that when God gives us something precious, the devil will come along to try to take it from us. Our response to God and to His ability will make the difference in whether or not the devil succeeds.

I Chronicles

"And Meonothai begat Ophrah: and Seraiah begat Joab, the father of the valley of Charashim; for they were craftsmen."
- 1 Chronicles 4:14

We have to admit this verse sent us searching. It was as if God was saying, "Let's see if you'll continue with this now!" It's one thing to have names and a contextual flow of scripture to go along with them to aid the understanding. It's quite another to have just names. First we traced the meanings of the names back to their root word meanings. What we found - in and of itself - was significant. But we needed to connect this verse, and we knew God had an intentional connection to the study as a whole. To find the spiritual significance of these names which would apply to our lives today, we had to go digging. Where else in Scripture did these names appear?

The first name, Meonothai, appears nowhere else in the Bible – only in this verse. There wasn't any great story of deliverance in which Meonothai participated. There was no mention of this person, except in this verse. The name Meonothai means "habitative." It is derived from a word which means, "abode of God, temple or tabernacle, retreat" and its base root word which means "dwell together, cohabitation, duty of marriage." This name, set apart and alone throughout the entire Bible, appeared almost as a theophany would appear. It's a plural word. It's a dwelling place of God, and it denotes a dwelling together in intimacy.

According to our verse, the offspring of Meonothai

(this dwelling together with God in intimacy) is Ophrah.

    Literally, the first meaning of Ophrah is female fawn (from its dusty color), and when you go back to the root words, you get a young roe or hart, and – this is a very interesting note – pulverize, be dust, cast dust, clay, earth and mud. In this verse of genealogy we see a symbolic connection between God and man. The dust of the earth being the dwelling place of God, a temple built without hands.

> *Mar 14:58 We heard him say, I will destroy this temple that is made with hands, and within three days I will build another made without hands.*

    There are several references in the Bible to the name Ophrah, and most are about the city of Ophrah, which was the home of Gideon. No problem making some deliverance connections there! We could draw a fair conclusion that Ophrah is representative of Gideon and the exploits relating to him. Truly, we could paint a very large canvas of connection between these two names and their meanings. The Spirit of God in the spirit of man, and so on. But I think one of the root words for Ophrah, "pulverize," is the one of greatest significance. There is a breaking, a crushing-to-powder of our soulish-ness that must take place in our lives for there to come forth the intimacy of cohabitation the Lord wants with us. We can't be His Bride when we're focused on ourselves, or on some other god.

    Here is a good example of this insight: After Gideon delivered Israel from the Midianites, the people wanted to make him ruler over them, but he said no, I won't do it and neither will my son. The Lord is your ruler. Gideon took the earrings of the conquered, which the Israelites willingly gave him, and made an ephod. He took it back to Ophrah and rather than being merely a symbol of God's victory, the ephod itself became a god to the people.

> *Jdg 8:27 And Gideon made an ephod thereof, and put it in his city, even in Ophrah: and all Israel went thither a whoring after it: which thing became a snare unto Gideon, and to his house.*

Another revelation in this genealogy of the 4:14 verse is found in the meaning of the other names, and in the reference to the valley of Charashim (craftsmen). Seraiah begat Joab. Seraiah means JAH has prevailed! It is a combination of two Hebrew words, one meaning father and the other JAH, the sacred name of the Lord, "most vehement." There are several Seraiahs in the Bible, but the others are named as sons of someone other than Kenaz. Again, the name is the focus, not the circumstance.

Joab means "Jehovah-fathered," and like Seraiah is a combination of two Hebrew words, father and the self-existent One. From a spiritual viewpoint, Joab can be said to be representative of our faith. When the Lord prevails, and He always does, our faith toward Him comes forth and grows. And in faith toward God is freedom. Faith is also a tool we use in the spirit to accomplish the works of God. And faith worketh by love. We have once again come full circle. It all comes back to the love of God.

Now let's look at this valley of craftsmen. The valley of Charashim mentioned in this verse - I Chronicles 4:14 - is the same as the valley of Ono, according to Nehemiah 11:35. The word "craftsmen" translates: fabricator of any material, artificer, carpenter, craftsman, engraver, maker, mason, skilful, smith, worker, workman, such as wrought."

It also means, "scratch, engrave, plough, fabricate, devise." A craftsman takes a material and creates something with it. It takes work, and it takes skill, to produce a new thing. God is the Master Craftsman, and from Him we receive the gifts and talents we need to take the materials we have and make something useful for His purpose.

Exo 31:1 And the LORD spake unto Moses, saying,

Exo 31:2 See, I have called by name Bezaleel the son of Uri, the son of Hur, of the tribe of Judah:

Exo 31:3 And I have filled him with the spirit of God, in wisdom, and in understanding, and in knowledge, and in all manner of workmanship,

Exo 31:4 To devise cunning works, to work in gold, and in silver, and in brass,

Exo 31:5 And in cutting of stones, to set them, and in carving of timber, to work in all manner of workmanship.

Exo 31:6 And I, behold, I have given with him Aholiab, the son of Ahisamach, of the tribe of Dan: and in the hearts of all that are wise hearted I have put wisdom, that they may make all that I have commanded thee;

A craftsman who is in his course in God, strategically positioned to advance the kingdom, is the one God will fill with His Spirit "in wisdom, and in understanding, and in knowledge, and in all manner of workmanship," in order to accomplish the plan of God. This is just another aspect of what can we glean and understand about this 4:14 reference. We have a responsibility and a part in the plan of God. He is our portion, and we are His.

In summary: In the name Meonothai, we can see God as our refuge, our dwelling place; and at the same time we see man meant to be the dwelling place of God. The Lord wants to join Himself to a Bride who will enter the duty of marriage – intimacy – with Him.

In Ophrah, we see the dusty, carnal man who must be pulverized and the dust cast off. The snare of our soulish desires will keep us in the dust, and make us unusable to the Lord. We can't be His craftsmen when we're busy making and worshipping images that are abominable to Him.

But praise God – JAH has prevailed! In the name Seraiah is the delivering God who has already prevailed and brought forth faith to carry us out of the dust and to cast the dust off of us! He makes us His craftsmen when we have turned our tools and our ways of doing things over to Him and ceased from trying to create our own thing. Then He returns to us the tools we need to create for His purpose and in His perfect plan, advancing His kingdom and not ours.

Is this deliverance? I'd say so. There is rest, peace and freedom in joining our prevailing God in His work of restoring all creation. Part of that restoration process is the purging and cleansing of our own souls.

Father God, I thank You for showing me Your greatness and Your love in so many ways. Lord, Help me realize my responsibility to work with You; and give me the willingness to yield to You every area and aspect of my life… so that I can rest in You, and also provide a suitable dwelling place for Your presence. I give You the sacrifice of thanksgiving and praise, Lord, and declare that You alone are God. There is no other. Father I ask Your correction where I need to be corrected, that I may have pure motives in my heart as I come alongside Your ministers with my support and service. Give me Your heart on the matter, Lord, whatever the matter is. Thank You for weaving such depth of meaning into Your Word, and giving me the understanding to apply Your wisdom into my life. To become the craftsmen You meant for me to be, not crafting my own plans, but joining You in Yours. Lord, get me out of the iniquity of pressing ahead without You, making plans without You and then asking You to bless me and join me in what I'm doing. Forgive me, Lord, for my independence and rebellion, and make me fully Yours. Develop the gifts and talents You've put within me, Lord, and direct them to Your purposes only. I declare today I want to be all of me – the me You created before the foundation of the world – completely immersed in all of You. AMEN.

BRASS
LAVER : Wash in the WORD

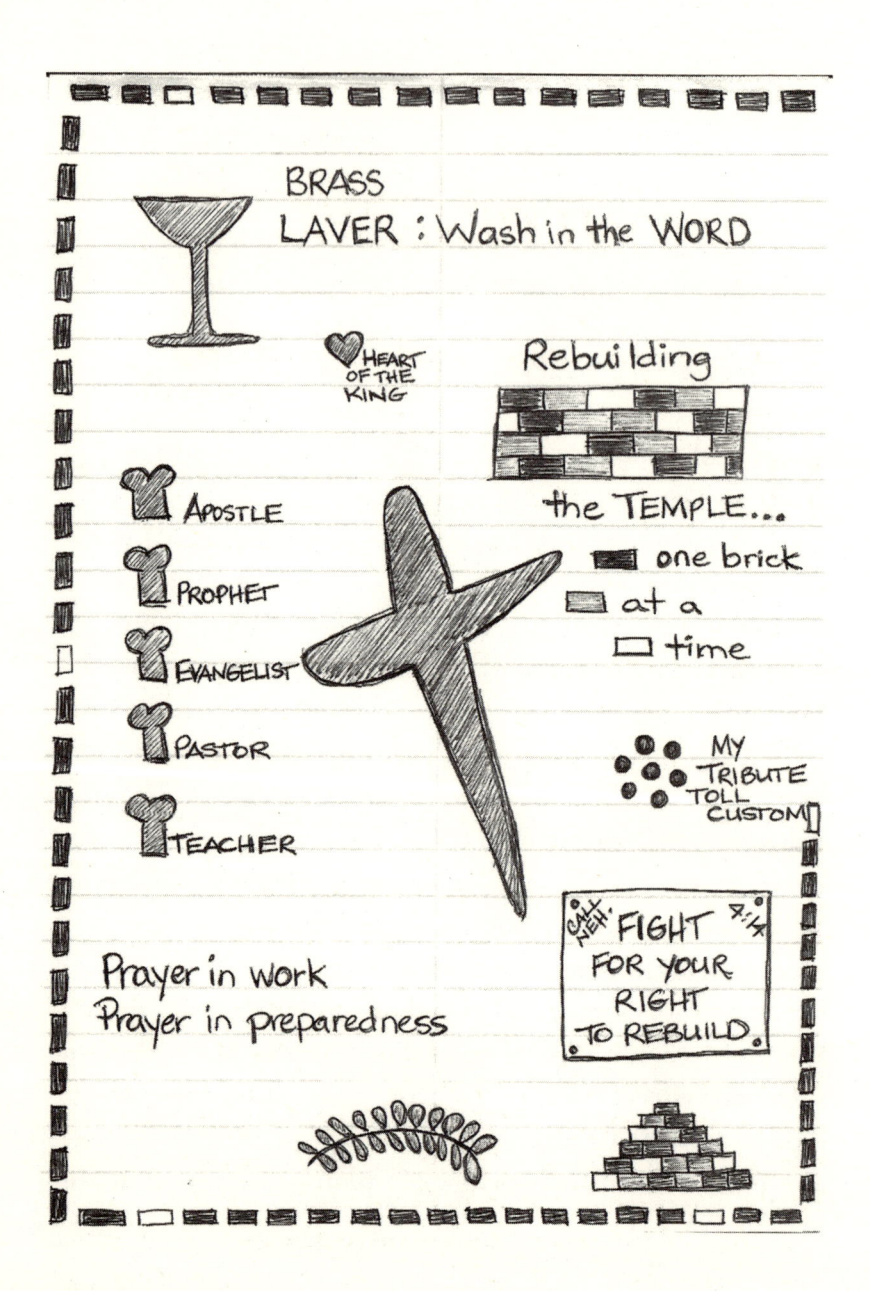

♥ HEART OF THE KING

Rebuilding the TEMPLE...

🍞 APOSTLE
🍞 PROPHET
🍞 EVANGELIST
🍞 PASTOR
🍞 TEACHER

▪ one brick
▬ at a
☐ time

MY TRIBUTE TOLL CUSTOM

Prayer in work
Prayer in preparedness

CALL NEXT FIGHT FOR YOUR RIGHT TO REBUILD

II Chronicles

"He made also bases, and lavers made he upon the bases;"
                                           - II Chronicles 4:14

Here in II Chronicles, King Solomon has commissioned workers to construct the temple and we are getting a picture of the magnificence of it. Solomon was fulfilling the dream that was in his father David's heart - the dream to build a house for the Lord. And of all the things to be highlighted and examined concerning Solomon's Temple, our study verse features the laver. So let's look at it briefly, with the understanding of its place in the process of moving into the Most Holy Place, which symbolizes entering into the "rest" of God, and also its function as it relates to the priesthood.

In the old covenant, the first step in the process of sanctification began at the altar of sacrifice, where the animal was killed. We saw in Numbers 4:14 the vessels, or tools, used in the sacrifice and how these instruments were to be packed up and carried along whenever the camp moved. There is a preparation for transition as we begin moving deeper into the things of God. The comparison of these instruments and the elements of our soul is a wonderful insight into one of the aspects of our responsibility to appropriate the freedom Jesus died to give us.

The next step in the progression toward the Holy Place is the laver. So here again, we see God connecting elements in Scripture to reinforce His love for us and His desire to have us be completely free to love Him. After the sacrifice is made, the priests had to wash up before entering the Holy Place, where the table was set with the shewbread, and the candlestick burned. The laver was made of brass, which speaks of judgment. We are commissioned to judge ourselves, to examine our hearts and rid ourselves of unclean thoughts and desires.

How do we do that? Again, the answer lies in the Bible's symbolisms. The laver was filled with water, which symbolizes the living Word. As the priests washed in water, we, the new covenant priests, are washed in the water of the word. The Lord cleanses His church, the Bride, by His word.

Eph 5:25 Husbands, love your wives, even as Christ also loved the church, and gave himself for it;

Eph 5:26 That he might sanctify and cleanse it with the washing of water by the word,

Eph 5:27 That he might present it to himself a glorious church, not having spot, or wrinkle, or any such thing; but that it should be holy and without blemish.

Joh 15:3 Now ye are clean through the word which I have spoken unto you.

The Word of God reproves us. It examines us. It instructs us. And just as the laver was not an optional piece of furniture in the temple, and the cleansing not an optional action of the priests, neither is the Bible to be an optional coffee table book in our homes and the reading of it an optional action in our lives. Scripture is the laver of the new covenant priests – you and me.

2Ti 3:16 All Scripture is given by inspiration of God, and is profitable for doctrine, for reproof, for correction, for instruction in righteousness:

2Ti 3:17 That the man of God may be perfect, thoroughly furnished unto all good works.

The cleansing that results from the washing of water by the word is another level of deliverance and "furnishes" us unto good works. That is the consequence – we are equipped for our destiny in the Kingdom, provided with all we need to accomplish our purpose in God and the advancement of HIS agenda, not ours.

Cleansing produces a sending. If we read the verse following, we see that Solomon had the laver put atop brass oxen. The bases that held the laver were these oxen.

2Ch 4:14 He made also bases, and lavers made he upon the bases;

2Ch 4:15 One sea, and twelve oxen under it.

These 12 oxen were not randomly placed as the pedestal of the laver. Twelve denotes government in Biblical imagery. Three oxen faced in each direction – north, south, east and west. Three is God's number for completion or fullness. Oxen often typify ministers or workers. Knowing the nuances and symbols God used to reveal Himself and His Word, this laver in Solomon's Temple speaks of the gospel – the living Word of God – going forth in fullness to the world. It goes out in every direction, carried by willing workers.

Certainly the Word of God is a delivering word. It frees us from sin, sickness, poverty and death as we allow ourselves to be washed in its living water. As we judge ourselves and examine our hearts, we can bathe in the living water of His word and be cleansed of all unrighteousness.

1Jo 1:9 If we confess our sins, he is faithful and just to forgive us our sins, and to cleanse us from all unrighteousness.

2Co 7:1 Having therefore these promises, dearly beloved, let us cleanse ourselves from all filthiness of the flesh and spirit, perfecting holiness in the fear of God.

Lord, I just take a moment right now to wash in this delivering word, Your laver of righteousness, Jesus Christ. Thank You for taking my burdens, generational curses, and the familiar spirits that would steal my peace and prosperity. Thank You for removing reproach and shame from my life as I judge and cleanse myself of all filthiness of the flesh and spirit.

Ezra

"Now because we have maintenance from the king's palace, and it was not meet for us to see the king's dishonor, therefore have we sent and certified the king;" - *Ezra 4:14*

As we dig into this verse, we find the message of balance between God's sovereignty and man's responsibility as a key element in our deliverance is continued. Again, we go to the context of the verse to find out what is going on here. The background is this: The Israelites are in the process of rebuilding the temple, and they have adversaries who are working to prevent that from happening.

This is a verse that explains, in part, the motivation of people who oppose the work of God. When we go about to accomplish something, to build and restore the things of God in our lives, there will always be those who don't understand and who will go about to stop what we're doing. Certainly, this is true when it comes to our freedom. There are people in our lives who like things the way they are – they don't want any changes that are not their own idea or changes that won't benefit them directly.

At first, these adversaries tried to join in the work. Look at it from the beginning of the chapter:

Ezr 4:1 Now when the adversaries of Judah and Benjamin heard that the children of the captivity built the temple unto the LORD God of Israel;

Ezr 4:2 Then they came to Zerubbabel, and to the chief of the fathers, and said unto them, Let us build with you: for we seek your God, as ye do; and we do sacrifice unto him since the days of Esar-haddon king of Assur, which brought us up hither.

Ezr 4:3 But Zerubbabel, and Jeshua, and the rest of the chief of the fathers of Israel, said unto them, Ye have nothing to do with us to build a house unto our God; but we ourselves together will build unto the LORD God of Israel, as king Cyrus the king of Persia hath commanded us.

When they were refused, these people began a systematic campaign to stop the building process. The word says they "weakened the hands of the people of Judah and troubled them." I think that means they found every possible way to aggravate and frustrate the effort. And this went on for many, many years, through the reign of several kings. Their subversive actions were both overt and covert, and culminated in a letter to King Artaxerxes accusing the Jews of undermining his reign.

Ezr 4:9 Then wrote Rehum the chancellor, and Shimshai the scribe, and the rest of their companions; the Dinaites, the Apharsathchites, the Tarpelites, the Apharsites, the Archevites, the Babylonians, the Susanchites, the Dehavites, and the Elamites,

Ezr 4:10 And the rest of the nations whom the great and noble Asnappar brought over, and set in the cities of Samaria, and the rest that are on this side the river, and at such a time.

The instigators of evil against the Jews gathered together different people from surrounding nations to thwart and delay the plan of God in the nation of Israel. That happens today, both in the natural and in the spirit realm. Someone is always stirring up trouble whenever there is a building up of God's people. Have you ever noticed how easily we fall into gossip and how quickly we can fall in line with a word of condemnation? The devil has trained most of us so well that it's comfortable for us to be swept up into a lynch-mob mentality. In this chapter of Ezra, all these nations banded together against the plan of God.

And how was their evil purpose accomplished? By speaking slander and instilling doubt in the mind of the king. Doubt about the character and intent of the Jews.

Ezr 4:12 Be it known unto the king, that the Jews which came up from thee to us are come unto Jerusalem, building the rebellious and the bad city, and have set up the walls thereof, and joined the foundations.

Ezr 4:13 Be it known now unto the king, that, if this city be built, and the walls set up again, then will they not pay toll, tribute, and custom, and so thou shalt endamage the revenue of the kings.

You need to know, King, that these are rebellious people – they have a history that doesn't look good. They've done some stuff. If you let them rebuild their hometown, things are not going to be good for you – they'll stop paying taxes and all those fees that keep your kingdom running.

That brings us to our featured verse, where the underlying motivation for the persecution is made clear. Because we receive our livelihood from your kingdom, it would be terrible for us to see you impoverished due to lack of tax and fee and customs revenue, so we're here to straighten you out about these Jews. If you don't believe us, go look it up for yourself – you'll see how they rebelled in times past and caused harm. They'll just do it again if you don't stop them.

Our 4:14 verse reveals the battle of the past, how the devil uses our past sins against us. How he moves people to judge us for who they think we are based on our past actions and attitudes, and how this kind of witchcraft works to delay fulfillment of the plan and purposes of God in our lives. But be not deceived, God is not mocked. His plan and purposes will surely come to pass, as they did in this instance, even though it was some years later that the temple in Jerusalem was rebuilt. This 4:14 verse closely correlates with the next one (in the Book of Nehemiah), where the victory is proclaimed. The study verse in Ezra and the one in Nehemiah should be connected as a natural course, so look at them together.

Nehemiah

"And I looked, and rose up, and said unto the nobles, and to the rulers, and to the rest of the people, Be not ye afraid of them: remember the Lord, which is great and terrible, and fight for your brethren, your sons, and your daughters, your wives, and your houses." - Nehemiah 4:14

We are in the same era as Ezra, and many Biblical scholars believe the books of Ezra and Nehemiah were actually one book and should not have been separated into two. That's not for us to debate, and it isn't the focus of this study, just a bit of information that may help connect what's happening. If you go back and read from chapter one in Nehemiah, you discover Nehemiah served Artaxerxes in the palace and was favored by this king. Nehemiah was also an intercessor and prayed to the God of Heaven for favor on Jerusalem. He was grieved about the broken down condition of this beloved place.

In Ezra, we see the natural plot to stop the plan, of God and in Nehemiah we see the spiritual answer. Nehemiah's prayer penetrated heaven. Can God intervene at any time and for any reason? Yes, He can. Will He do that? Not likely. We are to work with the Lord. Why do we expect God to do the heavy lifting when we aren't even willing to show up at the job site?

Again, there is a balance between God's sovereignty and man's responsibility. We can stay in our stuff, looking at what we see in our lives and the lives of others instead of seeing the vision of what we know to be true; or we can begin to penetrate heaven – step into a place in God where the unseen becomes our reality. Here's a truth that will change your life, if you let it: We have to bring God something He can respond to. If God responded to our need, there would not be a Christian on the planet that needed anything!

God responds to many things, among them... faith, prayer and love for others, worship, praise, obedience, and His Word. Nehemiah sent up a prayer of deliverance for Jerusalem from a pure heart of love for his people and his land, and not to advance any personal agenda. God heard Nehemiah's prayer and turned the heart of Artaxerxes to allow the rebuilding to resume.

Pro 21:1 The king's heart is in the hand of the LORD, as the rivers of water: he turneth it whithersoever he will.

Nehemiah returned to Jerusalem to encourage the people to rebuild, and to oversee the work. There was still plenty of opposition from surrounding nations, and we can see their ridicule and Nehemiah's response in chapter two. Lots of tension is evident between these people groups.

Neh 2:19 But when Sanballat the Horonite, and Tobiah the servant, the Ammonite, and Geshem the Arabian, heard it, they laughed us to scorn, and despised us, and said, What is this thing that ye do? will ye rebel against the king?

Neh 2:20 Then answered I them, and said unto them, The God of heaven, he will prosper us; therefore we his servants will arise and build: but ye have no portion, nor right, nor memorial, in Jerusalem.

As the work progressed, the threats of the enemy became bolder and more frequent. At the same time, intercession grew stronger. Ridicule from other nations was overcome by prayer and work. The people were united in their efforts, they had one mind – to accomplish the purpose and will of God.

Neh 4:6 So built we the wall; and all the wall was joined together unto the half thereof: for the people had a mind to work.

Notice that prayer is with purpose, and faith has a following. The purpose of prayer is to touch heaven, to bring the presence of God into the situation; and the following of faith is action. If your prayer doesn't move you, it won't move God. We are co-laborers with God. We can't do it on our own, but we shouldn't expect things to just "happen" either.

There are times to stand and see the salvation of God, and there are times to bring it into reality by our actions. Here, as the Jews went about their work in spite of ridicule and threats, trusting in God to protect them from their enemies, the enemies grew in number and power. They were incensed against the Jews and formed a coalition of conspiracy to war. Again, prayer and preparedness overcame the threat.

Neh 4:9 Nevertheless we made our prayer unto our God, and set a watch against them day and night, because of them.

The Jews in Jerusalem set a watch around the clock. They made themselves ready to face the enemy and not be taken in surprise. We need to do that. The Lord does not want us ignorant of the enemy's devices. We need to be watchful over our lives, our words, our actions and our attitudes that the enemy of our soul cannot overtake and invade us. "Watch and pray" – I think that means not only to watch for outside forces, but for those that would rise up from within our own hearts to condemn us.

1Jo 3:20 For if our heart condemn us, God is greater than our heart, and knoweth all things.

As if it isn't enough to have an enemy coming after us, from within and without; those who are considered "friend," the ones we think should uphold and stand with us, begin to fall victim to the "walk by sight." Here in Nehemiah we read that the Jews who lived in outlying areas began to "warn" their brothers of their impending doom.

Neh 4:12 And it came to pass, that when the Jews which dwelt by them came, they said unto us ten times, From all places whence ye shall return unto us they will be upon you.

Neh 4:13 Therefore set I in the lower places behind the wall, and on the higher places, I even set the people after their families with their swords, their spears, and their bows.

    It is still true today, as it was with Nehemiah, that there will always be those around you to let you know how bad things look for you; and telling you once is not enough. Their Jewish brothers who lived nearby told the rebuilders 10 times, over and over and over again, "They're going to get you!" But Nehemiah responded with greater preparation, and with words of encouragement.

    That's what he did in the 4:14 verse. Let's read it again: "And I looked, and rose up, and said to the nobles, and to the rulers, and to the rest of the people, Be you not afraid of them; remember the Lord, which is great and terrible, and fight for your brethren, your sons, and your daughters, and your houses."

    In other words, when we have our focus on the Conqueror, we can fight without fear because He is with us. But we must fight! Nehemiah goes on to tell us in verse 15 God brought the counsel of the enemy to naught – the threats of the enemy fell on deaf ears. There is a great lesson to be learned from this. When we refuse to listen to the enemy, he cannot hinder us. It is only when we agree with the evil word of fear that we are subject to it!

    Does this mean we foolishly lumber our way into whatever is ahead of us? No. It means we prepare for the worst natural circumstance and trust in the Lord to guide us and deliver us from the evil one. Sometimes we may have to go through some stuff, but we never go through it alone. God is always with us, when we step into Him. When we listen to the voice and Word of the Living God, the enemy cannot hinder us. When we listen to the voice and the word of the devil, we get to live in the curses of doing it our own way, and trying to preserve our own lives.

Pro 1:29 *For that they hated knowledge, and did not choose the fear of the LORD:*

Pro 1:30 *They would none of my counsel: they despised all my reproof.*

Pro 1:31 *Therefore shall they eat of the fruit of their own way, and be filled with their own devices.*

Pro 1:32 *For the turning away of the simple shall slay them, and the prosperity of fools shall destroy them.*

Pro 1:33 *But whoso hearkeneth unto me shall dwell safely, and shall be quiet from fear of evil.*

This is what Nehemiah is saying to the people – Be not afraid, remember the Lord. Hearken to His counsel and not the words of your own heart. Not the words of the people around you. Not the words of the enemy that would destroy you. Remember the Lord. Be not afraid. If we remember the Lord, we dwell in safety. We are free of fear of evil. It's a choice, and often when things are looking really bad, we need to make a conscious and conscientious effort to put our minds on God and His goodness. That's where the victory lies.

Isa 26:3 *Thou wilt keep him in perfect peace, whose mind is stayed on thee: because he trusteth in thee.*

Isa 26:4 *Trust ye in the LORD forever: for in the LORD JEHOVAH is everlasting strength:*

The verses in Ezra 4:14 and Nehemiah 4:14 flow together. They tell of the same circumstance, and they point out both the problem and the solution. When we read them together this becomes clear.

Ezr 4:14 Now because we have maintenance from the king's palace, and it was not meet for us to see the king's dishonor, therefore have we sent and certified the king;

Neh 4:14 And I looked, and rose up, and said unto the nobles, and to the rulers, and to the rest of the people, Be not ye afraid of them: remember the Lord, which is great and terrible, and fight for your brethren, your sons, and your daughters, your wives, and your houses.

The enemy uses people around us in his attempt to thwart the plan of God for our lives. He wants to render useless the gifts and talents and abilities God has placed within us, by whatever means necessary. Maybe there are people in your life who feel if you succeed they'll lose something, so they use manipulation and lies of the devil to bring up your past… one more time. That seems to be the case in Ezra. The trouble started because those who are self-focused feared loss.

There seems to be a pervasive attitude in the church today that says, "If you get something, it might take away from what I'm getting. If you succeed in your ministry, it might take something away from mine." This is destructive thinking that can destroy both the one with the attitude and the one to whom the attitude is directed. It's been proven over and over again that you can never make yourself look good by making someone else look bad. It might seem to work for a season, but then it falls apart.

There are lots of self-appointed apostles who are not sent, and are not sending others. Jesus divided Himself into five loaves – apostle, prophet, evangelist, pastor, and teacher. I believe He meant for every one of us to partake of Him and to be released into our purpose in Him in some area of His ministry. Not necessarily as a fulfill time vocation, but as a fulfillment of personal destiny within His Corporate Body. When we thwart the purpose of God in someone else, we are attacking the Body of Christ. Ouch.

I think most of us have probably been on both sides of these verses at one time or another, which may be why God has it as a part of this study in deliverance. We need to be loosed from the idea that someone else's ministry gift or calling will somehow diminish ours. And we need to be bound to the truth of the Word of God, that although we battle, we have already won. There is no place for fear in our lives.

The message of deliverance we get in Ezra and Nehemiah is first of all a deliverance from ourselves and our own selfish wants and desires that prevent us from embracing others in the Body of Christ in what they are doing. And it is a message that the Lord's presence as our Deliverer is the strength we need, providing the power to fight and to continue in the work He has wrought for us. In Him, we can push through the conspiracies, the threats of war, the ridicule and the opposition of the enemy.

I've included yet another prayer of deliverance that will free you and release you with renewed boldness to accomplish the work God has put in your heart to advance His kingdom. Maybe you don't even know what that is, but you can ask and believe God to bring you into it, to begin the rebuilding process of that which has been torn down and burned, that which looks destroyed and without hope. Our God is a God of hope. He is the Deliverer.

I encourage you to speak the following prayer out loud, and make a confession of faith that may rid you of some stuff that has held you back.

Father God, I come to You right now in the precious name of the Lord Jesus Christ, and I thank you again for this opportunity to cleanse myself from filthiness of the flesh and spirit in the laver of Your Living Word, Jesus Christ. As an act of my will I choose to forgive all those who have thwarted me in my walk with You and have been a part of preventing me from fulfilling my purpose in You and the destiny You put within me. I forgive my family, my friends, leaders in the church, coworkers, anyone at all, Lord, who has spoken against me, who has been used by the devil to steal my joy or my vision, who has been used to tear down what You meant for me to have, the place in You where I am meant to dwell. I forgive and release them now in Jesus name from responsibility for any curse that has attached itself to me. I take those curses now and I give them to the Lord Jesus Christ, who is my curse bearer.

And Lord, I recognize I have done the same thing to others. I repent to You, Father, for any time I knowingly or unknowingly thwarted Your plan and purpose for my brother or sister by my words of discouragement, manipulation, envy, or fear. I am sorry, Lord, that I allowed the lie of the devil to take authority from me, and to rule my life in ungodly ways. Please forgive me, Father, for any harm I have caused in Your Body, and cleanse my heart from fear of loss. Help me realize that when I help others succeed in their purpose in You, I succeed in mine.

Father, forgive me for believing the lie of the devil and putting aside Your word for my life and the vision You gave me. Bring it back, Lord, and give me the courage to walk in it, to fight for it, to remember You and keep my focus on You. I repent of allowing the devil to hinder me, and I ask to be delivered from all fear, discouragement, envy, manipulation and every other unholy thing that has pervaded my attitude or my actions.

    In the name of the Lord Jesus Christ, I utterly break agreement with spirits of fear, discouragement, witchcraft and rebellion, manipulation and control, envy and jealousy, and I declare I don't want these things in my life. I will not participate with them, I will not allow myself to be used by them against others, and I will not allow them access to me through my taking offense when they use others against me. Free me, Lord God, as only You can do. I want to work effectively in Your Kingdom. I want to move into the vision, the destiny and the purpose You have put within me, unencumbered by the things of world, the opinions of others, or the fear of man. I declare that the blood of the Lord Jesus Christ is all powerful and effective to free me from these ungodly things, Lord, and I receive what You have for me. AMEN

    If you prayed this prayer, it's a good idea to spend the next 15-20 minutes or more praising God for what He's done for you, and ask Him to fill you with more of Him. Ask Him to grow every fruit of His Holy Spirit in you in greater measure… love, joy, peace, patience, faith, gentleness, goodness, meekness and self-control. Fill up your heart with thanksgiving and your mind with His word - that is how you will keep the deliverance you've experienced!

I am born for a specific purpose!!!

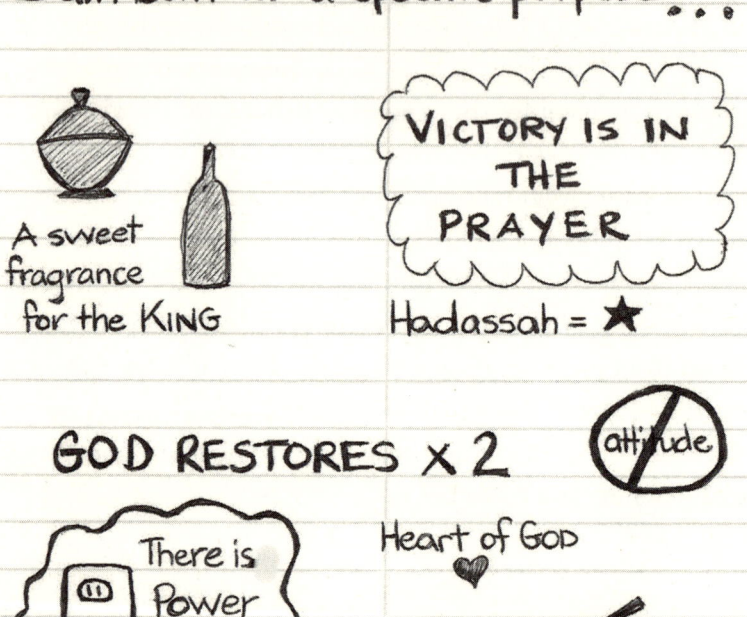

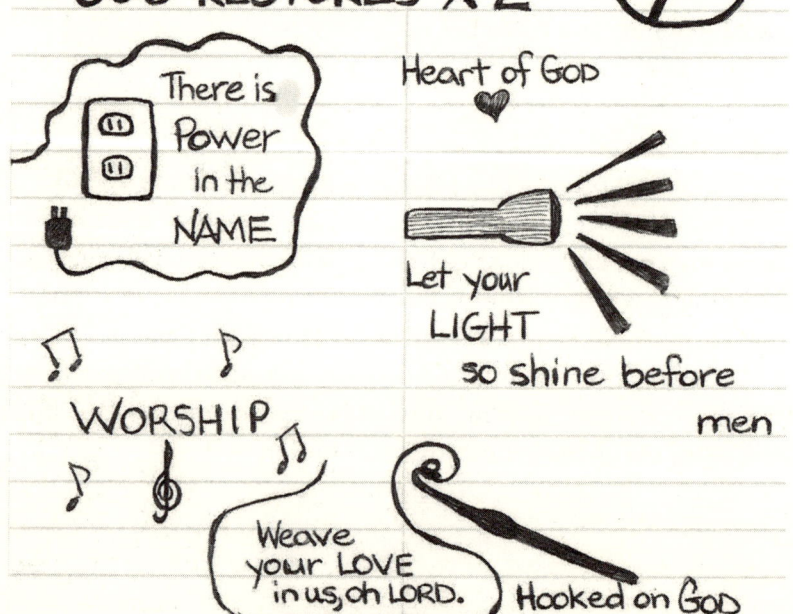

A sweet fragrance for the KING

VICTORY IS IN THE PRAYER

Hadassah = ★

GOD RESTORES × 2

🚫 attitude

There is Power in the NAME

Heart of God ♥

Let your LIGHT so shine before men

♪ ♪ WORSHIP ♪

Weave your LOVE in us, oh LORD.

Hooked on God

Esther

"For if you altogether hold your peace at this time, then shall there enlargement and deliverance arise to the Jews from another place; but you and your father's house shall be destroyed: and who knows whether you are come to the kingdom for such a time as this?" - Esther 4:14

This is actually one of the verses God spoke to me as a "4:14" reminder during those early days of wondering what He was trying to tell me to do. As I was studying – and I don't even remember what book I was reading at the time – this verse leaped off the page because of its Scripture reference. The author was exhorting his readers that each of us has a purpose in God, that each of us is born in God's time and for HIS purpose, that no birth and no life is accidental or incidental, and that each one of us must step into what God has for us, realizing no matter what it may look like around us, when we walk with Him we will walk into our destiny. And if we refuse to step out, we'll miss out.

This is one of the most powerful verses relating to deliverance, and our part in it, in all Scripture. "Who knows whether you are come to the kingdom for such a time as this?" In the story of Esther, King Ahasuerus, who reigned in Persia, held a great feast and called for his queen, Vashti, to be brought to him so he could show her off to the visiting princes and nobles of the 127 provinces he ruled. She refused to come, and so Ahasuerus asked, "What should be done to her?" His advisors pointed out that if the word got out to the provinces that the queen said "no" to the king and got away with it, it would set a precedent and all the wives would think they could do the same thing with their own husbands. So King Ahasuerus "dethroned" the queen. She was deposed and stripped of her royal privileges and forbidden to come before the king ever again.

Then a search was made throughout the land for beautiful young virgins, so that the king could choose a new queen. And these young women were rounded up and brought to the palace in Shushan. Among the virgins was a young Jewish girl named Hadassah. She was an orphan who was taken into the family of Mordecai after her parents' death. Hadassah was Mordecai's uncle's daughter, so they were actually cousins, and Mordecai worked in the palace. Scripture indicates that although they were of the tribe of Benjamin, their Jewish heritage was not openly known. When the palace guards were gathering young virgins, they spotted Hadassah, who was fair and beautiful, and whisked her away. Mordecai advised her not to reveal her heritage, and she became known as Esther, which is a name of Persian origin rather than Hebrew.

In short, Esther had great favor with Hegai, the eunuch who kept the virgins and helped them prepare for their night with the king. Once a virgin was taken in to the king, she became his concubine and was more or less kept in ward until such time as the king called for her, by name, again. That might never happen.

We can gain so much insight from Esther. First of all, we have an idea in our heads as to what life is supposed to be like, and then circumstances don't turn out the way we think. I don't have a doubt that little Hadassah had no desire to be orphaned. And after she was taken in by Mordecai, she probably had thoughts of marrying a nice Jewish boy and having a few children and maybe raise some goats or something. It may have been exciting to be chosen to audition for the position of queen, but I think it was probably more than a little disconcerting to be taken away from all she knew and loved. Esther not only adjusted, she prospered; and she prospered because she listened to instruction. Hegai, the eunuch and keeper of the king's women, symbolizes the Holy Spirit; and Esther listened to what he had to say.

Esther had to be prepared to meet the king. So do we. Esther underwent months of bathing and soaking in oils to soften her and infuse fragrance into her very being. Each one of the oils is representative of an aspect of our cleansing and sanctification. Esther went through the extensive preparation process and when it became time for her to go in to the king, she sought the advice of Hegai. Every one of the virgins was given the opportunity to adorn herself in whatever she wanted from the king's treasury for her big night, but Esther used wisdom and asked Hegai what to do. She gave us an example – to follow only the leading of the Holy Spirit - and she found favor with the king. Esther was made queen in Vashti's place, still keeping her Jewish heritage a secret.

The plot thickens as Mordecai overhears a conspiracy to take the king's life. He relates what he has heard to Queen Esther, who tells the king; and the conspirators were hanged. This is a significant piece that I believe relates directly to the 4:14 verse, so let's read it.

Est 2:17 And the king loved Esther above all the women, and she obtained grace and favor in his sight more than all the virgins; so that he set the royal crown upon her head, and made her queen instead of Vashti.

Est 2:18 Then the king made a great feast unto all his princes and his servants, even Esther's feast; and he made a release to the provinces, and gave gifts, according to the state of the king.

Est 2:19 And when the virgins were gathered together the second time, then Mordecai sat in the king's gate.

Est 2:20 Esther had not yet showed her kindred nor her people; as Mordecai had charged her: for Esther did the commandment of Mordecai, like as when she was brought up with him.

Est 2:21 In those days, while Mordecai sat in the king's gate, two of the king's chamberlains, Bigthan and Teresh, of those which kept the door, were wroth, and sought to lay hand on the king Ahasuerus.

Est 2:22 And the thing was known to Mordecai, who told it unto Esther the queen; and Esther certified the king thereof in Mordecai's name.

Est 2:23 And when inquisition was made of the matter, it was found out; therefore they were both hanged on a tree: and it was written in the book of the chronicles before the king.

In the next turn of events, King Ahasuerus elevated a man named Haman to a very high position in the kingdom – he was essentially second in command, over all the princes of the provinces – and the king commanded that the people bow before Haman. I think we all know that this kind of power is not something that many people can handle in humility. Haman certainly couldn't.

So here was Mordecai, a good Jew who would bow to no other god, being told to prostrate himself, along with the others who served in the palace, to this man Haman; and he wouldn't do it. Everybody was asking, why don't you do this thing? And Mordecai finally revealed that he was a Jew. The other palace staff members straightway told Haman, and in his wrath, Haman thought to punish not just Mordecai, but all Jews throughout all the provinces. He convinced the king that these people, the Jews, were a detriment to society and should be wiped out. King Ahasuerus gave Haman permission to do whatever he wanted; and Haman had a decree of destruction written against the Jews and sealed it with the king's seal.

Est 3:12 Then were the king's scribes called on the thirteenth day of the first month, and there was written according to all that Haman had commanded unto the king's lieutenants, and to the governors that were over every province, and to the rulers of every people of every province according to the writing thereof, and to every people after their language; in the name of king Ahasuerus was it written, and sealed with the king's ring.

Est 3:13 And the letters were sent by posts into all the king's provinces, to destroy, to kill, and to cause to perish, all Jews, both young and old, little children and women, in one day, even upon the thirteenth day of the twelfth month, which is the month Adar, and to take the spoil of them for a prey.

Est 3:14 The copy of the writing for a commandment to be given in every province was published unto all people, that they should be ready against that day.

When Mordecai heard of the king's decree, he clothed himself in sackcloth and lamented before the king's gate; and Esther sent him clothes so he could enter the palace grounds, but Mordecai refused. She sent a servant to find out why Mordecai was so distressed, and the answer came back that a decree had been issued to destroy all the Jews and that she should go to the king and entreat him to save the lives of her people. Her answer to Mordecai was, "Hey, you know the rules – I can't go to the king unless I'm called or else I could be executed, and I've not been called for a month now!"

This is where we are in chapter four when Mordecai says, "Girl, you may be queen but don't think you'll survive this decree. You're one of us!" (That's paraphrase, of course.)

Est 4:13 Then Mordecai commanded to answer Esther, Think not with thyself that thou shalt escape in the king's house, more than all the Jews.

This brings us to our verse, which should be read again…
Est 4:14 For if thou altogether holdest thy peace at this time, then shall there enlargement and deliverance arise to the Jews from another place; but thou and thy father's house shall be destroyed: and who knoweth whether thou art come to the kingdom for such a time as this?

By digging out the meanings of the Hebrew words, and their root meanings, we can understand the deeper significance of what Mordecai is saying to his cousin. All we see on the surface of his word to Esther is a threat. "If you don't speak out, you're going to die but God will find another way to deliver us." But when we examine the deeper meanings of the words, we see the urgency of the moment, and we see the picture of Jesus that is woven into the Hebrew text. For instance, "hold your peace" has a double intensity that goes beyond the idea of just being silent. It implies fabricating ways to play dumb about something, about being totally deaf to what you hear... on purpose.

Pro 31:8 Open thy mouth for the dumb in the cause of all such as are appointed to destruction.

  Mordecai wanted Esther to speak up for her people, but even more than that he was crying out for deliverance for Esther herself. He wanted to see her step into the destiny and purpose for which God had put her into position to achieve. "At this time" carries an urgency in the word "time" but the really interesting definition is of the word "this" which is the feminine form of another Hebrew word that translates "lamb." That gives us cause to pause.
  We see two implications, one in the natural and the other in the spiritual. In the natural, Mordecai seems to be comparing the nation of Israel, the Jewish people, to a lamb about to be sacrificed. In the spiritual sense, we can see Jesus, the Lamb of God, as the Deliverer, and Esther as the vehicle He desires to use in this situation. Mordecai says, in essence, "God will give us breathing room (that's the translation of enlargement) and freedom by His Lamb."
  Esther probably saw herself as the lamb about to be sacrificed as she made the decision to go to the king. But notice this: she did not go without support. She and her maidens, and all the Jews in the city knocked on heaven's door through prayer and fasting to seek the favor of God on Esther when she approached the king uninvited and unannounced. We need to realize that when we are facing a mighty challenge in the natural, it's a good idea to seek intercessors to agree in prayer with us about the outcome.

But also notice this: once Esther decided to step into her destiny, she didn't worry about the outcome. She would leave that to God. "If I perish, I perish."

> Est 4:16 Go, gather together all the Jews that are present in Shushan, and fast ye for me, and neither eat nor drink three days, night or day: I also and my maidens will fast likewise; and so will I go in unto the king, which is not according to the law: and if I perish, I perish.

How many of us can come to the level of decisiveness in God where we can say, "Okay, Lord, I'll do this no matter what the outcome. I'll follow what you've laid out for me to do." Esther realized she had been put in a position of power for a reason, and Mordecai points out – this is probably why you are where you are, Hadassah. There are many, many words that can be translated "know" and another interesting note about "who" and "whether," as in "who knows whether."

This last part of the 4:14 verse could easily be translated this way: "Would God! we can observe and recognize that Lo! you have been placed in a position of authority and dominion for the benefit of others and not yourself, to become a living sacrifice for God's people." That's a powerful observation that flows in the general theme of deliverance and builds on the foundations laid in Ezra and Nehemiah concerning the corporate application of deliverance and how we have a responsibility within the Body to defend and uphold and deliver our brothers and sisters in Christ. It's not about us and what we want – it's about HIM and what He wants. And He wants His creation, all of creation, to be free.

God took Hadassah, an orphaned Jewish girl and transformed her into Esther, a beloved and powerful queen. The one closest to the king. And He did it for His purpose, so that she would be in position to be used as deliverer. She was delivered, to be a deliverer!

Like Hadassah, we were taken out of our meager lives to be joined to the King. We were transformed. Esther's intimacy with the king made it possible to approach him, to make her request known and to see it fulfilled. Again, we learn of relationship with Christ as foundational to freedom. And our freedom is with purpose. It is a corporate purpose. As we make the decision to die to self, we can effect changes in the world around us. We can reach heaven with our prayers, and watch the hand of God move on our behalf and the behalf of those for whom we intercede. Listening to the instruction of the Holy Spirit, preparing and cleansing ourselves, submitting to the King, becoming intimate in our relationship with Him, fasting and prayer are all integral to our freedom. Who knows – would God! - that we all come into the knowledge of our destiny – that we step into God's purpose for our lives – to know that we know that we were born for such a time as now!

Job

"Fear came upon me, and trembling, which made all my bones to shake." - Job 4:14

As we go on in the 4:14 verses, we come to the Book of Job, and what appears at first to be yet another stumbling block to the primary theme of this work, which is God's heart and hand of deliverance, His great love and mercy to bring us freedom in every area of our lives. But as we examine this verse and the context of what's happening, we can see the Lord revealing wiles of the enemy, ways that the devil afflicts and affects us to prevent us from receiving from God, from stepping into our destiny and advancing His Kingdom. In this chapter, Job has already lost everything he had, including his health and his children. The enemy stripped him of his possessions and left him destitute and desolate and infirm. We should realize the devil had a right to do that, because of Job's fear. Fear broke down the hedge of protection that surrounded Job because of his uprightness with God.

The word tells us Job was a righteous man. Yet he allowed the spirit of fear to enter; and when it did, Satan had a legal right to afflict Job. II Timothy 1:7 tells us fear is more than an attitude of the mind, or a negative emotion; it is an evil spirit that is not given to us by God. When we actually read the word of God rather than depending on someone to tell us what it says, we see that God already knew Satan was working on Job and putting doubt into his heart. God questioned Satan, "Have you considered Job?" That translates, "Have you set your heart on Job?" The implication is, "I know what you're doing, Satan, because I can smell fear in the sacrifices Job is making to Me."

Because of Job's fear and doubt that his children might be transgressing against the Lord, the hedge of protection and favor around him had already been breached. Job never sinned outwardly, but the attitude of his heart was not pure in the sight of God. He worried, and he acted on his worry. He made sacrifices on behalf of his children, as if he not only suspected his children had been unfaithful in the things of God; but also, he expected them to. That left Job open and vulnerable to the attack of the enemy.

God restrained the devil from taking Job's life, but God didn't turn Job over to the devil. That's a religious idea. Let me repeat - it is a religious idea that God turned Job over to Satan, a conclusion born from carnal thinking brought in by an antichrist spirit. The antichrist spirit is one which causes man to attempt to understand the word of God by human reasoning rather than seeking the heart of God - the spirit of the word - revealed by His Holy Spirit. Trying to figure out what God means by using our own limited thinking always results in religion (tradition and legalism) that is void of relationship and love.

Even Job himself had the revelation that he had, in effect, brought on himself all the trouble he faced.

Job 3:25 *For the thing which I greatly feared is come upon me, and that which I was afraid of is come unto me.*

Job 3:26 *I was not in safety, neither had I rest, neither was I quiet; yet trouble came.*

Fear and faith are equal in the spirit realm in that they both project into the future, and they both demand to be fulfilled. In the verses you just read, Job admitted he was beyond uneasy, he didn't feel secure or relaxed. "I only thought I was doing all right with God, but I can see now that I opened a door to the devil." In spite of all his upright ways, Job was not truly trusting his Creator.

A lot of us are much the same way. We do all the right things because we reverence God, but we hold on to a nagging doubt that "everything's okay." We aren't really sure God is watching over us in a good way. We think we have to perform for Him, make sacrifices of good works to Him; when all He really wants is our love and trust. He is looking for people of worship and intimacy, people who will enter His presence, people who seek His face, not His hand.

In the religious view, this book of Job has been used to reinforce the idea that God is mean and cruel and a God of punishment. That's just not true. God is a God of judgment, but His judgments are always tempered with His mercy. So many of us in the Body of Christ have been taught that God punishes us for our transgressions. No, our transgressions open a door for the devil to afflict us, not God. We live in a cursed world, and when we choose the way of the world, we get to live in the midst of its curses. Going astray, stepping out from under God's umbrella of safety, precedes trouble.

Psa 119:67 Before I was afflicted I went astray: but now have I kept thy word.

When we repent of our sin, God is quick and faithful to forgive us and to restore us to righteousness, to cleanse us of all unrighteousness.

1Jo 1:9 If we confess our sins, he is faithful and just to forgive us our sins, and to cleanse us from all unrighteousness.

That does not mean there will not be an earthly consequence for committing an act of sin. If you sleep around and get pregnant out of wedlock, repentance takes away the sin, but not the pregnancy. If you're caught robbing a bank, repentance removes the sin, but not the prison sentence. When we love him, God in His great mercy will take every situation we've caused ourselves and turn it to our good.

No child is a mistake and God puts great purpose in those of us who were "inconvenient" to our parents. Being in prison is often a place of safety for many who would continue on a path of destruction unto death. It can be a wilderness experience where God can speak to people and put them back on track.

Our point is simply this: Job, by the attitude of his heart, opened the door for the afflictions he suffered. But we all know the end of the story – God redeemed Job and restored to him double what he had previously.

Let's not take the religious view that God punishes us. If our relationship with the Lord Jesus Christ is true, we must realize that God poured out all His wrath for sin on Jesus, so that we don't have to bear it. Our afflictions result from our stubborn insistence to go our own way and our ignorance of the voice of God. We hear voices – every body hears voices – and too many times we are listening to the wrong voice. Job listened to doubt and fear, and it caused tremendous devastation in his life.

After all this trouble and destruction comes on Job, his friends hear about it and come to comfort him. This is where we are in chapter four of the Book of Job. Job has declared "the thing I feared has come upon me," and he is lamenting of his very life when his friend Eliphaz just can't contain himself anymore and speaks out. This is the kind of friend we can do without in times of trouble, because Eliphaz is telling Job, "you're not so righteous, because if you were this wouldn't be happening to you. Isn't this God punishing you? These wicked things that have happened to you are because of your own wickedness."

Boy, that will make a person feel a lot better, won't it? These guys had come along to comfort Job, and instead they start right in judging him. We can see a similar thing in II Corinthians. Paul is upbraiding the church for their railing and ragging on the guy who messed up. Instead of encouraging and uplifting the one who erred, his brothers and sisters in the church made him feel worse.

2Co 2:6 Sufficient to such a man is this punishment, which was inflicted of many.

2Co 2:7 So that contrariwise ye ought rather to forgive him, and comfort him, lest perhaps such a one should be swallowed up with overmuch sorrow.

2Co 2:8 Wherefore I beseech you that ye would confirm your love toward him.

    Is there a truth in what Eliphaz was saying? Yes, but not the whole truth. The sin of Job was not an outward sin of action, it was one of attitude, as we said. And as Eliphaz continues, he reveals the source of his chastisement of Job.

Job 4:12 Now a thing was secretly brought to me, and mine ear received a little thereof.

Job 4:13 In thoughts from the visions of the night, when deep sleep falleth on men,

    I don't think Eliphaz even realized what he was saying. He was blinded by spiritual deception, a religious spirit, and seems to have believed what he received was from God. In the original language, "secretly brought" means to thieve or to deceive. Since we know God does not deceive, and Satan is the thief, the thing (the word) that Eliphaz heard in a dream and accepted was not from God. We further know this because in our study verse Eliphaz explains that the vision brought him fear.

Job 4:14 Fear came upon me, and trembling, which made all my bones to shake.

    Being afraid is the key that shows the hand of the devil at work. The enemy came to Eliphaz with a spirit of fear, and deceived him into believing the word he heard was from God. That's what happens to us. We take the word of the devil as a word from the Lord. Then we begin to accuse others, or withdraw into ourselves, or lose trust in God and start to think of our Creator as cruel and unloving.

How does that relate to deliverance and freedom? Does this verse teach us anything about our theme topic? Absolutely. It shows us how fear can rob us of faith and relationship and leave us with doubt and religion. We cannot be in faith and fear at the same time. It also teaches us that the devil will come to instill or empower fear while we are off guard, so to speak. Spirit never sleeps, and so dreams and night visions are received into our spirit. Like other thoughts, they are carried to the brain along the theta brain wave and processed. If our view of life is worldly and religious, they are processed to our detriment and the detriment of others. If our view of life is eternal and relational, we are able to process evil thoughts as evil and rid ourselves of them, to the benefit of ourselves and others.

The word tells us we can train our senses to discern both good and evil.

Heb 5:14 But strong meat belongeth to them that are of full age, even those who by reason of use have their senses exercised to discern both good and evil.

"Senses" refers to touch, taste, sight, smell and hearing. Those are all natural. If it's possible to train our natural, physical senses to that level of discernment, how much more can we train our spiritual senses by getting closer to God and to His heart? ...by listening to the Holy Spirit and not the spirit of the world?

Know this - we have the authority to rise up in the spirit while we sleep and take control of our dream life! In the spirit realm, you can actually change a dream from the devil. You can't change a God dream, but there is no need to have fear - at all. A God dream can be disturbing, but it will not cause you terror or panic or dread. Dreams will expose the plan of the devil. Even when you have an evil dream, there is God's mercy in it, because the devil will always show his hand.

You will not perish for lack of knowledge when you allow the Holy Spirit to interpret your dream, and not what you think you can figure out on your own, by the spirit of the world. When we use the psychic powers of the New Age, or the psychology of man to interpret dreams, we miss it. If you take the fear, you empower the fear and you get to live in it. If you take the knowledge, and use the wisdom of God you can live in the power of God.

From our study verse in Job, where Eliphaz is relating a spiritual encounter in the night, we learn that everything we dream is not from God, that well-meaning friends can be deceived, and that fear blocks freedom. Esther teaches us to depend on the Holy Spirit and Job shows us what happens when we don't.

Father, I come before You in thanksgiving for Your word and Your truth. Lord, make me know the season and the purpose of my life, that I can walk in the fullness of what You have for me! Send me a Mordecai to remind me of my position of power and authority because of my intimacy with the King of kings. Help me value my face-to-face relationship with You, Lord, and not to become complacent in my royal privileges and in the comforts I enjoy because of my place in Your Kingdom. Give me what I need, Lord, to make godly decisions, led only by Your Holy Spirit and not by the spirit of the world, and not by the voice of the enemy or my own stinking thinking.

Forgive me, Father, for those times I've disregarded Your message to me, when I've closed my ears and held my peace when You meant for me to speak out as Your oracle in the earth. I repent for holding on to my life and allowing fear to prevent me from stepping forth into my destiny. Forgive me, Father, for those times when I've brought a condemning word to a brother in distress, rather than uplifting him and expressing Your heart of love, Lord. Forgive me for listening to the voice of fear and spreading its vile corruption to my brothers and sisters in Christ. I repent to You, Lord, and declare Your love is triumphant over fear. Your perfect love casts out all fear, Lord, and I ask that You wash over me now with Your cleansing love. I break all agreement with the spirit of fear, night terror, dread and worry. I break agreement with the spirit of the world that would have me looking negatively at everything, and participating with an evil eye in every situation. I declare to that evil spirit, I do not want you in my life. I was bought with a price, and you didn't pay it. Thank You, Lord, that You free me of all fear and every evil spirit that would hold it in place.
AMEN

Proverbs

"Enter not into the path of the wicked, and go not in the way of evil men." - Proverbs 4:14

I have to admit, this verse in its simplicity and clarity made me feel as if I were getting a reward after having to dig for the treasure in many of the verses we've already examined. Basically, this verse tells us to steer clear of the bad stuff. Stay out of places where trouble brews, don't keep company with people who act like the devil, and avoid the road to destructive behavior. The word meanings in Hebrew, and the root words are also simple to comprehend. "Enter" means both "to come" and "to go," "path" is a well-trodden road, and can also mean "caravan." This implies that a great number of people are going this way and it would be easy to join in with them and find some sense of strength in numbers, or a sense of belonging to a group.

"Wicked" in this verse means "morally wrong… to be, do or <u>declare</u> wrong." The implication is an action or attitude meant to disturb or violate another, condemn, make trouble or vex. It's interesting that the tongue is brought into this definition of wicked. It isn't only our actions that can join us to this caravan of the wicked, it's our words!

Speaking "wrong" puts us on the well-trodden road. We do that when we speak evil of ourselves or others – "I can't do anything right" "He's such a loser" "So and so is a bitter old woman" "He's just plain mean" – I think you get the picture. God's heart is that we bless one another, and yet when we make these kinds of negative statements about ourselves and others, we are actually speaking a curse rather than a blessing. One of Scripture's best examples of how we curse others and speak "wrong" things is found in Psalm 41. When God revealed the spiritual significance of these verses, we were on our faces in repentance.

Psa 41:5 Mine enemies speak evil of me, When shall he die, and his name perish?

Psa 41:6 And if he come to see me, he speaketh vanity: his heart gathereth iniquity to itself; when he goeth abroad, he telleth it.

Psa 41:7 All that hate me whisper together against me: against me do they devise my hurt.

Psa 41:8 An evil disease, say they, cleaveth fast unto him: and now that he lieth he shall rise up no more.

Psa 41:9 Yea, mine own familiar friend, in whom I trusted, which did eat of my bread, hath lifted up his heel against me.

These verses refer to a person who is ill. Imagine the scene – there is a friend of yours who certainly appears to be dying of some sort of (what the doctors call) terminal disease. You go to see him. Verse 5 speaks of those in your friend's circle of acquaintances who have already heard about the problem and really don't care… maybe they believe they're better off without him, anyway. It's unfortunate, but there are a lot of children and grandchildren out there waiting for the old man to die so an inheritance can come their way. If they go see Grandpa at all, they tell him how much they love him, and then leave to spread the word about how bad he looks and how he doesn't have much time left. But guess what!?… you and I have done the same thing.

We make our hospital visit, tell the guy how good he looks and how much we're looking forward to having him home again; and then we leave and tell everybody what's wrong with him. "Oh, didn't Joe look bad. It won't be long, now. He has cancer, it's inoperable and spread all over his body. They went to take out a tumor and just closed him up again. There's nothing they can do. He's dying." The word says, my own familiar friend, the one I trusted, the one I fellowship with – he had dinner at my house not long ago – he's the one who has trampled my life in the dirt. Our words can actually hasten the demise of another person. The power of death and life are in the tongue. And when we speak death, we are declaring wrong and we enter the path of the wicked.

"Go not in the way of evil men" – the word "men" is not in the original Hebrew text. The translators added it so that the verse would make more sense to people. The original verse says, "Go not in the way of evil." Evil means bad or evil, to spoil by breaking to pieces, to make or be good for nothing. "Way" refers to our course of life or mode of action. It stems from a root word, "tread," which implies a walk, but also means to string a bow, from standing on the bow to bend it. This again confirms and connects the concept of our words as the vehicle we use to move through life, creating peace or causing havoc.

Psa 64:2 Hide me from the secret counsel of the wicked; from the insurrection of the workers of iniquity:

Psa 64:3 Who whet their tongue like a sword, and bend their bows to shoot their arrows, even bitter words:

The context of our study verse is an exhortation to embrace all three persons of the Godhead (the Father, Son and Holy Spirit). We are to accept and receive the understanding that is inherent in the love of the Father, walk in the wisdom of the Lord Jesus Christ and follow the instruction of the Holy Spirit.

One of the revelations from the Book of Proverbs that has proven most valuable to me is this picture of the Godhead: Anytime we see "understanding" we think of God the Father, when we see "wisdom" we think of Jesus Christ; and when we see "instruction, knowledge or reproof" we think of the Holy Spirit. This revelation opens a deeper level of relationship with God and a higher level of understanding the Godhead in Scripture.

We can see in this 4:14 verse in Proverbs another confirmation of our responsibility in achieving freedom in our lives. Deliverance is in our mouth, and so is bondage. We get to choose. Hallelujah!

Enter not into the path of the ★ wicked, and go not into the way of evil men. Prov 4:14

Cover us Lord

Garden of Healing

Song of Songs

The path of the just is as the shining light, that shines more and more unto the perfect day. Prov 4:18

our words our mouths

Because of love...

Romance

Ecclesiastes

"For out of prison he cometh to reign; whereas also he that is born in his kingdom becometh poor." - Ecclesiastes 4:14

Ecclesiastes, like Proverbs, is a book attributed to King Solomon. It is written from a worldly view, not from a heavenly perspective. This is how man without a relationship with his Living Creator looks at things. Ecclesiastes, as a whole, has a "what's the point" sort of feel to it. "All is vanity" says the preacher. In other words, there is nothing worthwhile "under the sun" or to put it plainly – in this natural world we live in. And so the book of Ecclesiastes becomes a sort of handbook for getting along in the world without God. At least, that's our view of it, and we are not alone in that assessment. Solomon is viewing the natural world from a natural perspective. Is there some practical advice to be gained from it? Absolutely! According to the Word of God, King Solomon was the wisest man who ever lived, apart from Jesus Christ. But his wisdom was not spiritual godly wisdom. It was worldly, and served him well in the world.

    The first verses of this chapter are a doom and gloom lamentation about how hard and oppressing life is, and how even when you do the right things there is always somebody to envy you and put you down. Then Solomon goes into a solution of sorts, "it's better to have a friend around who will lift you up when you fall," and so on.

    Our 4:14 verse is a strange verse, and along with

the verse before it seems quite out of place in this chapter. It's almost as if the Holy Ghost jumps into the middle of Solomon's discourse (on how much better it is to have a friend than to be alone) and totally reveals the paradox of salvation through grace. Seemingly out of nowhere, we have these rogue verses, our 4:14 verse and the one directly before it. They are interconnected, and so let's read them together:

Ecc 4:13 Better is a poor and a wise child than an old and foolish king, who will no more be admonished.

Ecc 4:14 For out of prison he cometh to reign; whereas also he that is born in his kingdom becometh poor.

On the surface, it looks easy to understand. In verse 13 we see a poor fellow who has wisdom being better off than a king who won't listen to counsel, and there is certainly truth in that. The verse stands on its own, like a proverb. But then we have this following verse where "he" comes out of prison and ascends to the throne, begging the question, "Who is the HE?" Digging into the root meanings of the words, we can glean the full understanding of God's heart as He interrupted Solomon's worldly viewpoint with a heavenly vision. First we see the "poor and wise" child. This is not simply a person without means who has intelligence.

The word "poor" means indigent, but its root translates "foolishness" and "silly." So apparently, this is the person whose own foolishness is at the root of his lack. Is there then a contradiction? How is this foolish person wise? We are not talking about two different children here, a foolish one and a wise one.

The answer is that we are talking about one who has undergone a transformation from foolishness to wisdom. From the ways of the world to the way of God. From the kingdom of darkness into the marvelous light of the Lord.

Col 1:13 Who hath delivered us from the power of darkness, and hath translated us into the kingdom of his dear Son:

There has been a transformation that takes the foolish and makes him wise. And this transformation comes about as we put on Christ.

1Pe 1:13 *Wherefore gird up the loins of your mind, be sober, and hope to the end for the grace that is to be brought unto you at the revelation of Jesus Christ;*

1Pe 1:14 *As obedient children, not fashioning yourselves according to the former lusts in your ignorance:*

1Co 2:12 *Now we have received, not the spirit of the world, but the Spirit which is of God; that we might know the things that are freely given to us of God.*

1Co 2:13 *Which things also we speak, not in the words which man's wisdom teacheth, but which the Holy Ghost teacheth; comparing spiritual things with spiritual.*

1Co 2:14 *But the natural man receiveth not the things of the Spirit of God: for they are foolishness unto him: neither can he know them, because they are spiritually discerned.*

1Co 2:15 *But he that is spiritual judgeth all things, yet he himself is judged of no man.*

1Co 2:16 *For who hath known the mind of the Lord, that he may instruct him? But we have the mind of Christ.*

These confirming verses speak not only to the poor, foolish man in Ecclesiastes who has become wise; but also to the king who remains foolish. In scripture, "king" often indicates a born-again believer (we are called kings and priests). But we have come to understand there are kings in the earth who have not received their kingdoms. In other words, there are those who have not stepped into the authority Jesus died to give us! There are born-again believers who have no interest in being taught or corrected, or going beyond where they are right now. They cling to the things of the world, the natural things, comfortable in their salvation experience but unwilling to move farther into the things of God and the intimacy of "knowing" Jesus Christ.

Our study verse tells us the "he" is that foolish one who is now wise. The "he" is the "whosoever will" – you and me, if that's our choice. "Out of prison he comes to reign," is translated "from a house or family in bondage, he ascends to a place of authority and rulership." The renewing of our minds – from my way of thinking to HIS way of thinking – will lift me from my state of poverty and indigence and carry me all the way to the throne room, where I can rule and reign with the Lord Jesus Christ… in THIS life.

We're not talking about someday in the great by and by, pie in the sky, religious Christianity. We're talking about living in the Kingdom of God as kings, right now. Making the turn (re-turning) to the Lord and away from iniquity puts us in a special place of power in the earth. And then there is the comparison to the one who does not turn. This is the foolish king who goes on still in his trespasses and becomes destitute, lacking and needy. These are the kings of the earth spoken of in Revelation 17. They are kings, but they have no dominion in the Kingdom of God.

Rev 17:1 And there came one of the seven angels which had the seven vials, and talked with me, saying unto me, Come hither; I will show unto thee the judgment of the great whore that sitteth upon many waters:

Rev 17:2 With whom the kings of the earth have committed fornication, and the inhabitants of the earth have been made drunk with the wine of her fornication.

Compromise and complacency prevent us from ruling with Christ. Being comfortable in our "religion" does not give us a place of authority in the Kingdom of God. When we allow the Lord to take us out of our foolishness and into His wisdom, He then takes us out of our bondage and into His reign over all things. Out of prison and into rulership!

Gen 39:20 And Joseph's master took him, and put him into the prison, a place where the king's prisoners were bound: and he was there in the prison.

Gen 41:14 Then Pharaoh sent and called Joseph, and they brought him hastily out of the dungeon: and he shaved himself, and changed his raiment, and came in unto Pharaoh.

Gen 41:38 And Pharaoh said unto his servants, Can we find such a one as this is, a man in whom the Spirit of God is?

Gen 41:39 And Pharaoh said unto Joseph, Forasmuch as God hath showed thee all this, there is none so discreet and wise as thou art:

Gen 41:40 Thou shalt be over my house, and according unto thy word shall all my people be ruled: only in the throne will I be greater than thou.

    Once again we are shown a clear picture of moving into our freedom in Christ, and something about what that looks like. It looks like dominion and authority through the relationship we develop with our Lord Jesus. That relationship is meant to be one of great intimacy, as we will see in Song of Solomon, where our study verse further describes our part in God's great plan. WHO we are in Him!

Father, thank you for the insights You are revealing to me. Thank You for Your love, Lord, that heals me and sets me free. Thank You for putting a watch over my words, Father, that I speak only good to edifying, that I do not fall victim to a lying spirit which would have me speak curses over my brothers and sisters – agreeing with the facts of the world rather than the truth that is Your word. Transform me, Lord, from foolishness into wisdom… Your wisdom, not the wisdom of the world. I declare I need You and cannot make the transition on my own. Take away my rebellion and independence, Father, as I declare to You: I don't want to go my own way, Lord. I want to go Your way. I break all agreement with lying spirits and every unclean thing that would bring a curse through words I have spoken over myself or others, and words that have been spoken over me by others. I break agreement with all spirits of rebellion and independence, self-protection and self-preservation. I ask Your forgiveness for participating with these things, and I ask that the curse be broken. I forgive all my ancestors for anytime they opened the door to these unclean spirits, and I release them from responsibility for any curse that has attached itself to me. I take those curses and I give them to the Lord Jesus Christ, who is my curse bearer. I declare that the blood of the Lord Jesus Christ is all powerful and effective to free me from this evil, and I thank You Lord for closing these doors to the devil. AMEN

Song of Solomon

"Spikenard and saffron; calamus and cinnamon, with all trees of frankincense; myrrh and aloes, with all the chief spices:"
- Song of Solomon 4:14

This Book, the Song of Solomon, is a beautiful love story of Jesus and His Bride, the church. It is a book that religion most often won't touch because it's viewed by religious minds as X-rated material. The truth is, most religious people have never glimpsed the heart of God for relationship, and so can only see what's happening in Song of Solomon as a carnal thing. I believe we should read the verses before and after this one, to give us a canvas on which to paint what the Holy Spirit has for us.

Son 4:9 Thou hast ravished my heart, my sister, my spouse; thou hast ravished my heart with one of thine eyes, with one chain of thy neck.

Son 4:10 How fair is thy love, my sister, my spouse! how much better is thy love than wine! and the smell of thine ointments than all spices!

Son 4:11 Thy lips, O my spouse, drop as the honeycomb: honey and milk are under thy tongue; and the smell of thy garments is like the smell of Lebanon.

Son 4:12 A garden enclosed is my sister, my spouse; a spring shut up, a fountain sealed.

Son 4:13 Thy plants are an orchard of pomegranates, with pleasant fruits; camphire, with spikenard,

Son 4:14 Spikenard and saffron; calamus and cinnamon, with all trees of frankincense; myrrh and aloes, with all the chief spices:

Son 4:15 A fountain of gardens, a well of living waters, and streams from Lebanon.

Son 4:16 Awake, O north wind; and come, thou south; blow upon my garden, that the spices thereof may flow out. Let my beloved come into his garden, and eat his pleasant fruits.

    The Lord is expressing His great love for us, and telling us clearly He doesn't see us as we see ourselves. He looks at us through the eyes of pure love, not conditional love. He can't contain Himself any longer, He is crying out to His Bride to come away with Him – come on, you're beautiful! We encourage you to study the heart of God in just these few verses, and discover yourself in them!

    In verse 12, the Lord compares His beloved to a garden enclosed (this word means "protected but bound up" and comes from a root word meaning "refusing to marry") a spring shut up, a fountain sealed. In other words, we're supposed to be fragrant and flowing, but we're stopped up; and God is saying – you're beautiful, get over yourself and your insecurities and your self-rejection, let Me tell you about you... who you really are!

    The Lord names the plants in this garden... the garden that is His church, His bride, you and me. He names eight things – spikenard, saffron, calamus, cinnamon, frankincense, myrrh, aloes and spices. Eight is the number for a new beginning! The Lord wants us to recognize what He has put in us, and the significance of each one of these plants that yield essential oils. As you see the depth and meaning in each of these spices, and realize this is what God has put within you, you will be very encouraged!

Spikenard

Spikenard is very aromatic, and yields a fragrant ointment made from the dried roots and wooly stems of the plant. The perfume created from Spikenard was especially precious and is even today often transported in an alabaster box to preserve its fragrance. This is the ointment with which Jesus was anointed before going to the cross.

Mar 14:3 And being in Bethany in the house of Simon the leper, as he sat at meat, there came a woman having an alabaster box of ointment of spikenard very precious; and she broke the box, and poured it on his head.

Mar 14:4 And there were some that had indignation within themselves, and said, Why was this waste of the ointment made?

Mar 14:5 For it might have been sold for more than three hundred pence, and have been given to the poor. And they murmured against her.

Mar 14:6 And Jesus said, Let her alone; why trouble ye her? she hath wrought a good work on me.

Mar 14:7 For ye have the poor with you always, and whensoever ye will ye may do them good: but me ye have not always.

Mar 14:8 She hath done what she could: she is come aforehand to anoint my body to the burying.

Mar 14:9 Verily I say unto you, Wheresoever this gospel shall be preached throughout the whole world, this also that she hath done shall be spoken of for a memorial of her.

There were many ancient uses for Spikenard aside from perfume and incense. We find it used as a skin tonic, to reduce anxiety and also to heal scar tissue. Today, those who use the healing oils of the Bible find Spikenard useful for allergies, migraine, nausea, cardiovascular support, and tachycardia.

In its chemistry, the primary ingredient of spikenard is sesquitperpenes, and we should say something about this chemical. Sesquiterpene molecules deliver oxygen molecules to cells, like hemoglobin does in the blood. They may also erase or deprogram miswritten codes in cellular memory, and are thought to be especially effective in fighting cancer. Sesquiterpenes deliver cancer cells a double punch – one that disables their coded misbehavior and a second that stops their growth.

Saffron

The second plant mentioned in our 4:14 verse is saffron. The saffron plant yields an aromatic spice used in both cooking and medicine. One of the most interesting things we found about saffron is that the "rose" mentioned in Isaiah is likely a saffron plant, the meadow saffron.

Isa 35:1 *The wilderness and the solitary place shall be glad for them; and the desert shall rejoice, and blossom as the rose.*

Notice this – the meadow saffron is a desert plant. We are not meant to wither in our dry places, but to blossom and to bring forth a fragrance and substance good to eat and valuable for healing. Primary in the chemistry of saffron are monoterpenes, which reprogram cellular memory, promoting permanent healing.

Song of Solomon 4:14 connects spikenard and saffron, as if these two elements are joined and infused. Interestingly in the natural chemical application, one deprograms and the other reprograms. We have to loose ourselves from the bad stuff, and then bind ourselves to the good stuff. The result is healing, and carrying healing properties within us to flow out onto others, along with a sweet, inviting fragrance.

Calamus

The calamus plant is a reed, and its definition tells us "by resemblance a rod, especially for measuring." It is one of the chief ingredients of the holy anointing oil of Exodus chapter 30 which was created for exclusive use in anointing the tabernacle, the ark of testimony in the holy of holies, the table, candlestick and altar of incense in the holy place, the sacrificial altar and the laver in the outer court, and the priests who ministered before the Lord.

There was an interesting command associated with this combination of ingredients that became the holy oil – it was not to be used on flesh. This oil, set apart for the things of God, was not to make contact with things of the world. There should be no mingling of the holy and the common. (Other ingredients of this holy oil that also are derived from the plants in the enclosed garden of Song of Solomon - you and I - are myrrh and cinnamon.)

Exo 30:31 *And thou shalt speak unto the children of Israel, saying, This shall be a holy anointing oil unto me throughout your generations.*

Exo 30:32 *Upon man's flesh shall it not be poured, neither shall ye make any other like it, after the composition of it: it is holy, and it shall be holy unto you.*

Exo 30:33 *Whosoever compoundeth any like it, or whosoever putteth any of it upon a stranger, shall even be cut off from his people.*

The chemistry of calamus is mainly phenylpropanoids, which can create conditions where unfriendly viruses and bacteria cannot live; but that isn't their most valuable function. Phenols and phenylpropanoids clean the receptor sites on cells. When cells can't communicate, the body malfunctions and illness results. In ancient times, calamus provided a tonic for the digestive system. Today, calamus is found to soothe inflammation and relax muscles. It also is supportive of the respiratory system, and can help clear kidney congestion after a person has been intoxicated.

Cinnamon

Cinnamon is conjoined with calamus in Song of Solomon 4:14, much like spikenard was connected to saffron. In combination, calamus and cinnamon are not only fragrant, they are powerful agents to cleanse receptor sites in our body. In tests, cinnamon compares favorably to antibiotics, and has been applied to tropical diseases and typhoid.

Taken from the inner bark of the tall cinnamon tree, this spice carries the image of uprightness. Cinnamon trees grow to about 20-ft high and have stiff evergreen leaves.

The chemistry of cinnamon includes cinnamaldehyde and hydroxycinnamaldehyde along with esters, phenols, phenylpropanoids and coumarins, which are antibacterial and antiviral phenols. When these coumarins are combined with aldehydes, it produces one of the most powerful antibacterial oils of all.

Frankincense

One of the gifts brought to baby Jesus by the wise men was frankincense, which comes from the clear yellow resin that exudes from incisions made in the bark of the tree and hardens into small yellow tears. Frankincense was ground and burned as incense, producing a white smoke that spiritually is meant to denote a purity of the heart or motivation.

The same family of desert tree that yields frankincense, gives us myrrh and the balm of Gilead as well. In ancient times, frankincense was thought to assist in the transition of death and was used for embalming as well as perfume. It was also used to anoint the newborn sons of kings and priests, probably as symbolic of their giving up their lives for the kingdom or the priesthood. All these implications associated with frankincense speak of our dying to ourselves in order to advance the Kingdom of God.

Rom 12:1 I beseech you therefore, brethren, by the mercies of God, that ye present your bodies a living sacrifice, holy, acceptable unto God, which is your reasonable service.

Psa 116:12 What shall I render unto the LORD for all his benefits toward me?

Psa 116:13 I will take the cup of salvation, and call upon the name of the LORD.

Psa 116:14 I will pay my vows unto the LORD now in the presence of all his people.

Psa 116:15 Precious in the sight of the LORD is the death of his saints.

What is the "cup" spoken of here? What is its symbolism and significance? Most of us know the psalms are prophetic and speak of Jesus, both in the natural and in the spiritual sense. In the Garden of Gethsemane, as Jesus was praying before going to the cross, He basically said, "Father, I don't want to do this – if there is any way, let this cup pass from me. Nevertheless, not my will, but Your will be done."

At this time in history and culture, the Romans had a method of maintaining control of outlying villages and communities. Wherever there was a hint of uprising, the Roman soldiers would come in to stop the rebellion. They would line up everyone in the village, from the eldest to the youngest. Then they would fill a cup with deadly poison, and the cup would be passed down the line. Most people would take just a little sip, hoping they wouldn't die, and they died anyway. But if there was a person in the line who would drink the whole cup, everyone would go free.

That's the cup Jesus took. He drank it all, the cup of salvation. We are called to do the same thing and die to ourselves. Not just a little bit, but all the way. It is our expression of love toward Him, just as He expressed His love toward us. This death, the death of the saints, is not a physical death, but rather a voluntary killing off of the ways of the world in our lives, and of our own thinking. This death to self is precious in the sight of God. Frankincense is a symbol of the purity of heart that results from our truly dying to self and living in the newness of life in Jesus.

Here is an amazing observation: every root word of this Hebrew word "lebonah" (frankincense) means "heart." In its spiritual significance, frankincense is at the heart - the very center - of our being. It represents our feelings, will and even intellect, our desires, courage and understanding. The origin of this spice is the word "unheart," which actually means "to transport with love."

1Jn 4:16 And we have known and believed the love that God hath to us. God is love; and he that dwelleth in love dwelleth in God, and God in him.

1Jn 4:17 Herein is our love made perfect, that we may have boldness in the day of judgment: because as he is, so are we in this world.

1Jn 4:18 There is no fear in love; but perfect love casteth out fear: because fear hath torment. He that feareth is not made perfect in love.

1Jn 4:19 We love him, because he first loved us.

1Jn 4:20 If a man say, I love God, and hateth his brother, he is a liar: for he that loveth not his brother whom he hath seen, how can he love God whom he hath not seen?

1Jn 4:21 And this commandment have we from him, That he who loveth God love his brother also.

This is the very essence of frankincense – the heart ... transporting love, in our words, our actions and our attitudes. This is the Father's heart! There is freedom in this, and emotional healing as well. Here again is a another view of deliverance through love. That's the very first picture we saw in the 4:14 verse in Genesis – God's deliverance through His love. The difference is the progression. Now the deliverance comes to us not only because of God's love for us, but also it comes as God's love flows THROUGH us to others. When we forgive, we are forgiven. When we love the unlovely, we reflect the Lord who loved us when we were the unlovely.

Chemically, frankincense is primarily monoterpenes,

which we've already stated reprogram cellular memory. They also are immune-builders, stimulating the body's production of white corpuscles. This essential oil is used for cancer, depression, allergies, headaches, bronchitis, herpes, tonsillitis, typhoid, warts, brain damage, and massive head injuries – and as an expectorant.

We find frankincense mentioned as an integral part of sacrificial worship, both in the meat offering and also in incense burning before the entrance to the holy of holies. Spiritually, the condition of our hearts is integral to sacrificial worship. There are also many mentions of frankincense in both Isaiah and Jeremiah and other places, although the words used are translated as "incense." In each of them, the word translated as "incense" is the Hebrew word lebonah, or frankincense. This was likely the primary element burned by Aaron to stop the plague, and was certainly prophesied by Isaiah concerning the gifts brought by the wise men.

Frankincense – the gift of the heart, embraces the image of God in us, revealing the love that is at the very core of our being. God is love. We are love. As a reprogrammer, frankincense speaks of restoring us into His image.

Myrrh

Like frankincense, myrrh is also connected to death, and was a major ingredient in the mix of oils that were used to create the holy anointing oil used in the tabernacle. Myrrh means "distilling in drops, also bitter." Myrrh is taken from the rockrose plant which grows in rocks and sand in Palestine. The perfumed gum from this plant is translated in some places in the Old Testament as "myrrh," but this is not the true myrrh of the New Testament, which comes from the same family of desert tree as frankincense and the balm of Gilead.

It's interesting to note that every one of these precious oils is extracted from plants that grow in desert places. We should never forget that we are to bloom and grow and yield precious fruits and oils no matter where we are and no matter in whatever condition we find ourselves. Its main chemistry component is sesquiterpenes, which again we've already talked about as useful in de-programming cells, particularly useful in combating cancers.

That is very interesting, since the Hebrew and Greek definitions for "myrrh" speak of bitterness, and bitterness is at the root of most, if not all, cancers. It's as if within the bitter drops of our circumstances we can find the very thing that will heal us.

Heb 12:11 *Now no chastening for the present seemeth to be joyous, but grievous: nevertheless afterward it yieldeth the peaceable fruit of righteousness unto them which are exercised thereby.*

Heb 12:12 *Wherefore lift up the hands which hang down, and the feeble knees;*

Heb 12:13 *And make straight paths for your feet, lest that which is lame be turned out of the way; but let it rather be healed.*

Heb 12:14 *Follow peace with all men, and holiness, without which no man shall see the Lord:*

Heb 12:15 *Looking diligently lest any man fail of the grace of God; lest any root of bitterness springing up trouble you, and thereby many be defiled;*

We have to recognize the problem in order to address it! Uncle Arthur Burt taught us this – you have to own it before you can disown it! But, again, we have the choice to "let it be healed." In the throws of bitterness, we can find the precious oil that prepares us for the unpleasantness.

Even though myrrh was bitter, in ancient days, it was said to elevate feelings of well-being. Pregnant mothers would anoint themselves against infectious diseases, and they also believed myrrh would protect their unborn children from generational curses. Again, spiritually, that would relate to our taking responsibility for those curses, even though "it's not my fault." That in itself can be a bitter pill to swallow – to repent when you didn't do it.

Myrrh was also used in a variety of other applications, including massage to facilitate stretching in childbirth, and to prevent or remove stretch marks afterward. It was put on umbilical cords to protect the child's navel from infection. It was used for skin conditions, oral hygiene, embalming and even as an insect repellent. Myrrh was found to "fix" or preserve other substances, and so was blended with so many perfumes and ointments that the Greek word for myrrh (muron) was sometimes translated "ointment" without revealing its content contained myrrh.

In modern use, myrrh has found application as an antiseptic, to balance thyroid and endocrine issues, support the immune system and in the treatment of various ailments including bronchitis, diarrhea, thrush, athlete's foot, ring worm, viral hepatitis, chapped skin, and wrinkles. Bitter or not, bring it on!

Aloes

In our 4:14 Song of Solomon verse, myrrh is connected to aloes, which is the next plant in the garden God calls His church. This is not the aloe plant that we know as aloe today.

The Bible dictionary tells us aloes were from a large and spreading tree known as eagle wood or lign aloes. Eagle wood in a spiritual sense would indicate humanity that has been set free to soar. The inner wood of the tree, particularly when in a state of partial decay, is fragrant, according to the Bible dictionary. This tells us that when we are truly dying to self, we send up a sweet smelling savor to the Lord. In Old Testament times, there were certain oils always used in embalming methods, and these included frankincense, cedarwood, and myrrh. In New Testament days, aloes, which were (and still are) known as sandalwood was another oil in common usage for this purpose. After Christ was crucified, sandalwood (or aloes) was one of the ingredients brought to prepare his body for burial.

Joh 19:39 And there came also Nicodemus, which at the first came to Jesus by night, and brought a mixture of myrrh and aloes, about an hundred pound weight.

    Interestingly, the fragrance of sandalwood is an aphrodiastic, and was used as an assistance in meditation. In Song of Solomon, as the Lord extols His beloved and describes the fragrances that emanate from her being, this fragrance attracts to intimacy. As we meditate on the goodness of God and immerse ourselves in worship, it is this oil that creates the mutual drawing – the pull of love from one to another. James 4:8 tells us to draw near to God and He will draw near to you.

    In its chemistry, sandalwood is primarily sesquiterpenes. In the world of natural substances, terpenes, or molecules built of isoprene units, are what make essential oils unique. Let's go back to the physical world for a minute and talk about what is called the blood-brain barrier. This refers to tissues that serve as a barrier to keep damaging substances from reaching the neurons of the brain and the cerebrospinal fluid. Rather than a barrier, it would be better to say "filter," through which only molecules of certain size can pass. In chemotherapy, for example, most of the molecules of the substances used are too large to pass this blood-brain filter, and this is why they say this type treatment is not effective against brain cancer. Essential oils of every species cross the blood-brain barrier, making them uniquely able to address disease.

    Moving into deeper study of aloes, we found eaglewood properly is "agarwood;" and the fragrance that comes from the heart of a tree – it could be from a variety of different trees - is a result of response to an attack on the tree. Mold begins to grow on the tree, and in response, the tree produces a rich, dark resin from within the heart wood of the tree. It is this resin that gives off the perfume.

    Think about Agar – the New Testament name for Hagar, the concubine of Abraham who gave birth to Ishmael.

Sandalwood even speaks to the feminine, as it supportive of female reproductive and endrocrine systems. Hagar was on the tree, Abraham. She was the fungus He allowed – actually invited and embraced – because he did not trust in the Lord to fulfill his promise of a son. But God redeems all things. In Abraham's heart, he was true to the Lord, but he was attracted to Hagar. Agarwood, remember, is an aphrodisiac. Abraham's response was to put Hagar out, but he couldn't get rid of her. In the natural, the resin of the tree cannot remove the mold, but only suppresses it. Eventually, the mold can kill the tree; but in its dying, it emits a beautiful, rich fragrance and healing oil.

Chief Spices

The last of the plants mentioned in the Song of Solomon 4:14 verse is "chief spices." This is balsam wood, also known as the balm of Gilead. This was a cultivated hybrid, a species that could not survive in the wild; but had to be cared for by a skilled gardener. Isn't that interesting! Balm was one of the items the queen of Sheba brought to King Solomon. He was so impressed by its fragrance and healing properties, he asked her to send him some seeds and trees, which he grew outside Jericho.

The oil was described by Theophrastes (a Greek writer, circa 300 BC) as "yellow, tenacious and sticking to the fingers." When a few drops were rubbed into a wound, it was said to bring about rapid healing. Basically, we can conclude that the balsam resin drew the wound together, like stitches. It was also considered to strengthen a weakened stomach when taken internally in very small quantity. This would speak to strengthening the inner man, our human spirit. Now we can better understand what it means to "apply the balm of Gilead" when we pray for healing for a person.

In Jeremiah, he asks, "Is there no balm in Gilead? Is there no physician there?"

Who is the great physician? The balm is Jesus Christ! The merchants who came by and purchased Joseph from his brothers, were from Gilead, and carried balm among their goods. Theirs was essentially a rescue mission, though they didn't know it. Joseph was redeemed. So are we. Although we don't always see the redemption or the blessing in the circumstance at the moment, there is a balm in the situation, whatever the situation may be. When we allow the balm – Jesus Christ - to be applied, we experience a healing. When the balm enters the wound, it is a preventative against infection, and it pulls the wound together, sealing it closed and creating the opportunity for rapid healing.

All these essential oils spoken of in Song of Solomon 4:14 are within us. When we are pressed, squeezed, attacked and otherwise challenged, this is what should be produced in us and should exude from us. In this passage, the Lord is revealing our potential and value in the healing of the nations. Again, we are involved in the deliverance not only of ourselves, but of others. It is only through our intimacy with the Lord that we can come forth in the fullness of what God intended to gather from His garden, which is us.

Certainly we can see that what the Lord has planted in us is more than just a sweet-smelling flower. This garden to which He likens His beloved is filled with healing plants. His Bride, His church, is meant to bring forth these fruits, to flow living waters as a fountain.

It is amazing at the healing properties each plant possesses – and remember, God is saying these properties are IN us. We are the garden – the garden protected, but bound up, refusing to enter our spiritual marriage. The Lord knows us so well! We have within us wondrous things, things that can only be realized and expressed when the walls and fences come down; but in so many ways we fear the intimacy of marriage to the Lord, of submitting completely to Him as our spouse. He also compares us to a spring shut up and a fountain sealed. God is about to break up the fountain within us! He wants us to flow in the compassion and power of His healing and love.

But so often, we don't know who we are – who HE has made us to be. The Lord wants to give us a picture, to have <u>us</u> see what <u>He</u> sees in us. This perspective is vital to our freedom. We can't become who God created us to be if we can't catch His vision of us. And He's giving us His vision of us in a declaration of love and admiration designed to make us leave the bondage in which we've become comfortable, and step out with Him.

In previous verses, we've seen how our words are integral to our freedom; and we recognize the power of our declarations. How much more powerful is HIS declaration over us! When we choose to turn from foolishness to wisdom, to receive a word of correction in love and change our way of thinking into His way of thinking, He brings us out of prison and elevates us to a position of authority and dominion, ruling in His kingdom. In this Song of Solomon verse, there is even more understanding of our place beside the Lord.

One of the methods our Heavenly Father gently uses to woo us into agreeing with Him in His plan for our lives lies in how He reveals to us who we really are… that we are not the dirty old sinners we've been taught we are. We're not unlovely and without value, but instead are loved and valued by the only One whose opinion matters - God Almighty! He tells us what He has put within us that He wants to bring out, and shows us how awesome and important we really are in the overall plan of creation and particularly in its restoration.

We are loved and valued!! ♥

THE FATHER'S LOVE LETTER

TAKE THE CUP... DIE DAILY.

OIL and PERFUME REJOICE the HEART...
PROV 27:9

BALM of GILEAD FOR THE HEALING OF THE NATIONS

THE MARRIAGE COVENANT

★ SOS 4:14 ★

Blow UPON MY GARDEN, that the SPICES MIGHT FLOW OUT

Father God, thank You again for marvelous insights into Your word, insights which speak of Your love for me, and tell me who I am. I love You, Lord, and I repent to You today for refusing to let You heal the hurts I've suffered, and for not truly entering into the intimacy of Your marriage covenant. Lord, I declare to You – I don't want to be a garden enclosed, I want to be a garden opened… so that others may come and partake of the fruit You've planted in me. I don't want to be a spring shut and a fountain sealed, Lord. Break open the well of living water within me. I want to flow, Father, with Your love and compassion, with Your healing power. I want to cultivate the seeds and trees and plants within me that yield healing oils. Lord, when I'm pressed I want the oil to be pure and sweet and useful. Help me die to myself, Lord, and live unto You. I break all agreement now with all spirits of bitterness that would spring up and defile many. I break agreement with fear of intimacy with You, Lord, and fear of relationships with others. I break agreement with fear of loving and being loved. I break agreement with rebellion – the iniquity of going my own way. Father, search me and know me. If there is any wicked way in me, Lord, reveal it so that I can rid myself of all filthiness of the flesh and the spirit; and lead me in the way everlasting. I don't want to live with secret sin, Lord, those evil things that hide and work, and hide their work. I want only to be the person You created me to be from before the foundation of the world… Your precious child. I want only to live from You and for You and not in and for myself. Help me die the proper death, Lord, a daily sacrifice of love toward You and others, so that I can be resurrected daily in the power of the Holy Spirit, bringing a heart and hands of healing to all who are oppressed by the devil in body, soul or spirit because You, God, are with me. I send this prayer in the precious name of Jesus Christ, my Redeemer, my Messiah, my Risen Lord, and I ask to be set free from any demonic influence that prevents me from moving in the resurrection power that raised Jesus from the dead. AMEN

POINT OF NO RETURN
STOP
ALTO
Israel,
This is not Burger King. You cannot have it your way!
Love,
God
XOXO
PRIZE
I WON!
Report Card
Nation of Israel
Whoredom F Adultery
MERCY
TRUTH
I PROMISE U

The Voice of the Prophets

As we become free of the fears and insecurities and compromise and lies and other demonic influences that have kept us bound, we see the Lord has laid a strong foundation of love and relationship with Him and within the Body. It's His heart's desire that we love Him, and each other, and ourselves. LOVE is His commandment. That is a prerequisite to understanding God and to our own deliverance from evil. As we listen to and heed the voice of love, we are loosed from the bonds and snares and webs of the enemy.

Pro 1:33 But whoso hearkeneth unto me shall dwell safely, and shall be quiet from fear of evil.

Moving into the 4:14 verses of the prophets, we will get a picture of our condition without God and what happens when we refuse to hearken to the voice of Love. There is a passage in Isaiah that serves as a good transition into this part of our study. It speaks of a people who are going their own way, what happens when they do, and how God's mercy is waiting to comfort and heal them when they return to the ways of the Lord and once again worship Him rather than their own minds and strengths and ways of doing things.

Isa 30:15 For thus saith the Lord GOD, the Holy One of Israel; In returning and rest shall ye be saved; in quietness and in confidence shall be your strength: and ye would not.

Isa 30:16 But ye said, No; for we will flee upon horses; therefore shall ye flee: and, We will ride upon the swift; therefore shall they that pursue you be swift.

Isa 30:17 One thousand shall flee at the rebuke of one; at the rebuke of five shall ye flee: till ye be left as a beacon upon the top of a mountain, and as an ensign on a hill.

Isa 30:18 And therefore will the LORD wait, that he may be gracious unto you, and therefore will he be exalted, that he may have mercy upon you: for the LORD is a God of judgment: blessed are all they that wait for him.

As we go along, we'll find the 4:14 verses in the books of the prophets to be more demanding of us, and they may even seem harsh, until we see the mercy of God's love interwoven into this thing called judgment. God is a God of judgment, but we must recognize and have a true awareness that God's judgments are always tempered with His mercy. Judgment and mercy are directly connected throughout the Bible 21 times, which in God's Biblical numbering system is symbolic of exceeding sinfulness – that's what the number 21 represents. Exceeding sinfulness demands God's judgment, but God's judgment is always administered in mercy. When the Lord steps into our lives and begins to cut away the evil, judgment is wrought on the evil spirit and justice is brought to the person – that's the mercy in judgment for the believer.

Psa 89:14 Justice and judgment are the habitation of thy throne: mercy and truth shall go before thy face.

Mercy and judgment are inextricably intertwined, and were married at the cross. The crucifixion of Jesus was a marvelous marriage of God's judgment and His mercy. The cross of Calvary speaks of judgment on all evil; but it also speaks of radical mercy poured out in the blood of Jesus on all who will accept it.

It is interesting that the book of Isaiah does not have a fourteenth verse in chapter four, since Isaiah is perhaps the most vocal and clearly understood of all the prophesies concerning the Messiah, our Lord Jesus Christ. After thinking it through, I decided that is precisely the reason there is not a 4:14 verse in Isaiah – the book is focused primarily on the natural appearing of the Lord – in the flesh.

Jesus' birth, ministry, crucifixion and resurrection are all there. While certainly there is spiritual significance and symbolism concerning the manifestation of Christ IN us, Jesus working in and through His people, the entire book is about our Deliverer. The revelations of Jesus in Isaiah are shown in the New Testament, from the very first 4:14 verse in Matthew; but we need to stay in sequence.

Here is the backdrop for the 4:14 verses we will examine in the books of the prophets: the nation of Israel is in trouble with God. There is a clear understanding in the writing of the prophets of the need for a Savior. This thread is woven throughout this section of the Bible. The true prophets of God were sent to tell the truth: to paint for Israel, in sometimes graphic methods, the error of their ways, and to condemn the false prophets and the priests who spoke peace when there was no peace, and (as stated in Jeremiah 8:11) had "healed the hurt of my people only slightly." The prophets and priests who were acceptable to the people were not acceptable to God. They were bringing forth a feel-good message of compromise that lulled the nation into complacency toward God and His statutes and turned them to worship other gods as a part of their daily lives.

That condition of God's church still seems true. In today's churches, there seems to be a lot of compromise and a mixing and mingling of truth and error, as in the days of the Hebrew prophets. People are being lulled into complacency; we are most assuredly worshipping other gods in our daily lives, with little or no awareness of what is happening or how we are being affected in the spirit realm. We really should gain some understanding about what's happening in the spirit from the things that befall us in the natural.

The situation with the priesthood, described by the prophets of old, is not a new thing. Even in the days of the tabernacle, there was a division of the priesthood. God had separated an entire tribe of people as the priesthood, in service to the Lord. These were the Levites, the tribe of Levi. But within the tribe of Levi there was a further separation, a setting apart of a people who would minister to the Lord rather than to the people. We can see this in Ezekiel 44:

Eze 44:10 And the Levites that are gone away far from me, when Israel went astray, which went astray away from me after their idols; they shall even bear their iniquity.

Eze 44:11 Yet they shall be ministers in my sanctuary, having charge at the gates of the house, and ministering to the house: they shall slay the burnt offering and the sacrifice for the people, and they shall stand before them to minister unto them.

Eze 44:12 Because they ministered unto them before their idols, and caused the house of Israel to fall into iniquity; therefore have I lifted up mine hand against them, saith the Lord GOD, and they shall bear their iniquity.

Eze 44:13 And they shall not come near unto me, to do the office of a priest unto me, nor to come near to any of my holy things, in the most holy place: but they shall bear their shame, and their abominations which they have committed.

Eze 44:14 But I will make them keepers of the charge of the house, for all the service thereof, and for all that shall be done therein.

Eze 44:15 But the priests the Levites, the sons of Zadok, that kept the charge of my sanctuary when the children of Israel went astray from me, they shall come near to me to minister unto me, and they shall stand before me to offer unto me the fat and the blood, saith the Lord GOD:

Eze 44:16 They shall enter into my sanctuary, and they shall come near to my table, to minister unto me, and they shall keep my charge.

What the Lord says by these prophets, which we should heed today, is that those who are set apart to minister to Him and yet have not fulfilled that assignment will be cut off from entering the deep things of God. They can minister to the people, but will likely not enter the Holy place, and certainly not the Most Holy place. Only those who remain steadfast in the faith, not performing the office of a priest unto other gods, but only to the true God, will live in His presence.

What does that mean? In essence, it means "no compromise" when it comes to the word of God, which is the word of love. We obey God out of our love for Him. Our love for God is the only thing that holds us in the Kingdom of God. When we fall back into loving ourselves or others above God, we are relegated to a lesser place of ministry where our true purpose in Him is hindered and we can't show forth the manifold wisdom of God. It's a dry, laborious place of mostly powerless works.

God doesn't want us there, and is in fact moving us toward the elimination of the outer court from our lives. There is coming a time when there will no longer be a place for sacrifice. In Revelation chapter 11 when the temple of God is measured, the outer court is omitted! Perhaps we would be wise to enter the holy place where we commune with God… where we come into common union with our Lord. The voice of the prophets is calling us into the deeper things of God. Will you enter?

Jeremiah 4:14

SOAP — Wash yourselves oh Israel

CELESTIAL GLORY

BAPTISM of SPIRIT SOUL BODY — HEB. 12

PURIFY YOUR HEART

VAIN THOUGHTS

Jeremiah

"O Jerusalem, wash thine heart from wickedness, that thou mayest be saved. How long shall thy vain thoughts lodge within thee?"
- Jeremiah 4:14

This verse in Jeremiah is pretty straight up. The prophet is bringing the word of the Lord that Israel has the opportunity to be saved, if only she will turn from her wicked ways. "Wash your heart" from wickedness translates "trample" the evil you hold in your hearts. The word "heart" in this verse speaks of the center of our being – at least, who we think we are - the mind, will, emotions and desires of the soulish realm. Jeremiah is warning the church, "There's a day of judgment coming, and you need to be ready to stand forth in righteousness. Get yourself clean!"

There are many witnesses to this same idea in the New Testament, and we're going to look at a couple of them. Paul tells the church at Corinth:

2Co 7:1 *Having therefore these promises, dearly beloved, let us cleanse ourselves from all filthiness of the flesh and spirit, perfecting holiness in the fear of God.*

To the church at Philippi, he writes:

Phi 2:12 *Wherefore, my beloved, as ye have always obeyed, not as in my presence only, but now much more in my absence, work out your own salvation with fear and trembling.*

"Working out" our own salvation brings up the doctrinal question of "once saved, always saved" – is it true? This is one of the biggest points of division within the Body of Christ, and has opened the door for a tremendous spirit of fear to infiltrate many denominational and even non-denominational churches throughout the world. It has also spawned a "works" mentality. This book is not meant to answer that question for you. However, the following insights may help you settle the question as you search the Scriptures for yourself, and live in what you find to be true.

Very briefly, the Bible is clear that we are saved by grace through faith in the Lord Jesus Christ, and not by any works which we may or may not accomplish.

Eph 2:8 For by grace are ye saved through faith; and that not of yourselves: it is the gift of God:

Eph 2:9 Not of works, lest any man should boast.

That being said, we need to remember we are a three part being – spirit, soul and body. And for our three-part being, God provided for us three baptisms for our complete and total salvation. Our born-again experience, that moment we confessed our sins and accepted the atoning blood of Jesus Christ for them, was the baptism for our spirit, and our spirit is forever preserved unto God.

Salvation is a many-faceted word. The Greek word translated "salvation" encompasses five key elements: preservation, healing, soundness, prosperity and deliverance from evil. Complete salvation was made available to us by the perfect sacrifice of Jesus Christ. When we accepted the gift by believing on Him, we got our preservation (the ticket to heaven). For all who are born again, our spirits are preserved. We are saved.

In addition to being a many-faceted word, salvation as used in the Greek text is progressive, showing an ongoing process: "I was saved, I am saved, I am being saved and I will be saved." This speaks of the purification and cleansing of our other "parts" – the soul and the body. For our soul, God provided the baptism of the Holy Spirit, where we can completely immerse our mind, will, emotions and desires into Him. The evidence of this baptism, according to Scripture, is a heavenly language personal to each individual soul. This is a different experience than the born-again experience. Having the Holy Spirit in us and receiving the baptism of the Holy Spirit are not the same. This is clearly shown in Acts:

Act 19:1 And it came to pass, that, while Apollos was at Corinth, Paul having passed through the upper coasts came to Ephesus: and finding certain disciples,

Act 19:2 He said unto them, Have ye received the Holy Ghost since ye believed? And they said unto him, We have not so much as heard whether there be any Holy Ghost.

Act 19:3 And he said unto them, Unto what then were ye baptized? And they said, Unto John's baptism.

Act 19:4 Then said Paul, John verily baptized with the baptism of repentance, saying unto the people, that they should believe on him which should come after him, that is, on Christ Jesus.

Act 19:5 When they heard this, they were baptized in the name of the Lord Jesus.

Act 19:6 And when Paul had laid his hands upon them, the Holy Ghost came on them; and they spake with tongues, and prophesied.

Receiving the baptism of the Holy Spirit gives us the tools we need to save our souls (remember your spirit is already preserved unto God when you receive Jesus as your Savior). The baptism of the Holy Spirit is what is being referred to in Ephesians when we read "work out our own salvation with fear and trembling." Our souls are being saved. We are in the process of the transforming and renewing – the saving - of our souls, and we have a responsibility to cooperate with the Holy Spirit in this cleansing and purging process.

Rom 12:2 And be not conformed to this world: but be ye transformed by the renewing of your mind, that ye may prove what is that good, and acceptable, and perfect, will of God.

The second part of the 4:14 verse in Jeremiah also refers to this process. "How long will your vain thoughts lodge within you?" or to put it more plainly, "How long are you going to keep your stinking thinking?"

2Co 10:3 For though we walk in the flesh, we do not war after the flesh:

2Co 10:4 (For the weapons of our warfare are not carnal, but mighty through God to the pulling down of strongholds;)

2Co 10:5 Casting down imaginations, and every high thing that exalteth itself against the knowledge of God, and bringing into captivity every thought to the obedience of Christ;

This is all part of saving our souls; and this, too, is not a "works" thing. It is a cleansing thing, and shows us once more God's heart to set us free. It also shows us once more that we have an assignment in the process. Our assignment is to participate with God by recognizing the demonic influence in our lives, repenting for entertaining it, and removing it from our mind, will, emotions and desires. It's not a shame for a Christian to have a demon, but it is a shame to keep it!

To complete our explanation of the total salvation concept, the third part of our being, the physical body, will be "saved" at the resurrection. The first aspect, the spirit, is saved when we accept the finished work of Christ, the second aspect, the soul, is being saved through our yielding to the Holy Spirit. The body, will receive its full salvation at the resurrection. Water baptism is symbolic of this aspect of our salvation. Be assured, if you go the way of the grave before the appearing of Christ, it's not over. That is not the end of you. You will get your body back, and you will receive in your body the rewards of your works.

This is where works have value. Works won't save you, and they won't give you faith. But works will flow naturally from your faith. You can have works without faith; but you can't have faith without works. Our actions and attitudes in this life from the time of our confession of salvation will be judged, and we will receive rewards and suffer losses, but we will not lose our salvation. The Word is clear on that point:

1Co 3:10 *According to the grace of God which is given unto me, as a wise masterbuilder, I have laid the foundation, and another buildeth thereon. But let every man take heed how he buildeth thereupon.*

1Co 3:11 *For other foundation can no man lay than that is laid, which is Jesus Christ.*

1Co 3:12 *Now if any man build upon this foundation gold, silver, precious stones, wood, hay, stubble;*

1Co 3:13 *Every man's work shall be made manifest: for the day shall declare it, because it shall be revealed by fire; and the fire shall try every man's work of what sort it is.*

1Co 3:14 *If any man's work abide which he hath built thereupon, he shall receive a reward.*

1Co 3:15 *If any man's work shall be burned, he shall suffer loss: but he himself shall be saved; yet so as by fire.*

Hopefully, that will ease your mind concerning whether or not you are really saved and going to heaven. Salvation is a gift, and God does not take it back. You can refuse the gift, and you can return the gift, but it is a gift nonetheless. In other words, God does not remove salvation from us, but we can walk away from it and give it up.

Is our born again experience the end? No, it's the beginning. Is there more to be done on our part? Yes, absolutely, but our works have to do with the rewards we will enjoy for eternity, not where we will spend it. Working out our salvation has to do with the brightness of the glory we will wear – how much Jesus will shine forth in and through each one of us. This is the final piece of salvation, the saving of our physical bodies. The Bible gives a comparison in II Corinthians to expalin that in the resurrection, some will shine brihgter than others.

1Co 15:40 There are also celestial bodies, and bodies terrestrial: but the glory of the celestial is one, and the glory of the terrestrial is another.

1Co 15:41 There is one glory of the sun, and another glory of the moon, and another glory of the stars: for one star differeth from another star in glory.

1Co 15:42 So also is the resurrection of the dead. It is sown in corruption; it is raised in incorruption:

This basic information is valuable for our full understanding of the warnings and admonitions of the Old Testament prophets. These men had a glimpse of all these things, but they were not given the opportunity, as we are, to be partakers of the glory of God and His divine nature. They are a part of the cloud of witnesses Paul speaks of who are cheering us on, hoping we are the generation who will truly believe God and step into the power and authority Jesus died to give us. If we do, the earth can be restored, death can be subdued under our feet and these waiting saints who have gone before can receive their glorified bodies and return with Jesus in physical form.

Heb 12:1 Wherefore seeing we also are compassed about with so great a cloud of witnesses, let us lay aside every weight, and the sin which doth so easily beset us, and let us run with patience the race that is set before us,

Heb 12:2 Looking unto Jesus the author and finisher of our faith; who for the joy that was set before him endured the cross, despising the shame, and is set down at the right hand of the throne of God.

Psa 110:1 A Psalm of David. The LORD said unto my Lord, Sit thou at my right hand, until I make thine enemies thy footstool.

1Co 15:26 The last enemy that shall be destroyed is death.

We've got our work cut out for us, saints! Fortunately, it's not entirely up to us. We have a part in it and a responsibility - to respond to God and to His ability. We don't have to make the plan, just agree with His plan and allow Him to use us for His purposes, to fulfill His plan of salvation, not only for each one individually but also for the earth itself – all of creation. Jeremiah tells us the trumpet is sounding. Are we listening? In this fourth chapter of Jeremiah, the prophet pleads with the nation to repent, for the people of God to return to God and stop going their own way. Let's reread the 4:14 verse and go just a little farther.

Jer 4:14 O Jerusalem, wash thine heart from wickedness, that thou mayest be saved. How long shall thy vain thoughts lodge within thee?

Jer 4:15 For a voice declareth from Dan, and publisheth affliction from mount Ephraim.

Dan means "judge" and so Jeremiah is telling the people, judgment is being called for and reason is made clear -

Jer 4:18 Thy way and thy doings have procured these things unto thee; this is thy wickedness, because it is bitter, because it reacheth unto thine heart.

Jer 4:19 My bowels, my bowels! I am pained at my very heart; my heart maketh a noise in me; I cannot hold my peace, because thou hast heard, O my soul, the sound of the trumpet, the alarm of war.

Jer 4:20 Destruction upon destruction is cried; for the whole land is spoiled: suddenly are my tents spoiled, and my curtains in a moment.

Jer 4:21 How long shall I see the standard, and hear the sound of the trumpet?

Jer 4:22 For my people is foolish, they have not known me; they are sottish children, and they have none understanding: they are wise to do evil, but to do good they have no knowledge.

How long? How long will we hear the sound of the trumpet and the alarm of war and sit in our complacency and comfort, waiting to be whisked away and believing there is nothing we can do? Most of the church is not looking for the appearing of Christ, they are looking for the appearing of antichrist! We can learn from this verse in Jeremiah that the Lord is ready to deliver us from evil, but we have a part in the deliverance. Are we going to accept it and walk in it? We don't battle for a victory, folks, we battle because of one! Does the Lord need our help? No. Does He expect it? Yes.

Jdg 5:23 Curse ye Meroz, said the angel of the LORD, curse ye bitterly the inhabitants thereof; because they came not to the help of the LORD, to the help of the LORD against the mighty.

Is there a mighty problem in your life? Marriage? Children? Job? Addictions? It's time to pick up the sword of the Word of the Living God and go forth into the realm of the spirit and draw blood on the enemy. It's time for us to destroy the works of the enemy by coupling our faith with the sword of the Spirit of God - His Word - in our prayers of intercession, in our praises of His wondrous works, and in our everyday conservation. This is how we draw blood on the enemy in the spirit realm.

Jer 48:10 Cursed be he that doeth the work of the LORD deceitfully, and cursed be he that keepeth back his sword from blood.

We're not waiting for a physical return of Jesus to sit back and watch Him straighten everything out for us... He's already here, and He wants to work through us to straighten it all out right now. Many of us are waiting for Jesus to come back and reign, while He's waiting for us to reign so He can come back! This is the deliverance message we get from this 4:14 verse – we are to wash ourselves from wickedness, and trample down the evil out of our own hearts. That's the first order of business.

Jer 4:14 O Jerusalem, wash thine heart from wickedness, that thou mayest be saved. How long shall thy vain thoughts lodge within thee?

II Cor 7:1 Having therefore these promises, dearly beloved, let us cleanse ourselves from all filthiness of the flesh and spirit, perfecting holiness in the fear of God.

Father God, here I am again to seek Your face. I know, Lord, that I can do nothing without You, but with You there is nothing I can't do. I'm sorry, Lord, for the way I've neglected and even refused to follow Your ways, and have stubbornly gone my own way. Your word is true, Father – my way has a snare. Thank You, Lord, that You are faithful even when I'm not. Thank You that You are standing ready to forgive and to cleanse me of all unrighteousness as I confess my sins to You. Father, I ask in the name of the Lord Jesus Christ to reveal to me any wickedness in my heart – those hidden sins and secret faults, Lord, that ensnare and entrap me. (take just a moment to let the Lord speak to you). **Lord, I want clean hands and a pure heart.**

 I repent to You, Lord, for allowing fear to infiltrate my soul and bring doubt into my heart about my salvation. I ask You to forgive me, Lord, and I ask that the curse be broken. I break all agreement with fear and doubt and unbelief. I confess I have trusted in my own understanding and my own strength and have been afraid to let go of

some things in my life and allow You to handle them. Help me know the truth, Lord, the truth that You can run my life better than I can. Lord, I ask for help with my thought life. I repent to You for allowing the devil to lie to me and lead me into unacceptable thoughts, fears of the future and regrets of the past. I declare to You today – I want to live in today, to trust You in all things, and to step out of past hurts and unmet needs. I repent for allowing those hurts and unmet needs to influence my walk with You in the present. Lord, I bind myself now to Your will, Your way, Your plans, Your purpose and direction for me, and I ask to be loosed from any hindering spirit that would keep me from trampling under the evil that so easily besets me from within my own heart. I declare Your word is true… if my heart condemn me, YOU God are greater than my heart. Thank You for freeing me from rebellion, distrust, disobedience, fear, and self preservation. I break agreement with those spirits now and I declare I do not want them in my life, in Jesus' name. They must leave me now and never return. AMEN.

Lamentations

"They have wandered as blind men in the streets, they have polluted themselves with blood, so that men could not touch their garments." - Lamentations 4:14

As previously noted, that our 4:14 verses in the books of the prophets would likely be more demanding and could even seem harsh, we find that to be true in the next few books. In Lamentations, the prophet Jeremiah is bemoaning the destruction of Jerusalem and the downfall of Israel. He gives the reason for the coming fall of the city and prophesies the sacrifice of Jesus and change of priesthood.

If we read the prophets without an understanding of Biblical imagery or Hebrew word meanings, we can miss a lot. This 4:14 verse, which refers to the prophets and priests, is a bit befuddling without its context, so we need to examine the verses before it in order to get the deeper meaning of what's happening here.

Lam 4:12 *The kings of the earth, and all the inhabitants of the world, would not have believed that the adversary and the enemy should have entered into the gates of Jerusalem.*

Lam 4:13 *For the sins of her prophets, and the iniquities of her priests, that have shed the blood of the just in the midst of her,*

These are the two verses which immediately precede our study verse. Who are the kings of the earth? That these people are called kings denotes authority and power. God calls us kings, so in the spiritual sense, these people are believers. But notice this – the verse says "kings of the earth." We can surmise that kings of the earth, although they are believers, have not yet entered their place of authority in the Kingdom of God.

In today's vernacular, we would call these people "carnal Christians," those who are still "of the earth" and not walking in the Spirit. There is a general feeling of complacency evident in the Body of Christ that says, "We're kings and nothing can touch us." There is a truth to that, but it is not THE truth. How many times are we caught unaware because of a compromising message or action or attitude from our priests and prophets, who comfort us with feel-good words that do little to prepare us for our assignments in God's Kingdom? In the parable Jesus told in Luke 19, we come to understand we are to "occupy" until He comes. Do we, as believers, sit back and sip tea and think we are an occupying force?

Luk 19:9 And Jesus said unto him, This day is salvation come to this house forsomuch as he also is a son of Abraham.

Luk 19:10 For the Son of man is come to seek and to save that which was lost.

Luk 19:11 And as they heard these things, he added and spake a parable, because he was nigh to Jerusalem, and because they thought that the kingdom of God should immediately appear.

Luk 19:12 He said therefore, A certain noble man went into a far country to receive for himself a kingdom, and to return.

Luk 19:13 And he called his ten servants, and delivered them ten pounds, and said unto them, Occupy till I come.

Notice a few things about this parable. "This day" salvation is come – Jesus is speaking of Himself. In His presence is salvation. Once we receive Him, He is ever with us. Next, after Jesus declares this salvation, He discerns that the people thought, "Hooray! It's over." They believed the freedom inherent in the Kingdom of God was going to magically and suddenly happen to them. Most of the church still thinks that way. We don't know exactly when this great escape will take place; but we think "suddenly" and magically, Jesus is going to come back. As long as that mentality is prevalent in the church, only a very small remnant of people will actually do what Jesus commanded in this parable - occupy.

In the parable in Luke 19, because He saw the people had a wrong idea about the Kingdom, Jesus explained – the noble man, the One with authority (again speaking of Himself), was going away to "receive" a kingdom and return. This speaks directly to the coronation celebration of the Lord in heaven. You can read in Daniel chapter 7 where Jesus received His Kingdom.

Dan 7:13 I saw in the night visions, and, behold, one like the Son of man came with the clouds of heaven, and came to the Ancient of days, and they brought him near before him.

Dan 7:14 And there was given him dominion, and glory, and a kingdom, that all people, nations, and languages, should serve him: his dominion is an everlasting dominion, which shall not pass away, and his kingdom that which shall not be destroyed.

Then in verse 18 of Daniel 7, Jesus does an interesting thing – He gives over the Kingdom to the saints.

Dan 7:18 But the saints of the most High shall take the kingdom, and possess the kingdom forever, even forever and ever.

That word "possess" in this verse in Daniel – "possess the kingdom" – means "to hold in occupancy," or occupy. In the parable in Luke, the One in authority gave the authority to his servants and said "occupy." Occupy is not a passive position. The Greek word means "busy oneself, work deeds," or in today's terms – get down to business. It comes from a root word meaning "practice" or "perform repeatedly or habitually, execute or accomplish." Now remember in the parable in Luke, the master gave his servants what they needed to do business on his behalf. Jesus gained a victory for us, and He wants us to maintain the land He bought with His blood. We have what we need to do that! He has already given it to us.

So the statement in Lamentations 4:12, that the kings of the earth would not believe the enemy has infiltrated the heart of the church, is applicable today because most of us think Jesus did it all, or will do it all, and we have nothing to do but wait around until he comes back and fixes everything. This is a subtle sin that holds our thought life in the two places God does not want us – the past and the future. Did He do it all? Yes. Will He do it all? Yes. But the vital piece we seem to miss is the NOW – He is doing it all now, for those who allow Him to work in and through us.

The next part of verses in their context (Lamentations 4:13) explains that the sins of the prophets and the iniquities of the priests are responsible for a condition of destruction coming upon the church. This can also be observed today. The enemy has infiltrated the heart of the church and even the believer, unchecked by many "prophets and priests" in spiritual leadership today.

The prophecy Jeremiah is bringing in these verses is a direct prophecy of the crucifixion of Jesus Christ; but it is also a spiritual prophecy of our condition today. Much of the leadership in the church today is going its own way, not listening for and following the leading of the Holy Spirit. Programs seem to be more important than people. You can sign up for a six or eight-week anger management class at church and that's acceptable. But when the Holy Spirit interrupts a Sunday meeting to heal you of that issue, others may be offended. It seems we have to keep the program going, even if it means cutting worship short, just as people are entering in and the Holy Spirit is moving on their hearts.

This isn't simply the fault of leadership. Each one of us needs to repent for the "what about me" attitude and fear of man and need for approval that permeates our church meetings. When the Holy Spirit begins to move on others, rather than quietly praying in the Spirit, we get bored and want to leave. The attitude of "If it's not happening for me I'm not interested" does not support the Body of Christ.

Equally unedifying is fear of man, where the Holy Spirit moves on us and we do not respond because we are afraid of what people will think of us. Truly abominable is the need for approval. Many times, leadership just wants to please everybody – let's please the people. Wanting to please people rather than God is an insult to God. Doing the wrong thing grieves the Holy Spirit; but not doing the right thing quenches the Holy Spirit!

When we don't do the right thing within the Body, we are committing the "sins of the prophets and the iniquities of the priests" spoken of by Jeremiah. It's the same as Christ being crucified again in the midst of Jerusalem. Within the church, religion hangs the Lord on the cross over again, and the blood of the just is being shed. Prophets and priests are going their own way. We have all the answers and are just fine with the way things are. How many of us are going to say, "I can't believe this is happening!" when the enemy storms our gates to steal our peace and prosperity? So now we can look at the 4:14 verse with greater understanding.

Lam 4:14 They have wandered as blind men in the streets, they have polluted themselves with blood, so that men could not touch their garments.

Jeremiah states that the priests (spiritual leaders) are blind. The root of the word "blind" implies that there is a film over their eyes. This is a direct reference to the Jewish priesthood of Jesus' time and the veil God put over their understanding so that the Gentiles – you and me – could be brought into our place as priests in the Kingdom.

We know that because of a certain understanding in the meaning of the word "polluted." On first reading this verse, we can see the slaughter of the daily sacrifice, and the blood of the sacrifice spattering their priestly garments. A word study gives us deeper spiritual understanding. The Strong's Exhaustive Concordance shows us the word "polluted," and also reveals an identical word and meaning:

H1351 gaw-al'

A primitive root, (rather identical with H1350, through the idea of freeing, that is, repudiating); to soil or (figuratively) desecrate: - defile, pollute, stain.

The first implication of the translation – through the idea of freeing – in conjunction with the meaning of the identical word reveals a prophecy of the Messiah:

gaw-al'

A primitive root, to redeem (according to the Oriental law of kinship), that is, to be the next of kin (and as such to buy back a relative's property, marry his widow, etc.): - X in any wise, X at all, avenger, deliver, (do, perform the part of near, next) kinsfolk (-man), purchase, ransom, redeem (-er), revenger.

Clearly, Jeremiah is referring in this verse to the sacrifice of Jesus Christ. The "pollution" of the priests who gave Him over to be crucified was in essence and in fact the solution for the world. It was the redemption of God's people, and the beginning of the Kingdom rule of Christ in the earth. This "pollution" brought in the better covenant.

Look at the end of our verse – "men could not touch their garments." The Old Covenant priests wore the covenant of God sewn into the hem of their robes. When the woman with the issue of blood reached out for Jesus, with the cry of her heart that she touch the hem of His garment, she was reaching for the covenant promise of God. There is great significance in this simple statement, "men could not touch their garments." The priests weren't entering in, and they wouldn't allow anyone else to enter in, either. They were pleased with themselves and the way they were doing things. They were happy with the incomplete atonement of their animal sacrifices, and so on. No one was able to touch the covenant. Then the blood of Jesus became their pollution, and the Old Covenant promise was made a benefit for those will believe and receive.

This 4:14 verse moves us from the letter of the law into the life of Christ. That's its message of deliverance to us today. Not only can we touch the covenant promise of God, we can convert it to a benefit in our lives, no longer walking in blindness, or following those who do. **Thank You, Lord, for Your redeeming blood.**

Lamentations / Ezekiel

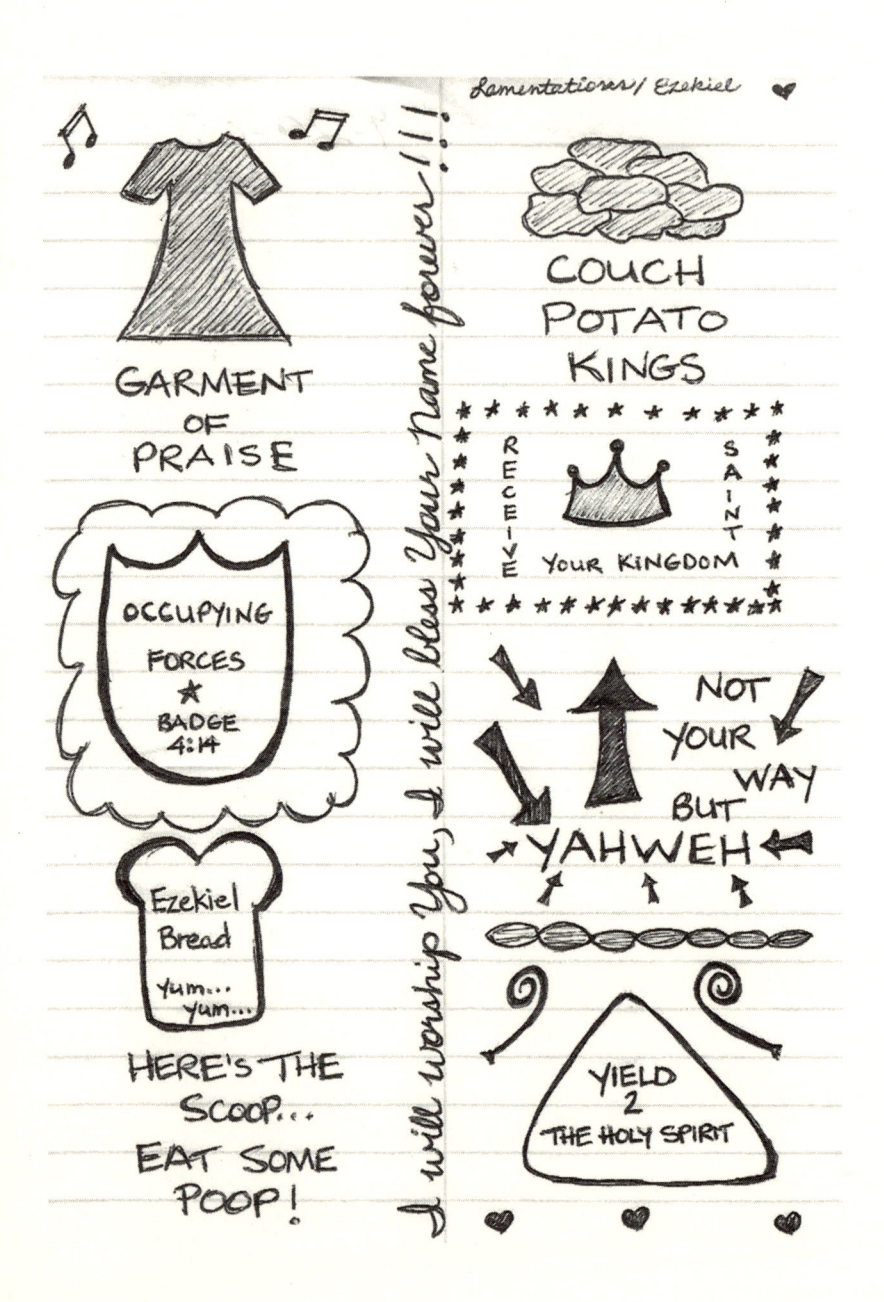

GARMENT OF PRAISE

COUCH POTATO KINGS

RECEIVE YOUR KINGDOM SAINT

OCCUPYING FORCES ★ BADGE 4:14

NOT YOUR WAY BUT YAHWEH

Ezekiel Bread yum... yum...

YIELD 2 THE HOLY SPIRIT

HERE'S THE SCOOP... EAT SOME POOP!

I will worship You, I will bless Your Name forever!!!

Ezekiel

"Then said I, Ah Lord GOD! behold, my soul hath not been polluted: for from my youth up even till now have I not eaten of that which dieth of itself, or is torn in pieces; neither came there abominable flesh into my mouth." - Ezekiel 4:14

As we move into the study verse in Ezekiel, we see another picture of God's description of Israel's defilement of itself. In chapter four of this book, the prophet is instructed by the Lord to become a natural example of the nation's spiritual condition. It is not a pretty picture. First, God tells Ezekiel to make a model of the city, and then to build up around it a fort and a camp and battering rams and a mountain to depict a siege of the city. Next, Ezekiel is to put an iron plate as a wall between himself and the model of the city to show the capture of the nation. And then comes the hard part. Ezekiel is to demonstrate the siege by lying on his left side for 390 days, symbolic of his bearing the iniquity of Israel, and another 40 days on his right side to bear the iniquity of Judah.

Then comes the REALLY hard part. God tells him what to eat and drink, bread and water; and what to put in the bread. It doesn't sound so bad at first, wheat and barley and beans and so on; but then comes the kicker - bake it with human dung. Disgusting. Anybody still long to be a prophet? Are you willing to obey God to that extent? This is the picture given in the verses leading to our 4:14 verse:

Eze 4:12 And thou shalt eat it as barley cakes, and thou shalt bake it with dung that cometh out of man, in their sight.

Eze 4:13 And the LORD said, Even thus shall the children of Israel eat their defiled bread among the Gentiles, whither I will drive them.

In my opinion, this is as strong a statement as could be made about how foul Israel had become as a nation. This example of watching the prophet of God use dung to bake the bread he will eat daily while facing off against a besieged city would certainly give one pause to consider how God is feeling about them and their actions. In verse 13, when the Lord declares the children of Israel will eat defiled bread, the spiritual indication from original word translation is that the people have defiled themselves by what they are consuming in a spiritual sense. They are <u>self-defiled</u> by their spiritual consumption. We can connect this to the previous verse in Lamentation. The priests and prophets have fed the people disgusting and sickening falsehoods – not the true word of God; and now the entire nation will pay for that in captivity. With that insight, look again at our 4:14 verse:

Eze 4:14 Then said I, Ah Lord GOD! behold, my soul hath not been polluted: for from my youth up even till now have I not eaten of that which dieth of itself, or is torn in pieces; neither came there abominable flesh into my mouth.

Here, Ezekiel is appealing to God, "Please don't make me do this!" He points out that he himself has lived righteously and not been defiled. The word "polluted" in this verse is different from the one we looked at in Lamentation. Here, polluted actually does mean to be foul or contaminated. Surely, Ezekiel is saying, "I've never eaten dung and I don't want to start now," but he is also saying something more. When we look up the word meanings Ezekiel 4:14, what Ezekiel is saying is this: "I've never defiled myself by consuming a doctrine of devils, participated in idol worship or partaken of sacrifices offered to idols, nor have I preyed on people and ripped them apart with my tongue."

God answers Ezekiel and takes him somewhat off the hook in that He allows the prophet to use the dung of cows rather than people.

Eze 4:15 Then he said unto me, Lo, I have given thee cow's dung for man's dung, and thou shalt prepare thy bread therewith.

Eze 4:16 Moreover he said unto me, Son of man, behold, I will break the staff of bread in Jerusalem: and they shall eat bread by weight, and with care; and they shall drink water by measure, and with astonishment:

Eze 4:17 That they may want bread and water, and be astonished one with another, and consume away for their iniquity.

Using cow dung may not seem to be much of a consolation; but don't lose sight of the mission of the prophet. Ezekiel was to be a living example to the nation to speak of a coming judgment from God. When Jerusalem was under siege at the end of the age, from AD 67 to AD 70, the prophecy represented by Ezekiel came to pass. According to the historical records of Josephus, the people of the city were in great famine. Their food and water were carefully measured, and there are historical reports of disgustingly sick actions – people scraping up and eating bird dung, mothers eating their own children and other abominations. No doubt there were those "kings of the earth" who could not believe what was happening.

Is this a dual prophecy for the natural world? Perhaps so. It came about then because of iniquity – a people going their own way. You've heard us say this before: God uses nations to judge nations. The good news is that once again, even in the midst of the horror of that time of great tribulation we can clearly see God's mercy in the judgment, how He protected His own and brought forth a remnant to carry on and advance His Kingdom in the earth. These first three 4:14 verses in the books of the prophets flow together. Jeremiah first tells us we have a choice - that we should choose to wash our hearts from wickedness and put away our stinking thinking. In Lamentation, he follows that admonition by placing the blame squarely on spiritual leadership and promising a new and better covenant because of their failure. The pollution became the solution.

Then Ezekiel demonstrates what happens to us spiritually as a body of believers, when we continue to go our own way. We end up hungry, self-defiled, and in bondage to ungodly captors. If we want to live in the presence and protection and provision of Almighty God, we must cleanse our hands and our hearts, separate ourselves from compromise, come out of complacency and move into commitment.

Psa 24:3 *Who shall ascend into the hill of the LORD? or who shall stand in his holy place?*

Psa 24:4 *He that hath clean hands, and a pure heart; who hath not lifted up his soul unto vanity, nor sworn deceitfully.*

Psa 24:5 *He shall receive the blessing from the LORD, and righteousness from the God of his salvation.*

Let's learn from Jeremiah and Ezekiel to honor the Lord by examining our hearts. What are the motivations behind our works? Where have we fallen into self-defilement by worshipping another god – the god of self, or work, or even family? Where have we sullied or soiled our garments by mixing and mingling truth and error, allowing compromise into our assemblies and services and even into our everyday lives under the guise of being tolerant or just trying to please everybody? Are we grieving the Holy Spirit in some area of our lives by doing the wrong thing? Are we quenching the Holy Spirit by NOT doing the right thing?

In verse four of Psalm 24 we have the witness to Ezekiel's cry – I've not defiled myself. When we refuse to elevate our intelligence and reasoning against God we have not lifted our soul to vanity; when we refuse to defraud God by pledging our allegiance to an idol we have not sworn deceitfully; and we can expect blessing from the Lord. Then <u>we will be able</u> to ascend the mountain of the Lord and step into the holy place of His abiding presence.

Father God, in the name of the Lord Jesus Christ I ask You to reveal my heart to me. I want to come into alignment with You, Lord, and stop going my own way. Give me clean hands and a pure heart that I may ascend to Your mountain and live in Your holy presence. Forgive me Father for compromising Your word, for mixing truth and error to suit my selfish needs, for falling into fear of man and need for approval. I know I am not here to please man, I am here to please You. I know that Your opinion is the only one that matters, and I repent for allowing the opinions of others, real or imagined, to guide me. Father, I ask You to forgive me for those times I've grieved Your Holy Spirit by doing the wrong thing, and forgive me for those times I've quenched Your Holy Spirit by not doing the right thing. Give me the courage to respond to You, and the wisdom to obey You. I break all agreement with pride, selfishness, fear of man, need for approval and the spirit of compromise. I declare I don't want any of these evil things in my life, and I ask to be loosed from their bondage tonight. I declare the blood of the Lord Jesus Christ, the blood that polluted the old priesthood, cleanses me. It is all powerful and effective to free me now, so that I am able perform my duties as a priest in the new priesthood, and perform them unto You acceptably in Your sight. AMEN.

vanity of vanities
ALL IS VANITY

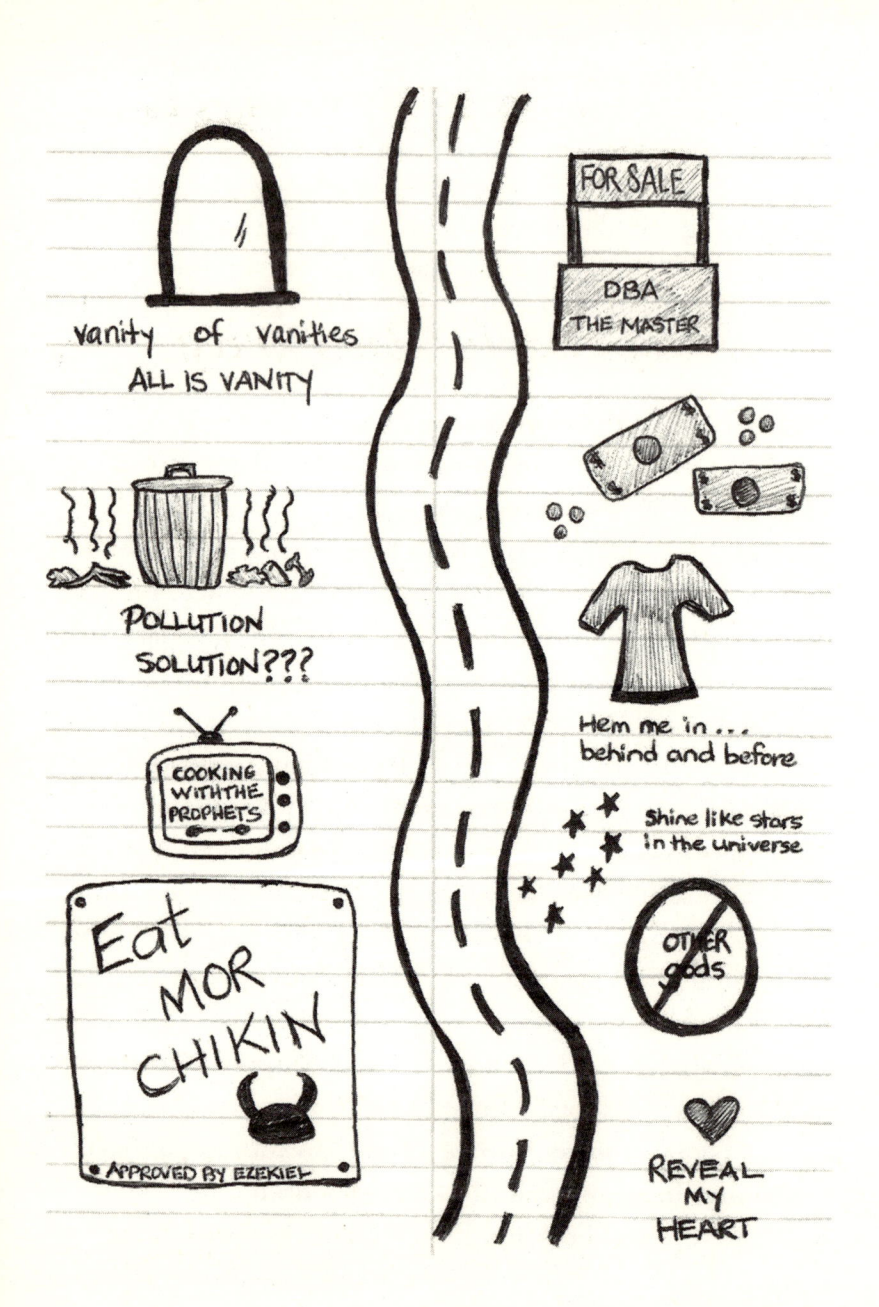

POLLUTION
SOLUTION???

COOKING
WITH THE
PROPHETS

Eat
MOR
CHIKIN
• APPROVED BY EZEKIEL

FOR SALE
DBA THE MASTER

Hem me in...
behind and before

Shine like stars
in the universe

OTHER gods

REVEAL
MY
HEART

All-powerful Authority

It is increasingly evident that we do, in fact, have an authority in Christ that is unquestionable and all-powerful to accomplish the task the set before us. God has given us in the person that is His Word, Jesus Christ, all things necessary to meet the challenges and overcome the obstacles. We just have to follow and obey. The Word and Truth of God tell us we do, indeeed, already have at our hand whatever we need.

First of all, we have strength available to us. God commands strength for us in what He has appointed for us to do. He instructs us to speak strength into ourselves, to use the voice of God in us to create strength. He says our strength is not for us, it's for others; and He very clearly teaches us our strength comes from and is found in Christ and not in ourselves.

Psa 68:28 Thy God hath commanded thy strength: strengthen, O God, that which thou hast wrought for us.

Joe 3:10 Beat your plowshares into swords, and your pruning hooks into spears: let the weak say, I am strong.

Rom 15:1 We then that are strong ought to bear the infirmities of the weak, and not to please ourselves.

2Co 12:10 Therefore I take pleasure in infirmities, in reproaches, in necessities, in persecutions, in distresses for Christ's sake: for when I am weak, then am I strong.

God has made wisdom available to us. He tells us we can get it, that He does not withhold wisdom, and it already belongs to us in and through Christ.

Pro 4:7 Wisdom is the principal thing; therefore get wisdom: and with all thy getting get understanding.

2Ti 1:7 For God hath not given us the spirit of fear; but of power, and of love, and of a sound mind.

1Co 2:16 For who hath known the mind of the Lord, that he may instruct him? But we have the mind of Christ.
Jam 1:5 If any of you lack wisdom, let him ask of God, that giveth to all men liberally, and upbraideth not; and it shall be given him.

With strength and wisdom, the challenges of the world seem very small and easily overcome. Those are just two attributes God has made available to us through the atoning blood of the Lord Jesus Christ. We also have courage, health, prosperity and even time. God has made available to us everything we need to accomplish His purposes in the earth. I think we should be about the Father's business, don't you?

Daniel

"He cried aloud, and said thus, Hew down the tree, and cut off his branches, shake off his leaves, and scatter his fruit: let the beasts get away from under it, and the fowls from his branches:"
- Daniel 4:14

Once more, we are entering a scene that needs explanation. Here in this chapter of Daniel, King Nebuchadnezzar is relating a former dream that came to pass in his life, and Daniel's correct interpretation of it. It is in this chapter that the king gives his testimony of God's greatness, and the life-lesson he learned. The dream was the one Nebuchadnezzar dreamed before he was struck mad and lived as a beast eating grass for seven years. Before we examine the verse, let's read Daniel's interpretation of King Nebuchadnezzar's dream.

Dan 4:20 The tree that thou sawest, which grew, and was strong, whose height reached unto the heaven, and the sight thereof to all the earth;

Dan 4:21 Whose leaves were fair, and the fruit thereof much, and in it was meat for all; under which the beasts of the field dwelt, and upon whose branches the fowls of the heaven had their habitation:

Dan 4:22 It is thou, O king, that art grown and become strong: for thy greatness is grown, and reacheth unto heaven, and thy dominion to the end of the earth.

Dan 4:23 And whereas the king saw a watcher and a holy one coming down from heaven, and saying, Hew the tree down, and destroy it; yet leave the stump of the roots thereof in the earth, even with a band of iron and brass, in the tender grass of the field; and let it be wet with the dew of heaven, and let his portion be with the beasts of the field, till seven times pass over him;

Dan 4:24 This is the interpretation, O king, and this is the decree of the most High, which is come upon my lord the king:

Dan 4:25 That they shall drive thee from men, and thy dwelling shall be with the beasts of the field, and they shall make thee to eat grass as oxen, and they shall wet thee with the dew of heaven, and seven times shall pass over thee, till thou know that the most High ruleth in the kingdom of men, and giveth it to whomsoever he will.

Dan 4:26 And whereas they commanded to leave the stump of the tree roots; thy kingdom shall be sure unto thee, after that thou shalt have known that the heavens do rule.

Dan 4:27 Wherefore, O king, let my counsel be acceptable unto thee, and break off thy sins by righteousness, and thine iniquities by showing mercy to the poor; if it may be a lengthening of thy tranquillity.

What Nebuchadnezzar dreamed was a warning from God, and Daniel made that clear to him when he advised the king to stop sinning and going his own way. But the king did not listen, and a year later his attitude was very prideful. He lifted himself up, saying, "I built all this kingdom by my own power and for my own glory." He made himself god instead of God.

There are dozens of stories in the Bible of those in positions of leadership and authority who begin to think they are in their elevated positions because of who they are and what they can do, rather than because of who God is and what He has done for them. Promotion can be a subtle trap, and it's been rightly said we will either practice humility or suffer humiliation. That's what happened to King Nebuchadnezzar. So now we can take our 4:14 verse and break it down to a deeper understanding.

Dan 4:14 He cried aloud, and said thus, Hew down the tree, and cut off his branches, shake off his leaves, and scatter his fruit: let the beasts get away from under it, and the fowls from his branches:

Nebuchadnezzar is speaking about the "watcher" he saw and heard in his dream...

Dan 4:13 I saw in the visions of my head upon my bed, and, behold, a watcher and a holy one came down from heaven;

    This watcher is an angel or guardian, and the king explains he believes this was a divine being because he says a "holy one" came down, which translates "sacred God." We can gather the king had already figured out that he was visited in the dream with a message from God... "Hew down the tree." This seems pretty clear cut; but this phrase has a couple of root meanings that give it a deeper dimension. One is "crowd" or "gash by pressing into," "Assemble selves by troops, gather selves together, cut selves." The other root meaning is "dig - husbandman."
    So while the dream was specific and individual for King Nebuchadnezzar, meaning God was pruning him as a good husbandman would; it also has a corporate implication in the spirit for each of us and for the body of Christ as a whole. Keep that in mind as we discover more about this hewing down concept later.
    Next, the watcher says to cut off the branches, shake off the leaves and scatter the fruit. This is a picture of complete exposure – stripping off all covering and removing any evidence of our own works. Not only is the dream warning Nebuchadnezzar his title as king will be removed, but also, that he will be stripped of all entitlement and privilege and become as a beast in the field.

Historically, the Assyrians were world conquerors, and Nebuchadnezzar was known as one of the most powerful world leaders who ever lived. In modern times, Saddam Hussein patterned himself after this king and some historians say Hussein actually considered himself Nebuchadnezzar reincarnated. Under his regime, Iraqi money portrayed Nebuchadnezzar's picture.

In the natural, the Babylonian kingdom of Nebuchadnezzar stretched forth in many directions, and these branches, too, were to be cut off. Branches cover the limbs of a tree, and speak of authority... think of the many places in Scripture Jesus is called a Branch.

Isa 11:1 And there shall come forth a rod out of the stem of Jesse, and a Branch shall grow out of his roots:

Jer 23:5 Behold, the days come, saith the LORD, that I will raise unto David a righteous Branch, and a King shall reign and prosper, and shall execute judgment and justice in the earth.

Jer 33:15 In those days, and at that time, will I cause the Branch of righteousness to grow up unto David; and he shall execute judgment and righteousness in the land.

Zec 3:8 Hear now, O Joshua the high priest, thou, and thy fellows that sit before thee: for they are men wondered at: for, behold, I will bring forth my servant the BRANCH.

Nebuchadnezzar was to lose all authority, the branches, because of his pride. Leaves give the tree its fullness and beauty, and in the natural, leaves are indicative of a change in season. The root meaning for shake off is "jump, to be violently agitated, untie." When a tree loses its leaves, it is in a time of dormancy, a time when no fruit can come forth. We call this a winter season, or a dry season when it happens to us. And notice this – later in the chapter it says the king was driven from men. In other words, there was no comfort for him from people, most of whom were likely his friends when he had power and money and influence. I'm sure all of us have experienced a time like this, when our friends and those who once supported us turned their backs and fell away when the season changed. King Nebuchadnezzar's winter season was forced, but many of us go through the same thing due to our own pride and other issues. When we do, we find ourselves pretty much alone.

It doesn't have to be that way. We are in the time in history - the time after the crucifixion and resurrection of Jesus - when there should be no winter season in a Christian's life. We understand this truth from the parable of the fig tree. Jesus cursed the tree because it had no fruit, even though the word says it was not the time for fruit. We think that was a cruel thing for the Lord to do – poor little tree, it was just living its life according to the natural order of things. That's precisely the point – we are to live our lives according to the spiritual order of things, not the natural order of things; and in the presence of the Creator is the ability to produce! No winter season. No falling leaves. Continual and abundant fruit. That's the call on our lives.

The fruit in the king's dream was "scattered." Fruit, of course, speaks of productivity. And the root of scatter means to "break through, spread or separate oneself." The fruit of this tree which represented the life and reign of King Nebuchadnezzar was separated from the tree and not fit for beast or bird. The dream and its interpretation are clearly meant to be a warning – King Nebuchadnezzar, there is a shaking coming that will strip you of your authority, bring down your high-mindedness and remove you from your place of favor. But Daniel tells the king, "If you repent and change your ways, giving glory to God and not yourself, it may be the Lord will allow you to live in peace for a while longer."

Once a tree is cut down, its branches cut off and it's been stripped of its leaves and fruit, it isn't good for much. Animals can't rest under it, birds can't make their nests in it, no one can eat of the fruit. It is no longer able to provide shade from the heat of the day or anything else.

We know that in Biblical imagery, trees speak of

people; and in dreams, trees often denote leadership – people who are in a place of natural or spiritual authority. Daniel says, "You're the tree, king, and you're going down."

> Eze 17:24 And all the trees of the field shall know that I the LORD have brought down the high tree, have exalted the low tree, have dried up the green tree, and have made the dry tree to flourish: I the LORD have spoken and have done it.

The whole purpose of taking this tree down was to get rid of pride, that sense of self that caused King Nebuchadnezzar to exalt himself and the works of his hands (as if he really had anything to do with it!). There are numerous references to green trees, where the nation of Israel in its pride and arrogance played the harlot by sacrificing to other gods, setting their idols in the groves and high places under green trees. The result of this wickedness was never good. God warns Nebuchadnezzar that He will pass judgment on the wickedness in the king's life, and one of the chiefest acts of wickedness was that he did not give God glory for the favor he enjoyed.

> Psa 37:35 I have seen the wicked in great power, and spreading himself like a green bay tree.

The green bay tree speaks of pride. There is another tree in scripture we want to stay away from, and that is the tree of the knowledge of good and evil, which is also closely related to pride. It's our pride, the green bay tree, which takes us to the tree of judgment to partake of its fruit. Let's go back to the first part of the verse, where the tree (Nebuchadnezzar in his pride) is to be hewed down.

There are a couple of significant places in Scripture where trees are cut down. One is in Matthew and the other in Luke; and they say essentially the same thing. The word says if a tree isn't producing good fruit, it is to be cut down.

> Mat 3:10 And now also the axe is laid unto the root of the trees:

therefore every tree which bringeth not forth good fruit is hewn down, and cast into the fire.

Luk 3:9 And now also the axe is laid unto the root of the trees: every tree therefore which bringeth not forth good fruit is hewn down, and cast into the fire.

  King Nebuchadnezzar was a natural example of a spiritual principle we can apply to our own lives. His pride is what brought him low. The same thing is true of us. The good news is we can cut down the tree of pride, but not in our own strength or reasoning. That "I can do it myself" (through sheer will power or mind over matter or striving and determination) is a statement of pride.

  These verses in Matthew and Luke refer to an axe. What is this axe? We can find it in Revelation chapter 20.

Rev 20:4 And I saw thrones, and they sat upon them, and judgment was given unto them: and I saw the souls of them that were beheaded for the witness of Jesus, and for the word of God, and which had not worshiped the beast, neither his image, neither had received his mark upon their foreheads, or in their hands; and they lived and reigned with Christ a thousand years.

  If you're asking yourself "where did I see the axe?" You can find it in the word "beheaded." The word "beheaded" appears five times in the King James New Testament, and in four of those places it means "decapitated" (the head severed from the body). But that is not its original meaning in this verse. The translation of the word beheaded in this verse is "axe." It is a word compiled from the meanings of three roots, one which means formed or fabricated, one which means hammered or pummeled, and one which means smitten or straightened.

  In other words, the people being referred to as beheaded for the witness of Jesus in this verse in Revelation are not those who had their heads severed from their bodies, for if they were the word "beheaded" would mean decapitated. They are those who allowed God to mold them and make them into a tool useful for His purpose. They were pommelled and hammered and straightened and formed into an axe in the hand of God! They have given over the headship of their lives to the Lord, and are no longer using their own reasoning and carnal thinking.

And the axe – what is the axe used for? To hew down the trees of pride and the knowledge of good and evil! We allow God to make us into a weapon and a tool; and then we, as the axe, cut down the trees in our own lives that prevent us from fulfilling our purposes in God and advancing His Kingdom.

This is the only thing – being beheaded – that qualifies us to bring judgment in all kinds of situations, and restoration to the people and to the earth itself, all of creation, because we no longer use our own human reasoning where we judge by appearance. Think of the translation in our Daniel verse. "Hew down" had a corporate application (crowd) – the Body of Christ – and it meant assemble as a troop, pressing in, "cutting self." Once again, the Word is interpreting the Word. Hallelujah!

In our Daniel 4:14 verse, the husbandman cuts down the tree, severs its branches and shakes off its leaves to expose the prideful nature the king had exhibited. But notice in verse 15, the stump was left standing.

Dan 4:15 Nevertheless leave the stump of his roots in the earth, even with a band of iron and brass, in the tender grass of the field; and let it be wet with the dew of heaven, and let his portion be with the beasts in the grass of the earth:

This must mean there was some good fruit in there somewhere, or at least the potential for good fruit to come forth. Otherwise, the tree would have been thrown into the fire, according to Matthew and Luke. This potential to produce was bound up in iron and brass. Chasing those words back to their origin, we find iron is connected to "piercing" and brass to "prognostication." We all know what piercing is, and prognostication is foretelling the future. We can conclude that it is through the piercing of our pride that we can gain an understanding of our future in God.

Notice, too, the tree stump continues to be watered by the dew of heaven. The Lord will sustain us as we go through those times of shaping when He makes us into the axe, and those times of beheading as we give up our head for His. Through the dew of heaven, the water of the Word, while we are in a state of seeming destruction, God teaches us. King Nebuchadnezzar got the message – God is God, I'm not. He began his testimony with these words:

Dan 4:1 Nebuchadnezzar the king, unto all people, nations, and languages, that dwell in all the earth; Peace be multiplied unto you.

Dan 4:2 I thought it good to show the signs and wonders that the high God hath wrought toward me.

Dan 4:3 How great are his signs! and how mighty are his wonders! his kingdom is an everlasting kingdom, and his dominion is from generation to generation.

And Nebuchadnezzar ended his testimony like this:

Dan 4:34 And at the end of the days I Nebuchadnezzar lifted up mine eyes unto heaven, and mine understanding returned unto me, and I blessed the most High, and I praised and honored him that liveth forever, whose dominion is an everlasting dominion, and his kingdom is from generation to generation:

Dan 4:35 And all the inhabitants of the earth are reputed as nothing: and he doeth according to his will in the army of heaven, and among the inhabitants of the earth: and none can stay his hand, or say unto him, What doest thou?

Dan 4:36 At the same time my reason returned unto me; and for the glory of my kingdom, mine honor and brightness returned unto me; and my counselors and my lords sought unto me; and I was established in my kingdom, and excellent majesty was added unto me.

Dan 4:37 Now I Nebuchadnezzar praise and extol and honor the King of heaven, all whose works are truth, and his ways judgment: and those that walk in pride he is able to abase.

We can gain a lot of insight from this chapter in Daniel. That God resists the proud is evident. But there is also evidence of His mercy – God warns us when we are in danger of losing our place of favor. Sometimes that warning comes through others in the Body of Christ, sometimes we hear it in a message from the pulpit, sometimes it may come as a spark of revelation from the Holy Spirit as we read the word, or in our time of worship. And sometimes it can come to us in a prophetic dream. We need to value our dreams and not consider them just the result of something we ate or saw at the movies. God speaks to us in our sleep, as well as in our waking hours, and we need to be paying attention. Let us be mindful of God's love and mercy. He warns us. And if we forget the warning, or don't heed the warning, He still sustains us through the winter season.

We also need to take it to heart that whatever position or leadership or authority we hold, whatever mighty actions we've taken, whatever great works we've done, whatever kingdoms we've built, it's only because of the Lord's hand on our lives. Under the hand of God, we can outrun chariots. Running in our own strength, we can only get run over.

1Ki 18:46 And the hand of the LORD was on Elijah; and he girded up his loins, and ran before Ahab to the entrance of Jezreel.

God sets up kings, and He takes them down.
Psa 75:5 Lift not up your horn on high: speak not with a stiff neck.

Psa 75:6 For promotion cometh neither from the east, nor from the west, nor from the south.

Psa 75:7 But God is the judge: he putteth down one, and setteth up another.

Psalm 100 tells us there is no such thing as a self-made man or woman.

Psa 100:1 A Psalm of praise. Make a joyful noise unto the LORD, all ye lands.

Psa 100:2 Serve the LORD with gladness: come before his presence with singing.

Psa 100:3 Know ye that the LORD he is God: it is he that hath made us, and not we ourselves; we are his people, and the sheep of his pasture.

Psa 100:4 Enter into his gates with thanksgiving, and into his courts with praise: be thankful unto him, and bless his name.

Psa 100:5 For the LORD is good; his mercy is everlasting; and his truth endureth to all generations.

Father God, thank You for this word. I enter Your gates with a heart full of thankfulness for Your love and Your mercy and Your truth. I praise You for who You are, Lord, and who You are re-making me to be, the precious child You created from before the foundation of the world. The one You love. The one You instilled with gifts and talents to fill a need that no one else can fill. Thank You, Lord, that I am unique and necessary in Your plan of restoration. I ask You to forgive me, Father, for all the times I thought I had accomplished something on my own. Forgive me for not recognizing Your hand on me, and for not giving You the glory due You. Forgive me, Father for participating with spirits of pride and elitism, for not humbling myself and giving myself over to be molded and shaped by You, for telling You how I want things to be, as if You're the servant and I'm the master. God, I admit my sin before You, and I declare that You alone know what's best for me. You alone have the Master plan, because You are the Master.

In the name of the Lord Jesus Christ, who is come in the flesh, I break all agreement with pride and rebellion and self-sufficiency. I ask You to forgive me, and I ask that the curse be broken. I break all agreement with disobedience, manipulation and distrust. I admit I have not trusted You to take care of my life, Lord, and I'm sorry. I know You can do a better job at it than I have. I pull down every curse of self-preservation and self-sufficiency I've spoken over myself, and I break every ungodly covenant I've made with my words. I ask that every spiritual document that gives satan a legal right to hold curses of pride and rebellion in my life be burned by Your consuming fire, Lord. I put myself on the altar and ask that You send Your fire to purge me of these sins.

Make me an axe, Lord. I put my head on the chopping block and ask for a divine exchange – my head for Yours – I give up my lordship over my life so I can fully receive Your lordship over my life. Father, I send forth my supplication in the name of the Lord Jesus Christ, and I thank You that His precious blood is all powerful and effective to free me from these sins now and forever. **AMEN**

DARE TO DREAM but... HEED THE WARNING!!!

NOT THE PIZZA

KINGNER — HAVE IT YOUR WAY OR NOT!

7
7
7
7
7
7
7
7
7

HOSEA... NOT LACKING!!!

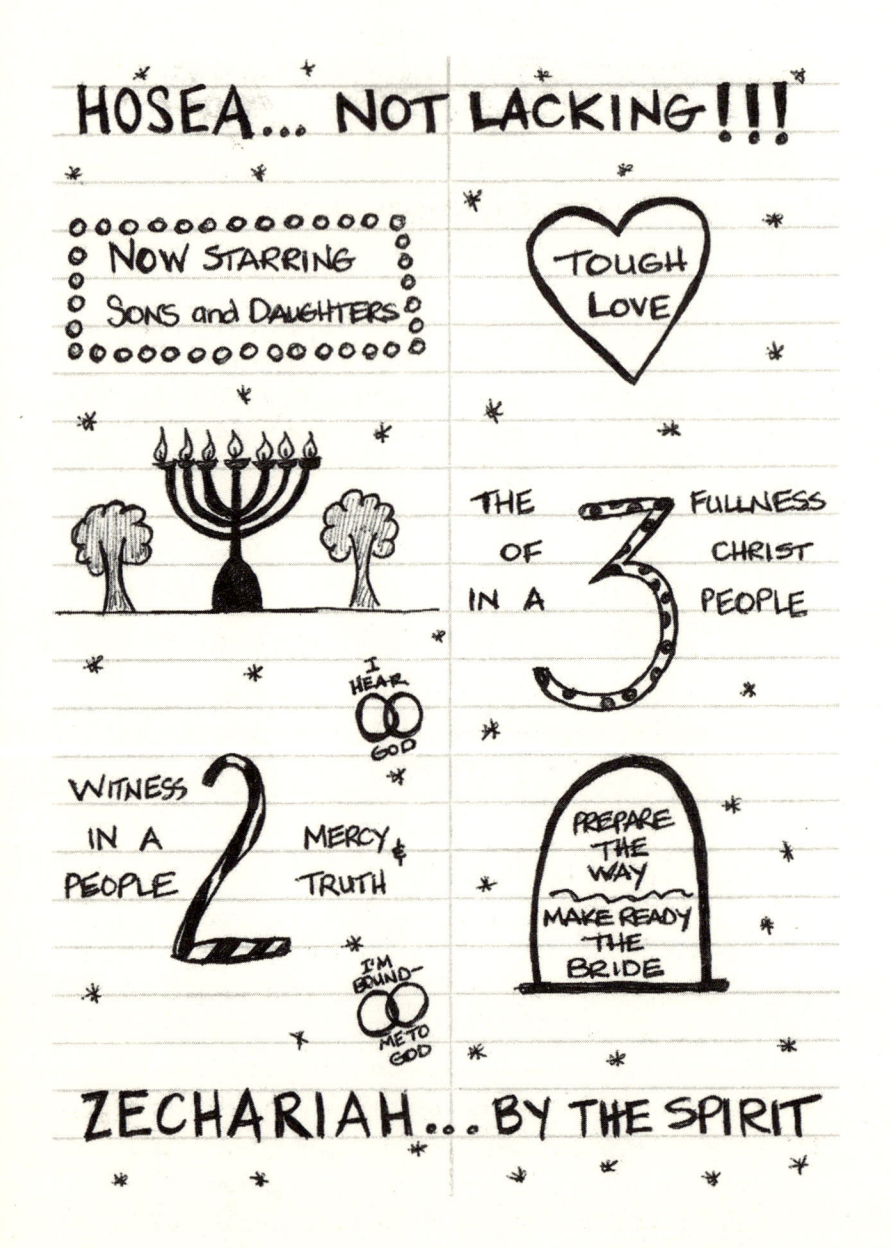

NOW STARRING SONS and DAUGHTERS

TOUGH LOVE

THE FULLNESS OF CHRIST IN A **3** PEOPLE

I HEAR GOD

WITNESS IN A PEOPLE **2** MERCY & TRUTH

I'M BOUND ME TO GOD

PREPARE THE WAY — MAKE READY THE BRIDE

ZECHARIAH... BY THE SPIRIT

Hosea

"I will not punish your daughters when they commit whoredom, nor your spouses when they commit adultery: for themselves are separated with whores, and they sacrifice with harlots: therefore the people that doth not understand shall fall." - Hosea 4:14

In this verse, The prophet Hosea clearly tells us there is a point of no return where our sins and iniquities catch up with us and bring their own shameful reward. This chapter in Hosea is the one where the prophet says:

Hos 4:6 My people are destroyed for lack of knowledge: because thou hast rejected knowledge, I will also reject thee, that thou shalt be no priest to me: seeing thou hast forgotten the law of thy God, I will also forget thy children.

    The prophecy is against the nation of Israel, and Hosea announces "there is no truth, nor mercy, nor knowledge of God" in the land. The people had altogether forgotten their God and were serving other gods and worshipping idols.
    God considers this adultery and fornication, and calls the nation a harlot. Apparently, this practice had been going on for a while, because the generation referred to as "daughters" had known no other way of doing things. That's the meaning in our verse where it says they are "separated with whores, and they sacrifice with harlots"… they grew up in the midst of abomination! The word "spouses" means bride, a son's wife. In the literal sense, these are ones who

married into spiritual abomination and knew nothing else.

God says, in the literal translation from the Hebrew, "I will not visit or have charge over you nor watch over the generation after you because you have chosen other gods to serve." Basically, God will let us have what we choose and He will step aside – as He said in Isaiah, "You trust in yourself and your intelligence, and in all manner of sorcerers, astrologers, magicians and soothsayers, so let them save you."

Isa 47:8 Therefore hear now this, thou that art given to pleasures, that dwellest carelessly, that sayest in thine heart, I am, and none else beside me; I shall not sit as a widow, neither shall I know the loss of children:

Isa 47:9 But these two things shall come to thee in a moment in one day, the loss of children, and widowhood: they shall come upon thee in their perfection for the multitude of thy sorceries, and for the great abundance of thine enchantments.

Isa 47:10 For thou hast trusted in thy wickedness: thou hast said, None seeth me. Thy wisdom and thy knowledge, it hath perverted thee; and thou hast said in thine heart, I am, and none else beside me.

Isa 47:11 Therefore shall evil come upon thee; thou shalt not know from whence it riseth: and mischief shall fall upon thee; thou shalt not be able to put it off: and desolation shall come upon thee suddenly, which thou shalt not know.

Isa 47:12 Stand now with thine enchantments, and with the multitude of thy sorceries, wherein thou hast labored from thy youth; if so be thou shalt be able to profit, if so be thou mayest prevail.

Isa 47:13 Thou art wearied in the multitude of thy counsels. Let now the astrologers, the stargazers, the monthly prognosticators, stand up, and save thee from these things that shall come upon thee.

God says essentially the same thing here in this 4:14 verse in Hosea. There is a point at which the Lord will no longer strive with us to keep us out of trouble and under His protection. He doesn't just throw His hands up in frustration and forget us; but He does allow us to discover the pains of our own rebellion. People say all the time that God is unlimited, but that's not scriptural. God can be limited, because He is true to His word and will not interfere with our will. He wants to free us, but we choose to remain bound up when we turn aside, turn back or turn our trust and our hope to other things.

Psa 78:40 How oft did they provoke him in the wilderness, and grieve him in the desert!

Psa 78:41 Yea, they turned back and tempted God, and limited the Holy One of Israel.

The very center verse of our Bible says this:

Psa 118:8 It is better to trust in the LORD than to put confidence in man.

Leaning to our own understanding and going our own way is putting trust in man. If all our hope is in the Lord, then all His mercy is toward us.

Psa 33:22 Let thy mercy, O LORD, be upon us, according as we hope in thee.

Still, in our verse in Hosea, the people obviously are not receiving the mercy of the Lord. Hopefully, we all will understand it is not God's decision to withhold His mercy, it's our decision to send it away by our iniquities.

Jon 2:8 They that observe lying vanities forsake their own mercy.

When we observe lying vanities... when we consider the worthless voice of the enemy and begin to worship the ways of the world, we forsake (the word forsake means "send away") God's mercy. This grieves the Lord, but He lets us find out for ourselves what a miserable existence we face without Him. People who "do not understand" will fall. And that is the lesson in this 4:14 verse in Hosea. Once again, we see we have a part to play in achieving freedom in our lives. We must not remain ignorant, but instead seek knowledge, mercy and truth.

God wants our hearts, but there are things of the world that He names in Hosea that are also after our hearts. The spirit of whoredoms wants to make us worship ourselves and things other than God, so that we are separated from God and without His protection and guidance. Verse 11 says whoredom, wine, and new wine take the heart. Whoredom is basically spiritual adultery or idolatry. When we say we're married to the Lord, and then go after our own lusts and comforts by trusting in other things, we have subjected ourselves to the spirit of whoredoms. Wine in this verse is basically the same thing – it means becoming intoxicated and overtaken by something other than the Holy Spirit. "Wine" here is a symbol of the confusion and carelessness we experience when we fall into the spirit of the world. It is a counterfeit to the Holy Spirit of God. "New wine" means driving out or dispossessing, expelling, robbing, seizing – this is a form of greed or covetousness. Any of these things can capture our hearts and leave us vulnerable to the curses that are already working in the world.

Hosea tells us God will not interfere if we choose to follow a spirit other than the Holy Spirit. The prophet speaks of the heartache we face when we do not allow the Lord to free us from feeling the pull of the world's enticements. Just as with everything else in the Kingdom, when it comes to deliverance, it's our choice. This 4:14 verse speaks of the result when we choose ways other than God's way. There really are not three ways of doing things. There is not God's way, the devil's way and <u>my</u> way; because if we are going "my way" we are in fact going the devil's way. Any disagreement with God, Satan takes as agreement with him; and we end up with the "blessings" of Satan (which are really curses) rather than the blessings of God.

Zechariah

"Then said he, These are the two anointed ones, that stand by the Lord of the whole earth." - Zechariah 4:14

The way God frees us from the world and its abominations can be seen in this, the last 4:14 verse of the Old Testament. This verse ties together the sum of what we've learned so far about God's heart of deliverance, and is a wonderful bridge into the 4:14 verses in the New Testament. This vision of Zechariah is the same as is given to John the Revelator. Again, we have to emphasize – let the Bible interpret the Bible. I want to read the whole chapter, so we can see the vision and relate it to John's.

Zec 4:1 And the angel that talked with me came again, and waked me, as a man that is wakened out of his sleep,

Zec 4:2 And said unto me, What seest thou? And I said, I have looked, and behold a candlestick all of gold, with a bowl upon the top of it, and his seven lamps thereon, and seven pipes to the seven lamps, which are upon the top thereof:

Zec 4:3 And two olive trees by it, one upon the right side of the bowl, and the other upon the left side thereof.

Zec 4:4 So I answered and spoke to the angel that talked with me, saying, What are these, my lord?

Zec 4:5 Then the angel that talked with me answered and said unto me, Knowest thou not what these be? And I said, No, my lord.

Zec 4:6 Then he answered and spoke unto me, saying, This is the word of the LORD unto Zerubbabel, saying, Not by might, nor by power, but by my spirit, saith the LORD of hosts.

Zec 4:7 Who art thou, O great mountain? before Zerubbabel thou shalt become a plain: and he shall bring forth the headstone thereof with shoutings, crying, Grace, grace unto it.

Zec 4:8 Moreover the word of the LORD came unto me, saying,

Zec 4:9 The hands of Zerubbabel have laid the foundation of this house; his hands shall also finish it; and thou shalt know that the LORD of hosts hath sent me unto you.

Zec 4:10 For who hath despised the day of small things? for they shall rejoice, and shall see the plummet in the hand of Zerubbabel with those seven; they are the eyes of the LORD, which run to and fro through the whole earth.

Zec 4:11 Then answered I, and said unto him, What are these two olive trees upon the right side of the candlestick and upon the left side thereof?

Zec 4:12 And I answered again, and said unto him, What be these two olive branches which through the two golden pipes empty the golden oil out of themselves?

Zec 4:13 And he answered me and said, Knowest thou not what these be? And I said, No, my lord.

Zec 4:14 Then said he, These are the two anointed ones, that stand by the Lord of the whole earth.

We can see the candlestick and the olive trees and the eyes of the Lord which run to and fro through the whole earth, and immediately connect with John's vision of the same things, written in the Book of Revelation; so we know we're talking about the end times, the last days, or whatever you want to call it. Though there may be a duality to end time prophecy, history clearly shows that the events of the "last days" were literally fulfilled in the generation following the death, resurrection and ascension of the Lord Jesus Christ.

There has already been a natural fulfillment of the

events of the Book of Revelation. Spiritually, these events are being fulfilled now; and when we come into the fullness of Christ as His Body, Jesus will return to receive His Kingdom. Spiritually, we are in the last days and they will continue until we come into His fullness.

It's not necessary for us to go through all the imagery of this vision; because what we really want to answer to the best of our ability as it has been revealed to us by the Holy Spirit is this – who or what are the two anointed ones spoken of here? We know the answer is the same as in Revelation. These two anointed ones are the two witnesses.

Rev 11:3 And I will give power unto my two witnesses, and they shall prophesy a thousand two hundred and threescore days, clothed in sackcloth.

Rev 11:4 These are the two olive trees, and the two candlesticks standing before the God of the earth.

In order to let the Bible interpret the Bible, we need to look at the basics. What is this Manufacturer's Handbook (the Bible) about? It's about the restoration of God's creation through the redemption of a Bride who will co-labor with the Son of God to accomplish that restoration. God's plan has always been "God in man, having dominion in the earth." His heart is for a joining together, an intimate relationship with us, His creation. The Bride has been chosen, but the Bride has not yet made herself ready. This is the message of the last days. Our Bridegroom gave His life, He has offered the cup of redemption, and we are to drink the whole thing, die to ourselves and allow His headship over us. Then He can present us, His bride, as the completion of Himself, to the Father (study Ephesians chapter 5).

What does that have to do with the two witnesses of Revelation and the two anointed ones of Zechariah?

From the word studies, going back to the original language and meanings of the words, we find "anointed ones" means "a son, a builder of the family name that glistens and produces light." Anointed also relates to oil, of course, and oil is obtained through a pressing process where the fruit itself is essentially crushed and unrecognizable from its previous form. Two is the Biblical number for witness, or literally, unity and division – in the natural, a witness causes both unity and division because a witness speaks in agreement with one and disagreement with another. In the prophetic sense, the number two also speaks of multiplication, a doubling. In the Greek, the word "witness" means martyr, one who bears record – by implication, through his life.

It's really easy to make the connection that these two witnesses are people, that the olive trees, the olive branches, the golden pipes that empty the golden oil out of themselves, are all the same people group. This group is known by many names: overcomers, the first fruits company, Joel's army, the elect Lady, the Bride of Christ, the manchild. And there is something more to understand about this spiritual connection.

We can conclude as we search deeper that this symbolism is meant to represent a united people group which witnesses both the nature and the ministry of Jesus Christ in the earth, a people of both mercy and truth. Two witnesses, mercy and truth, in one body of people. In Revelation chapter five, we see the nature and ministry of Christ in one scene:

Rev 5:5 *And one of the elders saith unto me, Weep not: behold, the Lion of the tribe of Judah, the Root of David, hath prevailed to open the book, and to loose the seven seals thereof.*

Rev 5:6 *And I beheld, and, lo, in the midst of the throne and of the four beasts, and in the midst of the elders, stood a Lamb as it had been slain, having seven horns and seven eyes, which are the seven Spirits of God sent forth into all the earth.*

Rev 5:7 *And he came and took the book out of the right hand of him that sat upon the throne.*

In verse five, we see the Lion – this is the nature of Jesus. He is not nor has He ever been a wimpy, weak-willed pushover. Having the nature of Christ means we have the boldness of the truth, to march through the ranks of the enemy with sword drawn to take blood, bringing judgment on evil and justice to people. Behold the Lion!

When John looked he saw, not a Lion, but a Lamb. This symbolizes the ministry of Jesus, the mercy of God fully manifested. Bringing the judgment of God (the truth) against evil always brings the mercy of God to the person who lacked the truth and was taken in the snare of the lies of the enemy. This is a powerful revelation, and I hope you're getting it.

We are connecting the witnesses, mercy and truth, to a people who witness and thus are the anointed ones that build the family name of God Almighty: those who have the Lion nature and the Lamb ministry of the Lord Jesus Christ manifesting in them and being demonstrated through their lives. There are many scriptural connections to confirm this revelation. Going by the law of first reference, we first see "mercy and truth" connected in Genesis chapter 24. This is the account of Abraham commissioning his servant to go and find a wife for Isaac – a woman of his own family. Abraham told the servant:

Gen 24:7 The LORD God of heaven, which took me from my father's house, and from the land of my kindred, and which spoke unto me, and that swore unto me, saying, Unto thy seed will I give this land; he shall send his angel before thee, and thou shalt take a wife unto my son from thence.

Most of us know the story. The servant swore his allegiance to Abraham in the task he'd been given, and set off to find the right woman. When he arrived at his destination, he waited outside the city and prayed that the Lord would show kindness and reveal the right woman. Really, he put out a fleece (study Judges chapter 6). He said:

Gen 24:13 Behold, I stand here by the well of water; and the daughters of the men of the city come out to draw water:

Gen 24:14 And let it come to pass, that the damsel to whom I shall say, Let down thy pitcher, I pray thee, that I may drink; and she shall say, Drink, and I will give thy camels drink also: let the same be she that thou hast appointed for thy servant Isaac; and thereby shall I know that thou hast showed kindness unto my master.

Rebekah came along and proved herself to be the one for Isaac by fulfilling the servant's request of God. She watered the camels and the servant discovered she was of Abraham's family. Then this servant of Abraham praised God and thanked Him for His goodness and faithfulness. This is where we see the elements of mercy and truth clearly connected to this type and shadow (symbol and imagery) of the Bride of Christ.

Gen 24:26 And the man bowed down his head, and worshiped the LORD.

Gen 24:27 And he said, Blessed be the LORD God of my master Abraham, who hath not left destitute my master of his mercy and his truth: I being in the way, the LORD led me to the house of my master's brethren.

Mercy and truth are the two witnesses of God's grace toward Abraham and Isaac, as He led the servant to the Bride of the Son of Promise. Notice the servant said, "I being in the way," meaning he was in obedience. God responds to our obedience in mercy and truth.

Psa 25:10 All the paths of the LORD are mercy and truth unto such as keep his covenant and his testimonies.

This faithful servant did not want to fail in his mission, and go home ashamed; and when he cried out to God, he received the answer by mercy and truth.

Psa 57:3 He shall send from heaven, and save me from the reproach of him that would swallow me up. Selah. God shall send forth his mercy and his truth.

Mercy and truth are the testimony of the Messiah, the promise of redemption.

Psa 85:9 Surely his salvation is nigh them that fear him; that glory may dwell in our land.

Psa 85:10 Mercy and truth are met together; righteousness and peace have kissed each other.

Psa 85:11 Truth shall spring out of the earth; and righteousness shall look down from heaven.

God did not leave Abraham destitute of His mercy and truth, but brought the bride. Notice this – the servant put on Rebekah an earring of gold, and two bracelets of gold. The imagery is this: her ear was commissioned to hear the voice of God, and her hands to do His work in the earth. Also, the numerical value of the Hebrew word for "bracelet" is 144, which is God's Biblical number of godly government. This woman was chosen to be the bride of the son of promise, as we the Body of Christ are chosen to be His Bride, appointed to hear His voice and to do His work in the earth.

Mercy and truth are the expression of the nature and ministry of our Lord and Savior Jesus Christ. Mercy and truth are directly connected in the Holy Scriptures 47 times. I think God wants us to know that connection, and to become His expression of, and His witnesses to mercy and truth in the earth.

Isa 16:5 And in mercy shall the throne be established: and he shall sit upon it in truth in the tabernacle of David, judging, and seeking judgment, and hasting righteousness.

This last 4:14 verse in the Old Testament has the anointed ones – the builder of the family name producing light – standing beside the Lord. His Bride, glistening with radiant righteousness, adorned with earring and bracelets that enable her to hear and to accomplish divine strategies, stands ready. That's the picture. We have to see it before we can see it! We are created to be the glistening bride, the glorious bride, the completion of our Bridegroom, pouring out of those pressed places within us anointed oils for healing and restoration, the oils of mercy and truth.

Father God, once again I am in awe of Your word, the depth and beauty and simplicity of Your word. I am awed, Lord, by the remarkable ways You reveal Yourself and Your plan for each one of Your children, and I thank You. Help me, Father, become what You have appointed me to be, an effective witness of Your mercy and truth.

Father, once more I thank You for revealing Yourself and Your plan. I thank You that it is Your good pleasure to give us the Kingdom, and in those places in my life where I have not been willing to trust You completely, where I have not been willing to give up the things and ways of the world, I ask to be made willing right now, Lord. I give over my will to You and ask to be bound to You and You alone, and to be loosed from the iniquities of my past and my generations. I repent to You, Father, for entertaining a spirit of whoredoms that has captured my heart in many areas and kept me from fully realizing Your love for me, and my purpose in You. I declare today that as an act of my will, I forgive all my ancestors or any other person in my life, for any time they participated with a spirit of whoredoms and opened the door for that spirit to affect and afflict me. I forgive them with my heart, my mind and my emotions, and I release them into Your hand. I ask Your forgiveness, Father, for my own participation with that unclean spirit, as well as the spirits of idolatry, pride, rebellion and disobedience that follow it. I break all agreement with these spirits now, in the name of the Lord Jesus Christ, and I ask to be delivered from them.

Father, I ask for an increase in knowledge and understanding, that I may make myself ready, and help others to become ready as well, to be the spotless Bride of the Lord Jesus Christ, fully capable of standing beside You and working with You. I ask to be adorned today with the golden earring that enables me to hear Your voice and Your instruction clearly, and with the golden bracelets that symbolize I am bound to You and which enable me to accomplish Your purposes and advance Your Kingdom in the earth. Do not leave me destitute of Your mercy and Your truth, Lord. Pour forth Your goodness so that it overflows my life and bathes the world around me with Your light. In the name of Jesus, I thank You, Father, for the freedom of Your abiding presence. AMEN.

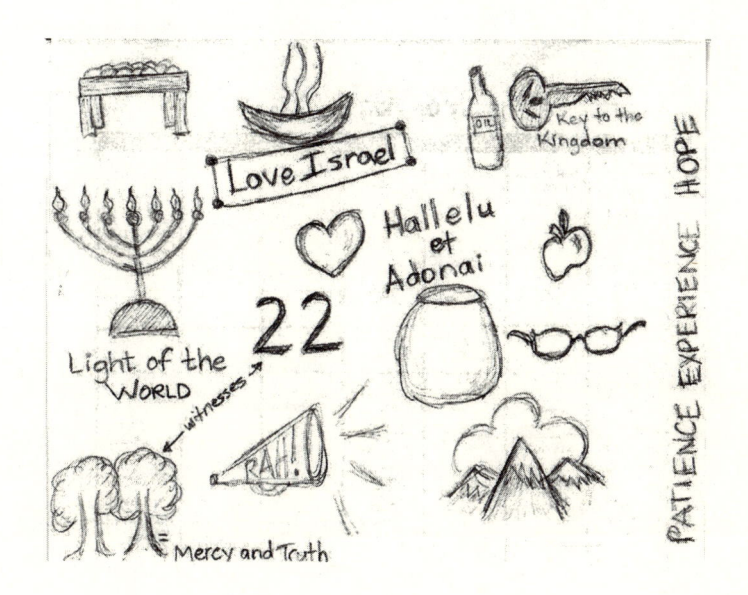

INTRODUCING...
THE NEW TESTAMENT
POP CORN
HEAR
Starring ISAIAH
LET YOUR LIGHT SHINE!
RECOVER
SALT
RESTORE
SEE
JOY
FAITH
SEEDS
30
60
100

4:14 Verses in the New Covenant

If this last section of our study doesn't light your fire for God and His Kingdom, your wood's too wet! After I figured out the Lord wanted me to write the revelations found in the verses numbered 4:14, I looked up every one and wrote them all out in sequence, to see if any sense could be made of it. After all, the Old Testament 4:14 verses seemed to flow nicely together, and they gave us a good picture of deliverance, the methods God uses to free us, our responsibility in the process, what we can expect when we don't follow the plan of God, and so on.

But nothing about these verses in their sequential order in the Old Testament scriptures compared to what was revealed in the sequential order of the 4:14 verses in the New Testament writings. What you are about to read now will absolutely confirm the hand of God in the book we call the Holy Bible – not only in the original manuscript writings, but in the King James translation and its numbering of chapters and verses as well. Even though the book was translated into English more than a thousand years after its writing, and the numbering of verses was added by the translators, God proves Himself once more as the Divine inspiration, even of the numbering!

God's heart on the matter of freedom and restoration, the deliverance of all His creation, is revealed throughout Scripture in the 4:14 verses, and nowhere does it come together in such clarity as in the books of the New Testament. Here now is every 4:14 verse in the New

Testament, in its sequential order, without the interruption of chapter and verse numbering:

> That it might be fulfilled which was spoken by Isaiah the prophet, saying,

> The sower soweth the word.

> And Jesus returned in the power of the Spirit into Galilee: and there went out a fame of him through all the region round about.

> But whosoever drinketh of the water that I shall give him shall never thirst; but the water that I shall give him shall be in him a well of water springing up into everlasting life.

> And beholding the man which was healed standing with them, they could say nothing against it.

> For if they which are of the law be heirs, faith is made void, and the promise made of none effect:

> I write not these things to shame you, but as my beloved sons I warn you.

> Knowing that he which raised up the Lord Jesus shall raise up us also by Jesus, and shall present us with you.

> And my temptation which was in my flesh ye despised not, nor rejected; but received me as an angel of God, even as Christ Jesus.

> That we henceforth be no more children, tossed to and fro, and carried about with every wind of doctrine, by the sleight of men, and cunning craftiness, whereby they lie in wait to deceive;

> Notwithstanding ye have well done, that ye did communicate with my affliction.

> Luke, the beloved physician, and Demas, greet you.

> For if we believe that Jesus died and rose again, even so them also which sleep in Jesus will God bring with him.

> Neglect not the gift that is in thee, which was given thee by prophecy, with the laying on of the hands of the presbytery.

> Alexander the coppersmith did me much evil: the Lord reward him according to his works:

Seeing then that we have a great high priest, that is passed into the heavens, Jesus the Son of God, let us hold fast our profession.

Whereas ye know not what shall be on the morrow. For what is your life? It is even a vapor, that appeareth for a little time, and then vanisheth away.

If ye be reproached for the name of Christ, happy are ye; for the Spirit of glory and of God resteth upon you: on their part he is evil spoken of, but on your part he is glorified.

And we have seen and do testify that the Father sent the Son to be the Savior of the world.

By stringing together the 4:14 verses of the New Testament in order, we get the full picture. If you feel a little overwhelmed at the awesomeness of our Creator, that's a good thing. The whole gospel of the Kingdom of God, the revelation of Jesus Christ, our walk with Him, the challenges we face and overcome, the victories we experience, and culmination of all things is contained in these verses. It begins with the revelation of Jesus Christ by the prophet Isaiah, and Jesus' words "the sower (God the Father) sows the word (Jesus Christ)" and ends with the uncompromising declaration "we have seen and do testify that the Father sent the Son to be the Savior of the world." Hallelujah!

This book could end right here and we'd all have a full meal under our spiritual belts, but don't put it down, because it's only going to get better as we look at each verse individually in its context, the same way we did in the Old Testament Hebrew writings. If you recall, there was not a fourteenth verse in the fourth chapter of Isaiah. Now that you see the New Testament verses, you probably understand why…. it's because the entire book of Isaiah is about the deliverance of God's creation through our Lord and Savior Jesus Christ – it's all about Him, it's not about me.

Hand of God in the NT...

Well of water — Springing up

GOD's WRESTLING FEDERATION

Everlasting Life

Expose the Unclean — Glorify the Father

Sound Off — YOU ANGEL NEW — Hear Ye! Hear Ye!

READ THE BOOK

† For Unto Us A Child Is Born

Broken Heart = SEEDS of Righteousness

→ UN 🍎 FULLNESS... NOT AN OPTION

Matthew

"That it might be fulfilled which was spoken by Isaiah the prophet, saying," - Matthew 4:14

To what reference in the writings of Isaiah is Matthew referring? Let's find out;

Mat 4:14 That it might be fulfilled which was spoken by Isaiah the prophet, saying,

Mat 4:15 The land of Zebulun, and the land of Naphtali, by the way of the sea, beyond Jordan, Galilee of the Gentiles;

Mat 4:16 The people which sat in darkness saw great light; and to them which sat in the region and shadow of death light is sprung up.

Even though the passage seems – and it is – pretty much self-explanatory, clearly declaring the light of the Lord Jesus Christ as having entered a dark and dying world, let's take the original meanings of the names in verse 15 and look at the deeper confirmation that this is a message of both personal and corporate deliverance. The land of Zebulon and the land of Naphtali speak of two of the tribes of Israel, but there is more to it than just that. Zebulon means habitation or dwelling, and Napthali means wrestling, a struggle. Isaiah's prophecy being referred to is for a people of God who are struggling within themselves.

We are the land of God's habitation, we are the temple of God, and there is a wrestling going on. We are beset by sin. Evil spirits are on assignment to carry us into attitudes and actions of sinning; and it is only by the grace of God, our faith in the truth and light of Jesus that we overcome.

Eph 6:12 *For we wrestle not against flesh and blood, but against principalities, against powers, against the rulers of the darkness of this world, against spiritual wickedness in high places.*

Rom 7:19 *For the good that I would I do not: but the evil which I would not, that I do.*

Rom 7:20 *Now if I do that I would not, it is no more I that do it, but sin that dwelleth in me.*

In verse 15 of Matthew chapter four, "by way of the sea" is an indication that we are indeed talking about people. In Biblical imagery, "sea" is one of those words used to symbolize God's people; so "by way of the sea" is not simply a geographical locator – it is a confirmation that Zebulon and Napthali describe a people, not just a place. The root meaning of "sea" is "salt." Jesus said we are the salt of the earth, and we need to keep our flavor. Think about salt for a minute, because there is a choice we make, even in being salted. We can allow ourselves to be salted on the outside, so that we are flavorful on a superficial or surface level only; or we can allow the salt to permeate our being so that we are flavorful throughout. Surface salt does not preserve, but salt that has penetrated is a preservative. There is a difference in being salted and being seasoned.

Mat 5:13 *Ye are the salt of the earth: but if the salt have lost his savor, wherewith shall it be salted? it is thenceforth good for nothing, but to be cast out, and to be trodden under foot of men.*

Continuing our examination of the meaning of Isaiah's prophecy, referred to in Matthew: "Galilee of the Gentiles" tells us what's coming next also includes the "circle of the heathen." A people who were no people are to be made partakers of the heavenly covenant made for Abraham.

1Pe 2:9 But ye are a chosen generation, a royal priesthood, a holy nation, a peculiar people; that ye should show forth the praises of him who hath called you out of darkness into his marvelous light:

1Pe 2:10 Which in time past were not a people, but are now the people of God: which had not obtained mercy, but now have obtained mercy.

According to the prophecy, the Gentiles sat in darkness, or obscurity. This word comes from a root word which is also used in this verse, shadow, which means "darkness of error." Region in this verse in Matthew means, "empty," and comes from the root word meaning "chasm or gulf." It is a vast emptiness. People who sat in obscure darkness of error, empty inside, void of hope or understanding, facing eternal death, were about to have great light come into their lives to enable them to win the wrestling match. Certainly, we can see how this scripture applies to us in our own lives today as the light and truth of the Lord Jesus illuminates our hearts and exposes every unclean thing so we can be rid of it.

There is much darkness of error still in our lives, and in the church body as a whole. Only the light of Jesus can dispel it. The good news is the prophecy of Isaiah has come to pass and the great light has entered the world. Now it's up to us to shine it forth!

Mat 5:14 Ye are the light of the world. A city that is set on a hill cannot be hid.

Mat 5:15 Neither do men light a candle, and put it under a bushel, but on a candlestick; and it giveth light unto all that are in the house.

Mat 5:16 Let your light so shine before men, that they may see your good works, and glorify your Father which is in heaven.

The question becomes "how do we do that?" How can we let the light of Jesus shine to the glory of God and not man? First, we must realize the truth that <u>we are the light</u>! <u>God works through us.</u>

Php 2:13 For it is God which worketh in you both to will and to do of His good pleasure.

God uses man to accomplish His purposes in the earth. We don't use God, He uses us, if we choose to allow Him to. The operative word is "let" – let your light shine – it's our choice. As we allow the Lord to move and work through us, the natural outflow is an exemplary life filled with what the Bible calls good works. We need to realize we can't "work up" good works, and doing good works will not grow our faith. But it is our faith that produces the good works that glorify the Father. Faith and works are connected in Scripture.

Jam 2:17 Even so faith, if it hath not works, is dead, being alone.

Jam 2:18 Yea, a man may say, Thou hast faith, and I have works: show me thy faith without thy works, and I will show thee my faith by my works.

James is saying if good works are not flowing out of faith, then our faith is dead… it is not faith TOWARD GOD, but faith toward something else. In other words, we can have good works in our lives without faith toward God, but we cannot have faith toward God without good works flowing as a natural result of that faith.

It is our faith in the Lord Jesus Christ that shines forth and expresses itself in actions and attitudes pleasing to God and endearing to men. It is our faith that draws people to us. Others see the strength in our everyday walk with the Lord, they notice the joy we have even in those times we are challenged and beset with obstacles. The joy of the Lord is our strength, and the joy of the Lord shining through us is the light of the world. It all comes from faith toward God, when we purposefully choose to believe Him and lean on

Him and trust in Him in all circumstances. That's when the joy comes and the light shines.

So if the light that produces good works comes from joy and joy stems from faith, we need to take a quick look at faith... Everybody believes something. There is no such thing as a non-believer. What we believe is a direct result of what we choose to hear. The voice we listen to is the voice we come to believe. When we choose to believe the bad report of the doctor, for example, we can quickly be overcome by the disease he has diagnosed.

When we choose to believe the curses spoken over us as children ("You're stupid, lazy, worthless, a loser, etc."), we will live a life void of victory because we have succumbed to the opinions of others rather than the opinion of God ("You're precious, valuable, smart, your life has purpose, etc."). When we choose to believe the world has the answer to our need, we will live a life of fear and lack. When we choose to believe the voices of independence, rebellion and self-preservation, we will undergo a long and lonely wilderness experience. Again, it's my choice as to what I hear, and what I believe.

Rom 10:13 For whosoever shall call upon the name of the Lord shall be saved.

Rom 10:14 How then shall they call on him in whom they have not believed? and how shall they believe in him of whom they have not heard? and how shall they hear without a preacher?

Rom 10:15 And how shall they preach, except they be sent? as it is written, How beautiful are the feet of them that preach the gospel of peace, and bring glad tidings of good things!

Rom 10:16 But they have not all obeyed the gospel. For Isaiah saith, Lord, who hath believed our report?

Rom 10:17 So then faith cometh by hearing, and hearing by the word of God.

Notice that we've come again to where we started in the 4:14 verse – the prophet Isaiah. Isaiah prophesied the gospel and then said, "who has believed our report?" There must be those who speak the gospel, and yet not all who hear the gospel will HEAR the gospel. **Lord, give us ears to hear!**

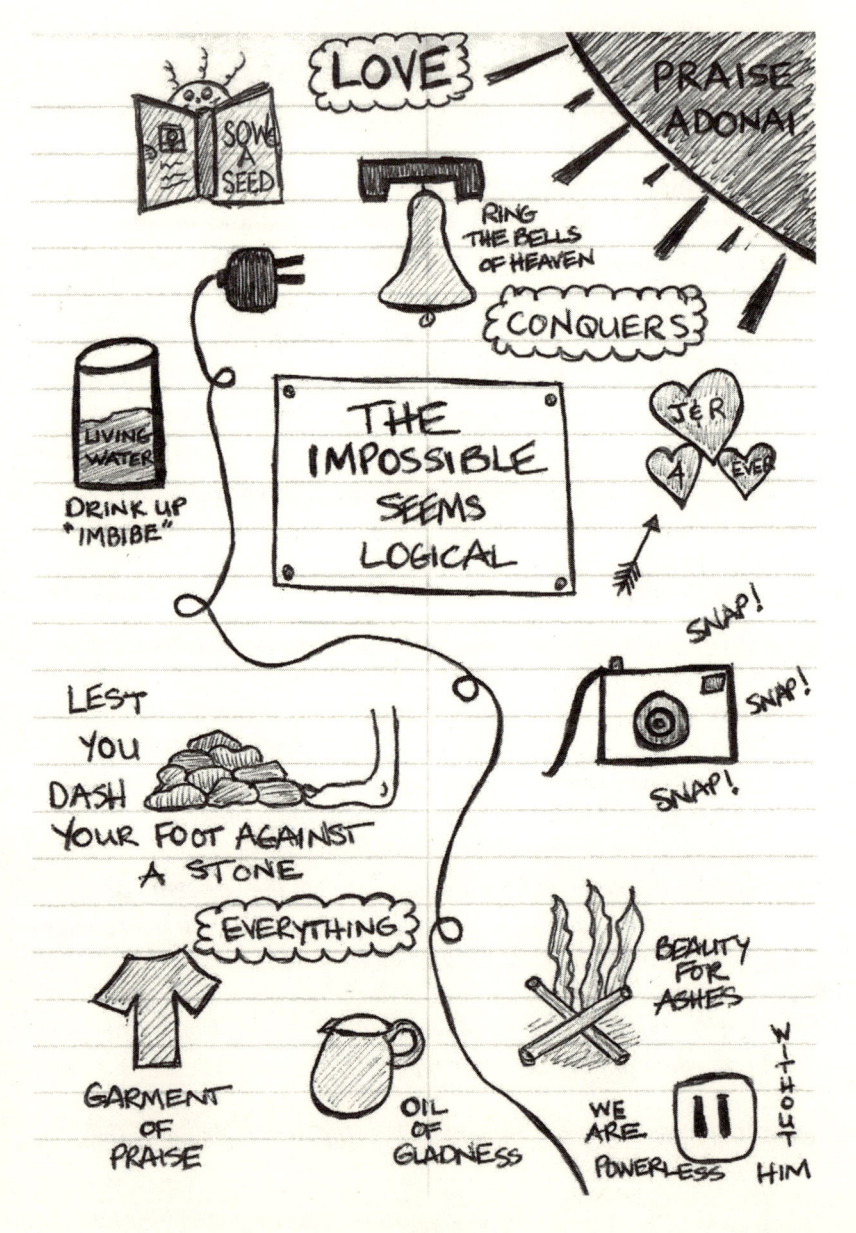

Mark

"The sower soweth the word." - Mark 4:14

Faith comes by hearing, and hearing by the word of God which is sown into our lives. There are many dimensions to this verse, which is the beginning of what may be Jesus' most well known parable, and one we all have heard preached dozens or even hundreds of times. But no matter how many times we've heard it, there is something more to hear. How shall they hear without a preacher? The sower sows the word.

Joh 1:1 In the beginning was the Word, and the Word was with God, and the Word was God.

Isa 7:14 Therefore the Lord himself shall give you a sign; Behold, a virgin shall conceive, and bear a son, and shall call his name Immanuel.

Luk 1:30 And the angel said unto her, Fear not, Mary: for thou hast found favor with God.

Luk 1:31 And, behold, thou shalt conceive in thy womb, and bring forth a son, and shalt call his name JESUS.

Luk 1:32 He shall be great, and shall be called the Son of the Highest: and the Lord God shall give unto him the throne of his father David:

Luk 1:33 And he shall reign over the house of Jacob forever; and of his kingdom there shall be no end.

Luk 1:34 Then said Mary unto the angel, How shall this be, seeing I know not a man?

Luk 1:35 And the angel answered and said unto her, The Holy Ghost shall come upon thee, and the power of the Highest shall overshadow thee: therefore also that holy thing which shall be born of thee shall be called the Son of God.

Isa 9:6 For unto us a child is born, unto us a son is given: and the government shall be upon his shoulder: and his name shall be called Wonderful, Counselor, The mighty God, The everlasting Father, The Prince of Peace.

Joh 1:14 And the Word was made flesh, and dwelt among us, (and we beheld his glory, the glory as of the only begotten of the Father,) full of grace and truth.

The sower sows the word. God the Father by His Holy Spirit sowed the word, His only begotten Son, and those with ears to hear, heard the Word. The Word, Jesus Christ, is still being spoken by the preachers, you and me, and the Word is still being heard by those with ears to hear. The Word we do not say speaks far louder and more clearly than the words we use. Our very life is the testimony of Christ, or should be. In order for that to be the case, the parable of the sower must be understood.

The Word, the very seed life of Jesus Christ is broadcast throughout the earth, and falls in every garden, the garden of the heart. Some falls near the garden path, some on stony ground, some among thorns and some in good ground. His disciples ask the Lord what the parable means and Jesus explains it to them. Notice this – Jesus tells the disciples that understanding is not given to everyone, but only to those who are willing to be taught so they can teach, to be fed so they can feed others, to partake of the kingdom so they can advance the kingdom.

Please don't skip over this, thinking you already know all about it. Perhaps there is a deeper understanding. Perhaps the Lord will open it here and share it with you.

Mar 4:14 The sower soweth the word.

Mar 4:15 And these are they by the way side, where the word is sown; but when they have heard, Satan cometh immediately, and taketh away the word that was sown in their hearts.

When we are not "in" the way, but are instead "by" the way, meaning we are <u>near but not on</u> the path of righteousness, we are compromised in our walk with the Lord. These are they who are by the wayside. In that place of compromise, the truth of the Word that is sown in our hearts can easily be stolen from us by the voice of the enemy.

Psa 44:15 My confusion is continually before me, and the shame of my face hath covered me,

Psa 44:16 For the voice of him that reproacheth and blasphemeth; by reason of the enemy and avenger.

The second positional place of danger is one with no root in itself.

Mar 4:16 And these are they likewise which are sown on stony ground; who, when they have heard the word, immediately receive it with gladness;

Mar 4:17 And have no root in themselves, and so endure but for a time: afterward, when affliction or persecution ariseth for the word's sake, immediately they are offended.

This is a Pharisaical spirit which takes offense at the truth. It brings with it doubt and unbelief. We begin to hold on to bitterness, closing ourselves off and hardening our hearts. Usually, we do this in an attempt to defend ourselves from hurt, and we operate from a spirit of self-preservation. In this position, we can receive a word from the Lord, but will let go of it at the first sign of personal discomfort. In other words, if it's convenient for us, we take it; but when the word becomes hard, we forsake it.

Mat 11:4 Jesus answered and said unto them, Go and show John again those things which ye do hear and see:

Mat 11:5 The blind receive their sight, and the lame walk, the lepers are cleansed, and the deaf hear, the dead are raised up, and the poor have the gospel preached to them.

Mat 11:6 And blessed is he, whosoever shall not be offended in me.

The third position of danger is one of becoming immersed in the ways of the world.

Mar 4:18 And these are they which are sown among thorns; such as hear the word,

Mar 4:19 And the cares of this world, and the deceitfulness of riches, and the lusts of other things entering in, choke the word, and it becometh unfruitful.

In this scenario, the seed is sown, the word enters, and then is overcome by all the distractions and temporal pleasures the world offers. Again, it's our choice as to whether or not we allow ourselves to be ruled by the world or by the Word. The ways of the world have a way of enticing us, luring us into giving up our time and talents to vain pursuits that profit us nothing. In Leviticus, God warns of how not caring for His word leads to unfruitfulness.

Lev 26:18 And if ye will not yet for all this hearken unto me, then I will punish you seven times more for your sins.

Lev 26:19 And I will break the pride of your power; and I will make your heaven as iron, and your earth as brass:

Lev 26:20 And your strength shall be spent in vain: for your land shall not yield her increase, neither shall the trees of the land yield their fruits.

Finally, we have the word that falls on good ground, which is a prepared heart.

Mar 4:20 And these are they which are sown on good ground; such as hear the word, and receive it, and bring forth fruit, some thirtyfold, some sixty, and some a hundred.

How do we prepare our hearts? Both Jeremiah and Hosea tell us to "break up the fallow ground." David tells us in Psalms "a broken and contrite heart" the Lord will not despise. Contrite literally means "crushed to powder." So if you've been through some stuff that has left you feeling crushed, be very encouraged! The crushing process is part of the preparation of our hearts that enables us to receive good seed into good ground. Part of the process is sowing in righteousness.

Hos 10:12 Sow to yourselves in righteousness, reap in mercy; break up your fallow ground: for it is time to seek the LORD, till he come and rain righteousness upon you.

Father God, I come to You in the precious name of the Lord Jesus Christ and I thank You for the truth of Your Word and the revelation of Your divine guidance in this book we call the Bible. Thank You, Father, for sowing the Word into the earth, Your Son Jesus, who is the light of the world. Thank You for the great light that shines in the darkness, shining through each one of us. Help me, Lord God, to be the light You created me to be. Expose any darkness in my heart, Lord. Bring into Your marvelous light the enemies that beset me. I want to be salted through and through, not just sprinkled with a surface flavor, Lord, but permeated with flavor in every part of my being. As an act of my will, I choose to forgive my ancestors, and every other person in my life who opened a door for spiritual error to take occasion to deceive me. I ask Your forgiveness, Father, for participating with spiritual error, and spirits of religion. I recognize I have allowed bitterness in my heart, and I repent to You, Father. Lord, I have experienced spiritual deafness and spiritual blindness, and I ask that You open my ears to Your truth, and that You expel all spiritual deafness and all spiritual blindness from me. I break all agreement with these evil things, Lord, and I break agreement with doubt and unbelief. I declare the blood of the Lord Jesus Christ is all powerful and effective to free me from doubt and unbelief, spiritual error, spiritual deafness, spiritual blindness, the spirit of Pharisees and all other religious spirits. Thank You for Your freedom, Lord, that You died to give me. AMEN.

Luke

"And Jesus returned in the power of the Spirit into Galilee: and there went out a fame of him through all the region round about." - Luke 4:14

In our sequence of verses that flow so beautifully together in the New Testament, this verse follows the sowing of the word. When the Word is sown in our hearts in good ground, we are strengthened in the power of the Spirit and enabled to take the Word to the unsaved effectively. The result is a lot of talk about Jesus everywhere we go, and beyond where we've been. The Word is spread throughout all the region round about us – our families, our co-workers, our neighbors, those we do business with, even casual acquaintances begin to hear the Word spoken through us and especially by the way we live our lives. Remember, the words we do not say are heard more clearly than those we speak. When we are walking in the power of the Spirit of God, people notice, and Jesus is glorified!

Looking at the meanings of the words in this 4:14 verse in Luke, we see that at the end of Satan's temptation of the Lord, because Jesus withstood the temptations, He "returned in the power of the Spirit into Galilee." The word returned means to go back again or come back again, and "power" means "miracle power." The root of this word "power" is "to be able or to be possible."

One of our goals is the renewed mind. Bill Johnson (Bethel Church in Redding, CA) says this – and we agree

– "you'll know you have a renewed mind when the impossible seems logical to you." That is really when we have the mind of Christ! There are many verses that speak of this miracle power - God's ability and His possibility. In other words, no matter what, it is possible, and He is able.

Mar 10:27 And Jesus looking upon them saith, With men it is impossible, but not with God: for with God all things are possible.

Mar 9:23 Jesus said unto him, If thou canst believe, all things are possible to him that believeth.

Mat 9:28 And when he was come into the house, the blind men came to him: and Jesus saith unto them, Believe ye that I am able to do this? They said unto him, Yea, Lord.

Mat 9:29 Then touched he their eyes, saying, According to your faith be it unto you.

Eph 3:20 Now unto him that is able to do exceeding abundantly above all that we ask or think, according to the power that worketh in us,

Eph 3:21 Unto him be glory in the church by Christ Jesus throughout all ages, world without end. Amen.

We see in Luke 4:14 that Jesus, in the ability of miracle power, returned to the "circle of the heathen" (that's Galilee) and began to make realities out of possibilities. And we know that is what happened, because everybody was talking about Him. If Jesus had not demonstrated the miracle power of God, His reputation would not have spread throughout the region. The word "fame" literally means everybody was talking!

There were rumors flying about everywhere concerning this man and the miracle power of God flowing through Him. Those who were healed and set free didn't even have to say so – the testimony of their lives was the evidence of the miracle power of God working through Jesus.

The miracle power Jesus had was born out of the Word of God. In the temptations Satan brought before Jesus, the Lord answered two times, "It is written." At the third temptation, Satan himself used the word of God, showing how the Word can be twisted.

People are still doing that today. Rather than allowing the Word to come alive with the plan of God and our part in God's plan, we have a tendency to make our own plan and then find a scripture to validate what we want to do. For most of us, at some time or another, it's not the plan _of_ God, it's our plan _for_ God. We want to change things we don't understand, but the truth is: God's plan is more important than my understanding of it. I just need to agree and obey.

In the third temptation, Satan spoke something that made sense to a carnal mind, and even backed it up with the word of God.

Luk 4:9 And he brought him to Jerusalem, and set him on a pinnacle of the temple, and said unto him, If thou be the Son of God, cast thyself down from hence:

Luk 4:10 For it is written, He shall give his angels charge over thee, to keep thee:

Luk 4:11 And in their hands they shall bear thee up, lest at any time thou dash thy foot against a stone.

Luk 4:12 And Jesus answering said unto him, It is said, Thou shalt not tempt the Lord thy God.

People can "prove" most any doctrine you can think of by taking verses out of context, or stringing together scriptural concepts that are unrelated to the situation or problem at hand. What results becomes a tradition, a man-made teaching fashioned from the Word as it is understood by carnal thinking, and this then becomes a denominational doctrine that nullifies the Word of God.

Mar 7:13 Making the word of God of none effect through your tradition, which ye have delivered: and many such like things do ye.

Going back to the account in Luke, we see that the third time Satan tempted Jesus, supporting his suggestion with Scripture, Jesus made a declaration. The word "said" in Luke 4:12 indicates a pouring forth, either spoken or written. It is emphatic. Lots of things are written, but when we add our declaration to the word – our "amen" faith to God's "amen" faith – the temptations have to stop. Declaring the Word in faith is one way we submit ourselves to God, and the devil has to flee. At least for a season.

It is when we know the Word, depend on the Word, and speak the Word that the miracle power of the Holy Spirit can begin to use us in God's work. Jesus returned in the power of the Spirit, after He had answered the temptations of the devil with the living Word of God. It isn't glorifying to God for us to know His word as the letter of the law, to be used to manipulate people and "get stuff" from God. God's Word, without His Spirit in it, will not avail us of a victory. We must get His heart on the matter. The Word is both never-changing and ever-changing because it is so multi-faceted. The dimensions of God's Word are varied, and no matter how long we study it, we will not get it all. As we grow in Him, He can reveal more to us in His Word. (We see things now as we read a passage that we've never noticed before, in spite of the hundreds of times we've read it.)

It is amazing to hear people say, "I've read the Bible" and yet they do not continue to study or read it. It's as if they're saying, I've read it once, so I don't need to read it again. The only time some people open their Bibles is in church, and sometimes not even then. In too many homes, the Bible is nothing more than a coffee table book or a decorative furnishing.

We say we love the Lord, but how can we love someone we don't really know? How can we know someone we don't spend time with? Jesus Christ is the Word of God.

Spending time in the Word is one way we get to know Him better and love Him more.

     Jesus returned in the power of the Spirit and fame of Him was spread everywhere. This verse is the official start of Jesus' ministry, marking His victory over the lust of the eyes, the lust of the flesh and the pride of life. Immediately following this victory is His announcement of the vision and purpose for which He was sent from the Father. Jesus enters the synagogue and reads from the prophet Isaiah. Again, we see the connection of these New Testament verses as being a synopsis of the prophecy of Isaiah.

Luk 4:15 And he taught in their synagogues, being glorified of all.

Luk 4:16 And he came to Nazareth, where he had been brought up: and, as his custom was, he went into the synagogue on the sabbath day, and stood up for to read.

Luk 4:17 And there was delivered unto him the book of the prophet Isaiah. And when he had opened the book, he found the place where it was written,

Luk 4:18 The Spirit of the Lord is upon me, because he hath anointed me to preach the gospel to the poor; he hath sent me to heal the brokenhearted, to preach deliverance to the captives, and recovering of sight to the blind, to set at liberty them that are bruised,

Luk 4:19 To preach the acceptable year of the Lord.

Luk 4:20 And he closed the book, and he gave it again to the minister, and sat down. And the eyes of all them that were in the synagogue were fastened on him.

Luk 4:21 And he began to say unto them, This day is this Scripture fulfilled in your ears.

John

"But whosoever drinketh of the water that I shall give him shall never thirst; but the water that I shall give him shall be in him a well of water springing up into everlasting life." - John 4:14

Here is further confirmation of the miracle power of the Holy Spirit in Christ and His ministry to all people. Jesus Himself is speaking in this verse, and the scene is at Jacob's well, with the Samaritan woman. There is a comparison being made. Jesus first tells the woman, "The water you get from this well will satisfy you only for a little while, and then you're going to be thirsty again." Then He says, "But what I give you will remain in you and become a fountain that will refresh you always and even become a well from which others can be refreshed and brought into everlasting life and joy." <u>We are the wells of God</u>, meant to pour forth the life of the Lord into the lives of others.

Joh 7:38 He that believeth on me, as the scripture hath said, out of his belly shall flow rivers of living water.

Jacob's well was a symbol of the law of God as the Hebrews knew it and followed it. It was a picture of the religious culture and mindset of the day. This well that the patriarch Jacob had dug reminds us of another well associated with Jacob, the well where Jacob met Rachel. When he saw her, he loved her, and he opened the well to water her sheep even though it was the custom to wait until everyone had come together, and that had not yet happened.

Gen 29:7 And he said, Lo, it is yet high day, neither is it time that the cattle should be gathered together: water ye the sheep, and go and feed them.

Gen 29:8 And they said, We cannot, until all the flocks be gathered together, and till they roll the stone from the well's mouth; then we water the sheep.

According to the way things had always been done, it wasn't time. Jacob's love for Rachel was contrasted against the custom of the day. Here in Luke, the freedom and love of the Lord Jesus Christ is being contrasted against a backdrop of religious division on the outskirts of Samaria. Samaria represented the outcasts of Israel, those who were of questionable lineage. They were of mixed blood, and therefore not considered to be Jews, and were definitely unworthy. The custom of the day dictated that Jews were not permitted to interact with Samaritans.

Joh 4:9 Then saith the woman of Samaria unto him, How is it that thou, being a Jew, askest drink of me, which am a woman of Samaria? for the Jews have no dealings with the Samaritans.

But Jesus tells this woman, "whosoever" drinks. She was a Samaritan, and quite surprised that Jesus, a Jew, would even speak with her. The word "drinks" means to imbibe. Imbibing is drinking deeply, not just taking a sip or two. Jesus offers this woman, who is essentially a nobody in the Jewish culture of the day, the key to abundant natural life and eternal spiritual life.

He opened to her the well of salvation, not the well of religion. Our freedom will never be achieved through following a formula of religious activity. It is only through the saving grace inherent in the sacrifice of the Lord Jesus Christ – His blood – that we can be delivered from sin, sickness, poverty and death.

This well of life characterizes the healing ministry of Christ. Jesus began His ministry and worked for three and a half years healing the sick, raising the dead, casting out devils and teaching His disciples to do the same things. After His resurrection, Jesus commissioned the disciples to continue His ministry. He sent the Holy Spirit to empower them, and through the miracle power that raised Jesus from the dead, His disciples revealed Jesus. They continued His ministry, the Lord working with them.

Mar 16:20 And they went forth, and preached every where, the Lord working with them, and confirming the word with signs following. Amen.

Acts

"And beholding the man which was healed standing with them, they could say nothing against it." - Acts 4:14

The Book of Acts gives us an awesome insight into the lives of the disciples – not just those who walked with Jesus in His time on earth, but also of those who believed on Him after His death, resurrection and ascension. These men and women provide for us the same pattern Jesus did – heal the sick, raise the dead, cast out devils – it didn't stop with Jesus and it didn't stop with the original 12 disciples, or with the next 70, nor the 120 after those.

Acts 4:14 shows us that a man with an experience is never at the mercy of a man with an argument. When the gospel is demonstrated, not just talked about, signs and wonders confirm the Word is true. There is no denying it.

Just as the blind man who was harassed by the Pharisees responded, "I don't know whether the guy is a sinner or not – all I know is I was blind, but now I see!" Our lack of intelligence or experience or training – our checkered past or uncertain future - makes no difference to the one receiving a gift from God as it flows through our hands.

This verse in Acts follows the account in chapter three where Peter and John were asked for alms by a crippled man as they approached the temple. Rather than giving the man money, which they didn't have, they offered him a new life through the Lord Jesus Christ, which they had within them.

Act 3:6 Then Peter said, Silver and gold have I none; but such as I have give I thee: In the name of Jesus Christ of Nazareth rise up and walk.

Act 3:7 And he took him by the right hand, and lifted him up: and immediately his feet and ankle bones received strength.

Act 3:8 And he leaping up stood, and walked, and entered with them into the temple, walking, and leaping, and praising God.

Of course, this was an action unacceptable to the religious minds of the day. What Peter and John did was against the rules, and they gave glory to the Lord Jesus, boldly exclaiming His name and His power. But even though the Pharisees were upset, they could not speak against what happened because of the truth that was manifest in their midst. They could not deny the testimony evident in the life of the man who had formerly begged at the gate in a crippled state of being and who was now standing in their midst, whole and healthy. They could not refute or deny the reality of the healing power of Jesus.

Act 4:16 Saying, What shall we do to these men? for that indeed a notable miracle hath been done by them is manifest to all them that dwell in Jerusalem; and we cannot deny it.

The message is this – we must demonstrate the miracle power of the Holy Spirit in us, not just tell people they can have it. We can all doubt what we hear, but no one can deny tangible evidence. It may not be "explainable," but it is reality. The crucifixion and resurrection of the Lord was not just for us, but for everyone. It was not simply that I can be healed, but that I can allow God to work through me to heal others. It was not just to cleanse myself of all filthiness of the flesh and spirit, but to help others cleanse themselves as well. It was not just for me to stand under the spout where the blessings come out, but to rig up multiple shower heads for those around me.

Mat 10:7 And as ye go, preach, saying, The kingdom of heaven is at hand.

Mat 10:8 Heal the sick, cleanse the lepers, raise the dead, cast out devils: freely ye have received, freely give.

We are not meant to be alone and independent. We are not meant to be the "bless me" club of God. Every gift and talent God has given us is for His purpose, not ours. The special gifts of the Holy Spirit working in us and through us are not our gifts… the gift is from the Holy Spirit and belongs to the one who receives it, not the one it's being given through. If you want to say "I have the gift of healing" that is a wrong statement. It's not your gift. It is better to say, "God uses me in the gift of healing."

It is the Lord in us that accomplishes His purpose through us. We are co-laborers with Christ, and without Him we are totally powerless to effectuate any change in our own lives, or in the world around us.

Heb 13:20 Now the God of peace, that brought again from the dead our Lord Jesus, that great shepherd of the sheep, through the blood of the everlasting covenant,

Heb 13:21 Make you perfect in every good work to do his will, working in you that which is wellpleasing in his sight, through Jesus Christ; to whom be glory forever and ever. Amen.

Phi 2:13 For it is God which worketh in you both to will and to do of his good pleasure.

Peter and John gave glory to the Lord for the miracle healing that occurred at their hands – "don't look at us as if we're something great – it's the Lord." They knew clearly the working of the miracle power of the Holy Spirit and used a demonstration of that power to bring people into the knowledge of Jesus.

Act 3:12 And when Peter saw it, he answered unto the people, Ye men of Israel, why marvel ye at this? or why look ye so earnestly on us, as though by our own power or holiness we had made this man to walk?

Act 3:13 The God of Abraham, and of Isaac, and of Jacob, the God of our fathers, hath glorified his Son Jesus; whom ye delivered up, and denied him in the presence of Pilate, when he was determined to let him go.

    A demonstration of Holy Spirit power makes people sit up and take notice. Those who would not receive a word from us about the Lord will begin to listen when we move in words of knowledge, gifts of healing and miracles, and prophecy. When we can speak into a person's life something that only that person and God would know about, it causes ears and hearts to be opened to God and builds faith for others to receive the saving grace of Jesus Christ.

    The sower sows the word – we need to know the Word so we can receive the empowerment of the Holy Spirit. We need to speak the Word so others can hear and receive faith toward God. We need to live the word so we can fulfill the commission of the Lord and our purpose in it. Our demonstration of the Word, bringing to life the freedom Jesus died to give us, sets the atmosphere for others to believe and follow the pattern set by Jesus. It's not about me. It's about Him.

Father God, thank You for the miracle power of the Holy Spirit working in me. I ask that You teach me, Lord, how to walk in the Spirit, and how to speak Your word so that signs and wonders follow, confirming Your word. Lord, I repent for my iniquities, of going my own way, of taking glory due to You and Your name. I repent to You for claiming Your gifts as my own, and I ask Your forgiveness. I repent, Father, for making my own plans and asking You to bless them, rather than agreeing with Your plan and being blessed in it. Lord, I recognize that pride and fear have kept me from fulfilling my purpose in You in many ways, and I ask Your forgiveness. As an act of my will, I choose to forgive my ancestors for opening the door to pride and fear. I forgive my mother and father, my grandparents, parents by the spirit by adoption, godparents and all other ancestors living or dead who participated with those evil spirits. I break all agreement now with every familiar spirit, spirit guide and every other spirit of pride and fear that has taken occasion to afflict or affect me and my family. I speak to those spirits and declare I do not want you in my life, and will no longer entertain you. Father, I know that the blood of the Lord Jesus Christ is all powerful and effective to rid me of those hindering spirits, and I thank You for delivering me from the snare of the fowler, in Jesus name. AMEN.

MORE OF YOU...
MORE OF YOU...
WE ARE THIRSTY
FOR MORE OF YOU!!!

FISHIN'
4
FAITH

DOCTRINE

GOD
THRONE ROOM
HEAVEN
07/07/07 777
PAY TO Abraham $
All Blessings
FOR INHERITANCE   God
333777 555111

DANGER!
PELIGRO!
FOLLOW GOD!

Denomination?
100
WHO
CARES?
? 5 1
10

BIG STEPS   BIG SHOES
WALK ON

Romans

"For if they which are of the law be heirs, faith is made void, and the promise made of none effect: - Romans 4:14

Y̶ou may hear people say that Christianity is an exclusive religion; and that is true in the sense we believe there is only one way to achieve total salvation, and that is through faith in the blood of the Lord Jesus Christ. No other religion has the answer of eternal life. In most other major belief systems, people must physically die for their god. In Christianity, our God died for us. There is but One who has the words of eternal life.

Joh 6:66 From that time many of his disciples went back, and walked no more with him.

Joh 6:67 Then said Jesus unto the twelve, Will ye also go away?

Joh 6:68 Then Simon Peter answered him, Lord, to whom shall we go? thou hast the words of eternal life.

So, while it is true we have a faith like no other, at the same time, faith in the finished work of the Jesus Christ is not exclusive, in that all people are offered the same package and have the same opportunity to accept the truth. Jesus died for all. He died for each one, but not at the sacrifice of any other. The miracle power of the blood of Jesus, the living water that brings eternal life and flows from believers has been clearly seen flowing out of the disciples' faith.

Faith has been a central theme in the message of deliverance, and here we see the significance of believing in connection to the promises of God. In looking at the New Testament in terms of the progression of our Christian walk, the gospels – Matthew, Mark, Luke, John – and the Book of Acts, are about justification. The books of Romans through Jude are concerned with sanctification, and Revelation speaks of glorification.

With that in mind, we can conclude that our 4:14 verse in Paul's letter to the saints in Rome is a part of the sanctification process. Paul is reasoning with the church concerning faith and the law of Moses. He points out that the promise of blessing was given to Abraham because of his righteousness; and that Abraham was considered righteous because he believed God, not because he followed some prescribed method of ordinances. Faith has righteousness. Verse 13 tells us the righteousness of faith brought the promise of God to Abraham.

Rom 4:13 For the promise, that he should be the heir of the world, was not to Abraham, or to his seed, through the law, but through the righteousness of faith.

Abraham's FAITH toward God, not the sign of outward circumcision, was the deciding factor in making him heir of the world, heir of salvation and all it means; and through him as the example, the promise and inheritance of all things should be made available to the "whosoever wills" – you and me. All who follow the method of Abraham, in other words, those who believe God, will be counted righteous. Not those who follow the letter of the law, but those who follow the Spirit of Christ, are the heirs. If we could do it in our own strength, we would. Mankind has proven for thousands of years we cannot save ourselves through our good works or our own righteousness. It is only by the grace of God, through faith in the Lord Jesus Christ and His sacrificial love, that the promise is made into a benefit in our lives. The righteousness of faith is the only righteousness that can free us from the bondage of the world and release us into the fullness of the Word and freedom of the Spirit.

Paul is doing his best to make it clear to the church at Rome that salvation is for everyone who believes in the Lord Jesus Christ, not just the Jewish people. He states it is not the outward circumcision – the sign of following the law - that saves us, but the inward circumcision of the heart that brings the blessings of God into our lives. And circumcision of the heart is a result of having faith toward God and no other. "Verily, verily" is a phrase used by Jesus and translates "truly, surely, faithfulness, amen, so be it." The translators could have legitimately said "truth, truth" or "faith, faith" because the words have the same meaning and could easily interchange. Faith toward God is truth in action. It is faith that sets us free.

The Apostle Paul wrote a great deal of what we call the New Testament scriptures, and his writings were mostly in the form of letters to the churches throughout Asia and the Mediterranean. Each church dealt with different problems and circumstances, due in part to local cultures and customs. In Rome, it seems the saints were dealing with who's a Jew and who isn't – or more accurately, who are God's chosen people and who aren't. Isn't it interesting the way we still have these questions floating around? Most of the time, the controversy is centered in denominational issues. Who's right and who's wrong? Paul says, who cares? Follow God.

I Corinthians

"I write not these things to shame you, but as my beloved sons I warn you." - 1 Corinthians 4:14

What is it Paul writes as a warning to the Corinthian saints? To find out, we need to go back to chapter three. There, we find what today we call denominational issues. Division in the Body of Christ is nothing new. Paul preached against it 2000 years ago. He first tells the church, I would like to give you something substantial to grow on, but you're not ready to receive it. You're all still into carnal thinking.

1Co 3:1 And I, brethren, could not speak unto you as unto spiritual, but as unto carnal, even as unto babes in Christ.

1Co 3:2 I have fed you with milk, and not with meat: for hitherto ye were not able to bear it, neither yet now are ye able.

1Co 3:3 For ye are yet carnal: for whereas there is among you envying, and strife, and divisions, are ye not carnal, and walk as men?

Here is how Paul determined their carnality – they followed a man's teaching and not God's Spirit. How many of us do the same thing today by saying, "I'm a Baptist," and, "I'm a Methodist," and, "I'm a Lutheran," and so on. We are stuck in the doctrine of man rather than the Spirit of God.

1Co 3:4 For while one saith, I am of Paul; and another, I am of Apollos; are ye not carnal?

1Co 3:5 Who then is Paul, and who is Apollos, but ministers by whom ye believed, even as the Lord gave to every man?

1Co 3:6 I have planted, Apollos watered; but God gave the increase.

1Co 3:7 So then neither is he that planteth any thing, neither he that watereth; but God that giveth the increase.

1Co 3:8 Now he that planteth and he that watereth are one: and every man shall receive his own reward according to his own labor.

1Co 3:9 For we are laborers together with God: ye are God's husbandry, ye are God's building.

Back in the 1940s and '50s, William Branham felt and taught this same thing. He was grieved that the Body of Christ was so divided. According to a biography of Branham, during a healing campaign in California in 1955, Branham "explained that the Roman Catholic Church organized Christianity first, forcing its ideas on millions of illiterate people for hundreds of years. Martin Luther pulled away from Catholicism, following the Pillar of Fire. Luther preached people couldn't earn salvation; rather, it comes as a gift from God. Luther emphasized the Scripture *The just shall live by faith*. Unfortunately, Luther's followers organized into their own denomination. The Pillar of Fire moved on, shedding more light as It went, but the Lutherans couldn't move with It because they had already drawn up documents saying what they believed. Later John Wesley followed the Pillar of Fire into a message of sanctification and holiness, calling it a second work of grace. His preaching caused a revival in England that swept around the world. Unfortunately, his followers organized the Methodist church and carved their doctrines in stone. The Pillar of Fire moved on, but the Methodists couldn't move with It because they were already organized around their doctrines. In 1906 the Pillar of Fire shed more light on the baptism of the Holy Ghost, bringing forth gifts of the Spirit, such as speaking in tongues and prophecy. The people who received this light called themselves Pentecostals. It became the fastest growing Christian movement in the world. So, what did the devil do? He talked the Pentecostals into organizing, which made them draw boundary lines and build fences. They also carved their doctrines in stone, just like earlier movements did." Branham warned his audience, "The Pillar of Fire is moving out again, and the Pentecostal people are so organized they can't move with It. God's Fire will keep moving just like It did in every age. So don't ever draw boundary lines. It's all right to say, 'I believe this,' but don't end it with a period; end it with a comma, meaning, 'I believe this, <u>plus</u> as much more as God will reveal to my heart."

William Branham kept attempting to draw the Body together, which is what Paul was doing in Corinth. Paul tells the saints, "Look, we're all in this thing together. Not one of us is more important than another. We're all ministers, all "laborers together with God." What are we laboring together to accomplish? Building God's people. Paul finishes his exhortation by saying, let everyone who is a minister, called of God (and by, the way, that is every one of us), build on the proper foundation, the doctrines of Jesus Christ.

1Co 3:10 According to the grace of God which is given unto me, as a wise masterbuilder, I have laid the foundation, and another buildeth thereon. But let every man take heed how he buildeth thereupon.

1Co 3:11 For other foundation can no man lay than that is laid, which is Jesus Christ.

Branham echoed Paul's sentiments another time, when he said, "The basic flaw in every denomination is rigidity, which creates barriers. As soon as a group writes down their creeds, bylaws and articles of faith, they freeze God's Spirit of revelation. The Bible is perfect, but man's understanding of the Bible is not. If God gives someone deeper understanding, people who are bound to a denominational creed can't accept it. The hierarchy of leadership inside each denomination resists the spirit of revelation, as each man seeks to preserve his own position within the hierarchy and the overall, comfortable status quo."

This part of Paul's letter to the Corinthian church was meant to prevent division in the Body of Christ, to keep the people from separating into groups that followed one man or another. Paul goes on in chapter three with some great revelation concerning having an eternal eye, and then comes right back to "don't glory in man." Then in chapter four, Paul goes on in this same vein, saying none can glory in himself because each one has nothing he did not receive. In other words, all we have is God-given. It is He that has made us, and not we ourselves, as the psalmist says.

Psa 100:3 *Know ye that the LORD he is God: it is he that hath made us, and not we ourselves; we are his people, and the sheep of his pasture.*

Paul also points out that his position as an apostle is not an enviable one in the eyes of the world. These are the verses which immediately precede our study verse.

1Co 4:9 *For I think that God hath set forth us the apostles last, as it were appointed to death: for we are made a spectacle unto the world, and to angels, and to men.*

1Co 4:10 *We are fools for Christ's sake, but ye are wise in Christ; we are weak, but ye are strong; ye are honorable, but we are despised.*

1Co 4:11 *Even unto this present hour we both hunger, and thirst, and are naked, and are buffeted, and have no certain dwelling place;*

1Co 4:12 *And labor, working with our own hands: being reviled, we bless; being persecuted, we suffer it:*

1Co 4:13 *Being defamed, we entreat: we are made as the filth of the world, and are the offscouring of all things unto this day.*

Anybody still want to be called an apostle? If we are to successfully lead others, we must be willing to make the sacrifices Paul speaks of in this passage... Be a fool for Christ's sake, enduring rejection, hunger, uncertainty and persecution... and get ready to work really, really hard. Bless those who curse you, be nice to people who put you down, endure persecution without defending yourself. If you want people to see Christ in you, to model Jesus, you will likely have to go through some of this kind of thing, or all of it.

Then Paul says, "I'm not telling you all this to make you feel ashamed, or so that you'll feel sorry for me. I only want to give you a warning. Don't forsake what you know to be true. I love you like a father would love you, and so I'm going to give it to you straight. Stay in the way I've taught you as a father. Follow me." – and the implied ending to what Paul says here is - "I'm following Christ."

The message is clear. Don't get off into another doctrine, or make a tradition out of what one or another of us ministers are teaching you. Let the Lord in us lead you in His footsteps; trust those who truly love you and faithfully love the Lord.

You know, the Lord is never-changing and He is ever-changing. His truth remains truth, but His ways are changeable. God speaks to us in different ways, and begins to stretch us. We've said before, if you want to walk with the Lord, you'll have to learn to take big steps. His stride is wide.

II Corinthians

"Knowing that he which raised up the Lord Jesus shall raise up us also by Jesus, and shall present us with you." - 2 Corinthians 4:14

In his second letter to the Corinthian church, Paul continues teaching unity in the love of God and the sacrifice of Christ, as he corrects their skewed doctrinal problems. The focus is once again on the steadfastness of God's promises and the value of humble service in advancing the Kingdom Jesus died to establish for us. Paul reiterates his faithfulness through the trials, temptations and tribulations he had faced and overcome; and tells us how he and others like him could remain faithful to the gospel in spite of the difficulties.

Let's break down word meanings in our 4:14 verse. Knowing – that is a big word, and literally means "seeing." It comes from two other Greek words, one of which means "to gaze with wide open eyes" and the other "to stare at or clearly discern, to experience."

Paul <u>knew</u> by his own experience that the Lord lives. He had a personal encounter with the Lord Jesus, and so he was able to see with an eternal eye, and he saw the reward of resurrection and fullness. That is why he and others could endure the hardships they faced. Faithfulness to Kingdom principles is possible because of relationship with the Lord, and not for any other reason. If we have an intellectual conversion, but not a spiritual conversion, the enemy will not find it difficult to entice us back into the world, or simply to receive us when we come running back to a false peace or false security or false provision because life took a hard turn and we hit the rail. Each one of us needs a personal encounter with the Lord Jesus, and He is even more eager than we are for that to take place.

Let's talk practically for a moment. There are few of us who have had the kind of dramatic encounter Paul had. Not many have a "Damascus road experience" where the brilliant glory of the Lord descends and strikes us blind and He then speaks audibly, telling us clearly who He is and what we are to do. Our relationship with Jesus may be defined by a gentle knowing in our hearts, a peace that surrounds us in times of trouble, a gentle nudge to go a certain way. It may be an overpowering feeling of love, a weeping, a longing, an uncontrollable joy. Encountering Jesus can come about in any number of ways. He can visit us in the night in a dream or at any time through an open vision.

One thing is certain. No matter how we meet Him, the meeting will forever change us. And as we "follow on to know the Lord" we will begin to experience a deepening intimacy, a growing sense of security and peace, and a heightened discernment of spiritual matters. Eternal vision is the "knowing" Paul expressed. "I know Jesus is alive, He showed me clearly that is true. And I know because He lives, so do I. Because He was raised bodily from the dead, so will I be. This is why I do the things I do." The verse preceding our study verse gives us another confirmation of the significance of faith and how it manifests.

> 2Co 4:13 *We having the same spirit of faith, according as it is written, I believed, and therefore have I spoken; we also believe, and therefore speak;*

The spirit of faith works in each of us, according to what we believe and speak. When we believe the worst, and speak it, we get to experience it. When we believe God's promise, and speak it, we get to experience it. Paul is telling the saints: we believe we will receive the fulfillment of all God's promises toward us; and being fully convinced of what we believe, we testify boldly that our deliverance is from

God. He does not fail those who trust in Him, and He saves to the uttermost – spirit, soul and BODY – those who come to Him through Jesus Christ.

What do we believe, and what do we speak? Can we, as Paul did, know the end of the matter? Yes, absolutely. Paul shared his testimony of the Damascus road encounter, and also of the tribulations he went through. He testified so that those listening could respond to God's grace and goodness toward him with thanksgiving, to the glory of God, and so they could enter the same grace and goodness in their own lives. Each testimony is a "do it again, God."

I was saved when I accepted the Lord Jesus as my Redeemer, immersing my faith in His blood. I am saved today, preserved for all eternity as belonging to Him. I am being saved moment by moment and day by day as I grow in my relationship with the Lord and progress further in my purpose of advancing His Kingdom in the earth. And I will be saved at the resurrection when my Body is fully redeemed from the corruption of flesh. The process is this – I am justified, I am being sanctified and I will be glorified.

We serve an amazing God Who loves us so much He has given us not only the thousands of promises inherent in our salvation package, but also instruction in how to convert those promises into benefits in our lives. The mysteries of heaven are laid up _for_ us, not from us. As stewards of the mysteries, we have a responsibility to respond to God's ability. God never reveals something simply so we can have the knowledge of it. He wants us to apply that knowledge into our lives and move into wisdom. We must respond to the ability of God, and allow Him to do what only He can do. He reveals something to us, then says, "Now that you know this, allow Me to bring judgment and justice into this area of your life." We must allow God to bring judgment on those things that are not pleasing to Him or beneficial to us. When God brings judgment on a thing, it is an expression of His mercy because it carries justice – it rights the wrongs of the enemy against us and leaves us better off.

Father, thank You for this word. Thank You for the awesome way You reveal Yourself and for Your promise of total deliverance. Show me how to turn Your promise into a benefit, Lord. I declare to You this day I believe You. I believe Your Word is true, and I will speak it. From today, Father, I purpose to speak of Your goodness and Your grace, so that my testimony, like Paul's, will be a "do it again" for someone else. I ask Your forgiveness, Lord, for those times I've doubted You and turned back to the things of the world, seeking satisfaction that only You can provide. Forgive me for following the doctrine of man rather than Your Holy Spirit. Help me, Lord, to recognize Your leading, to hear only Your voice, to respond quickly and decisively to Your will and not my own. I break all agreement with a spirit of division that would cause me to judge others who may not yet understand the revelations I've been given, and those who have revelations I've not yet understood. Give me Your heart on the matter, Lord, whatever the matter is. I know that You alone have the Word of eternal life. I break all agreement with a spirit of confusion that would lead me hither and yon in a vain search for truth that is easily available in You. Give me the Spirit of Your Word, Lord, and not the letter only. I break all agreement with spiritual deception, spiritual error and spiritual bondage, Lord, and I ask that You free me from those evils and release me into Your perfect will for my life. In the name of Jesus, I ask these things; and I declare the blood of the Lord Jesus Christ is all powerful and effective to accomplish all I ask. AMEN

Galatians

"And my temptation which was in my flesh ye despised not, nor rejected; but received me as an angel of God, even as Christ Jesus." - Galatians 4:14

Now we move with Paul to Galatia and his message to the churches there. Paul's tone is one of disappointment, I think, that those converts in Galatia would slip away from the true gospel, and that they would begin to doubt his own credibility in the doctrines of Christ that he had taught them. Paul seems to be a bit angry, and frustrated as well, that those he had so diligently taught, and who had so eagerly accepted him and what he had to say, turned back to other gods and to the law.

Gal 4:8 Howbeit then, when ye knew not God, ye did service unto them which by nature are no gods.

Gal 4:9 But now, after that ye have known God, or rather are known of God, how turn ye again to the weak and beggarly elements, whereunto ye desire again to be in bondage?

Gal 4:10 Ye observe days, and months, and times, and years.

Gal 4:11 I am afraid of you, lest I have bestowed upon you labor in vain.

Paul says, "You know, I understand that before you knew God you were serving other gods, but now that you know the truth, how could you do that? You're putting yourselves back into bondage with your trust in astrology; and it looks as if I've taught you and loved you and guided you for nothing." Then he changes the tone somewhat and begins to reason with them – "Please realize we're all in this together, and your actions are hurting you, not me." That is the background of our verse. Read it again.

Gal 4:14 And my temptation which was in my flesh ye despised not, nor rejected; but received me as an angel of God, even as Christ Jesus.

There is some controversy over this text in the scholarly world, and some translators say "your temptation" instead of "my temptation." But it really doesn't matter because it doesn't change the meaning of what Paul is trying to convey here. The word "temptation" indicates a trial of any kind. He says the people did not consider him less anointed or less an apostle of God because he had an affliction. The affliction is likely the same "thorn in the flesh" Paul spoke of in II Corinthians, or it could have been any other infirmity he suffered under the weight of the workload of his ministry (which was certainly very great).

Paul basically reminded this church at Galatia if they had not thought him credible, they would have used his infirmity to revile him – "Look at him, he's no apostle. If God had sent him, surely He would have sustained him. He's no extraordinary messenger because if he were, he'd be in perfect health." People who choose not to believe the truth use any number of reasons why it isn't true. It's a good example of how our reasoning can destroy our faith. "Well, this guy's got so many problems in his life, his ministry must be false." That is a self-righteous, religious attitude. God can, and does, speak through and work through all kinds of people (even the unsaved) to accomplish His purposes.

One of the reasons people don't receive a word from the Lord is the way it's packaged. Unless the messenger "looks" the part, we tend to discredit the word he brings. We have our own pre-conceived ideas of what an apostle is – certain age, certain education, certain mannerisms, certain clothes, and so on. The same thing is true with the other vocational offices – prophet, evangelist, pastor, and teacher. We are the ones who practice respect of persons, not God. Paul makes this point when he says, "You didn't act this way toward me before." As a matter of fact, Paul goes on to say they had shown the highest affection for him, and had previously accepted him as God's messenger.

This is the lesson we can gain from this verse. Even though a person has problems, it doesn't mean he or she is not anointed or has somehow lost the anointing of God in what he or she is doing or saying. We may have an awesome experience with the Lord, because of the insights we're given by a certain minister, and then later find out the minister is flawed. Does that negate what the Lord did through him? Does that make the minister an outcast, or his anointing no longer valid? I think not. Don't give up your deliverance – your healing and freedom – because a minister stumbles or falls or seems to have a weakness. God's plan (and whom He chooses to use in it) is bigger than our understanding of it!

Clearly, we are to trust God and not man. Judge the message, not the messenger. One is not more anointed than another because he has the right appearance, money, position, power or health.

Jam 2:9 But if ye have respect to persons, ye commit sin, and are convinced of the law as transgressors.

If we receive the word of the Lord only when it suits us, and then condemn the messenger when the word is not soft and pleasing, we're in trouble. Those of us in full-time ministry know a little about how Paul felt. Many times in ministry – and if you haven't already discovered this, you will – many times, a person will love you and appreciate the wonderful way you've given them insight and helped them overcome some obstacle in their lives. Then later they fall back for one reason or another; and suddenly the word you have for them is despised.

It's not easy to give someone a hard word, knowing it may not be received, and you will be thrown out right along with the word of the Lord. The good news is: God knows our hearts, and He redeems our time. Whenever you minister the Word of the Lord to someone, imparting an understanding they may not yet have, you are walking in wisdom; and God will restore to you whatever time you spent with that person. There is never an excuse of "I don't have time" to pray for someone, or to give wise counsel, or to share the Word. The Lord Himself will see to it that all those other things you think you have to do get done! He redeems our time when we spend it advancing His Kingdom.

Col 4:5 Walk in wisdom toward them that are without, redeeming the time.

Ephesians

"That we henceforth be no more children, tossed to and fro, and carried about with every wind of doctrine, by the sleight of men, and cunning craftiness, whereby they lie in wait to deceive;" - Ephesians 4:14

This is the verse in which Paul gives the reason for the Body of Christ having in its structure the five-fold ministry – apostles, prophets, evangelists, pastors and teachers. Let's get the understanding in the full context of this verse, and come into a deeper revelation of God's heart on the matter.

Eph 4:4 There is one body, and one Spirit, even as ye are called in one hope of your calling;

Eph 4:5 One Lord, one faith, one baptism,

Eph 4:6 One God and Father of all, who is above all, and through all, and in you all.

Eph 4:7 But unto every one of us is given grace according to the measure of the gift of Christ.

Eph 4:8 Wherefore he saith, When he ascended up on high, he led captivity captive, and gave gifts unto men.

Eph 4:9 (Now that he ascended, what is it but that he also descended first into the lower parts of the earth?

Eph 4:10 He that descended is the same also that ascended up far above all heavens, that he might fill all things.)

Eph 4:11 And he gave some, apostles; and some, prophets; and some, evangelists; and some, pastors and teachers;

Eph 4:12 For the perfecting of the saints, for the work of the ministry, for the edifying of the body of Christ:

Eph 4:13 Till we all come in the unity of the faith, and of the knowledge of the Son of God, unto a perfect man, unto the measure of the stature of the fullness of Christ:

 Jesus gave "gifts" unto men, and to every man grace according to those gifts. Five is God's Biblical number symbolizing grace; and in these verses we see another confirmation of the grace of God shown through these five-fold gifts. Every person in ministry is a gift to the Body, whether that ministry is vocational or not. Most of us have been taught that the five-fold ministry speaks only to vocational offices; but in truth, every single member of the Body of Christ is called into one of these areas of Jesus' ministry in some way. Everyone is not vocational in one of these areas, but everyone has a place in the Body, with a function designed to help fulfill these areas.

 There is a comparison to be made between these gifts and the feeding of the five thousand in Matthew, where the people were gathered in the wilderness to listen to Jesus, and there was nothing for them to eat. The disciples said "send them away" but Jesus said, "Oh, no. You feed them."

Mat 14:16 But Jesus said unto them, They need not depart; give ye them to eat.

Mat 14:17 And they say unto him, We have here but five loaves, and two fishes.

Mat 14:18 He said, Bring them hither to me.

Mat 14:19 And he commanded the multitude to sit down on the grass, and took the five loaves, and the two fishes, and looking up to heaven, he blessed, and broke, and gave the loaves to his disciples, and the disciples to the multitude.

Now we're going back even farther, to make the connection in the Hebrew scriptures (what we call the Old Testament). By looking at what we call types and shadows (imagery that shows a spiritual picture through a natural account), we allow the Bible to interpret itself and we gain a deeper inderstanding and a greater revelation of God's heart.

> *1Sa 21:2 And David said unto Ahimelech the priest, The king hath commanded me a business, and hath said unto me, Let no man know any thing of the business whereabout I send thee, and what I have commanded thee: and I have appointed my servants to such and such a place.*

> *1Sa 21:3 Now therefore what is under thine hand? give me five loaves of bread in mine hand, or what there is present.*

> *1Sa 21:4 And the priest answered David, and said, There is no common bread under mine hand, but there is hallowed bread; if the young men have kept themselves at least from women.*

> *1Sa 21:5 And David answered the priest, and said unto him, Of a truth women have been kept from us about these three days, since I came out, and the vessels of the young men are holy, and the bread is in a manner common, yea, though it were sanctified this day in the vessel.*

> *1Sa 21:6 So the priest gave him hallowed bread: for there was no bread there but the shewbread, that was taken from before the LORD, to put hot bread in the day when it was taken away.*

Can you see the comparison? In Samuel, David says essentially the same thing to the priest that Jesus said to His disciples in Matthew – "Give me what you have." What David and Jesus both received were five loaves of bread. The bread was given to the servants, who were worthy by virtue of David's word in Samuel and Jesus' word in Matthew. The bread was hallowed – holy and set apart for God's purpose – in Samuel according to the priest and in Matthew according to our High Priest, who blessed the bread and set it apart for

God's purpose. Now consider another passage of scripture:

Joh 6:33 For the bread of God is he which cometh down from heaven, and giveth life unto the world.

Joh 6:34 Then said they unto him, Lord, evermore give us this bread.

Joh 6:35 And Jesus said unto them, I am the bread of life: he that cometh to me shall never hunger; and he that believeth on me shall never thirst.

When we return to Ephesians and look once again at the five-fold ministry, we find the essence of Jesus Christ. Everything He was and did is in these gifts to mankind. Jesus, the hallowed Bread of Life, divided Himself and gave to His disciples every element they needed to feed the church, which is His Body. He did it for a purpose, and the purpose is stated in our 4:14 verse.

"That we henceforth be no more children, tossed to and fro, and carried about with every wind of doctrine, by the sleight of men, and cunning craftiness, whereby they lie in wait to deceive;" (Ephesians 4:14)

We have in our midst the fullness of the Lord Jesus Christ and His ministry, expressed through those in the Body who operate in the five-fold ministry under the direction of the Holy Spirit, keeping their focus on Christ and not themselves. This fullness is provided so that we, the Body, can grow up. We are meant to be simple, but not simpletons, child-like, but not childish. Without the godly direction and administration of the apostolic anointing, without the clear word of the prophetic, without the enthusiastic truth of the evangelist, without the love of the pastor and the instruction of the teacher, God's children are subject to being swept away from truth and into error.

"Carried about with every wind of doctrine" indicates being taken hither and yon as a natural occurrence, like breathing. When you don't know the right way to go, chances are you will naturally go whichever way the winds blow, following whatever sounds good at the time.

The rest of this verse – sleight of men, cunning craftiness and lying in wait to deceive - all speak of fraud. Any word that does not come from the throne of heaven is fraudulent! Too often, men will speak from the soul and not from God's Spirit. It is easy to be misled by the voice of a soulish man or the voice of the devil, unless we are in tune with the voice of God. Jesus said, "My sheep hear my voice."

Did He mean that literally? Not many of us have heard the audible voice of God. Sometimes we hear Him as a still small voice inside – a knowing. But many times, the voice of the Lord comes most often through another member of the Body, who is operating in one of the offices – whether vocational or not. Jesus gave us Himself, divided into functional offices, to keep us tuned in to the heart of heaven. It's interesting that the meaning of "children" (that we be no more children) is "negating the word," or literally "not speaking." The verse following this one, which completes the thought, tells us that speaking God's word is a necessary part of growing up.

Eph 4:15 But speaking the truth in love, may grow up into him in all things, which is the head, even Christ:

How can we speak the truth in love? First, we have to know the truth, which is the heart of God, not the letter of the law. All of us could beat each other up with the word, because none of us is one hundred percent perfected. We make mistakes, we say the wrong thing, perhaps we've gotten off track in some area, or maybe we just haven't allowed God to fully heal us of past woundedness. Speaking the truth in love involves more love than truth – not that we should ever lie or withhold truth; but that we should follow the guideline given by Paul to Timothy for ministering to others.

2Ti 2:23 But foolish and unlearned questions avoid, knowing that they do engender strifes.

2Ti 2:24 And the servant of the Lord must not strive; but be gentle unto all men, apt to teach, patient,

2Ti 2:25 In meekness instructing those that oppose themselves; if God peradventure will give them repentance to the acknowledging of the truth;

2Ti 2:26 And that they may recover themselves out of the snare of the devil, who are taken captive by him at his will.

Truth can be spoken from a spirit of accusation very easily when we judge and begin to tell others what's wrong with them. People already know what's wrong, they need to be told what's right. Our foremost concern before we ever open our mouths should be, "What is the motivation of my heart?" If what you are about to say is not clearly motivated by love, keep your mouth shut. Many times, we are more effective at "speaking the truth in love" when we are silent in public and passionate in private intercession. The victory is in the prayer, not the preaching. Our goal in ministry should be to instill righteousness-consciousness, not sin-consciousness. I guarantee, if a person is busy doing the "dos" he will have very little time for the "don'ts."

Becoming free to develop into effective ministers who advance the Kingdom of God means we have to grow up and speak the truth in love, not accusation. The truth is Jesus Christ, the Bread that came down from heaven and ascended there again, dividing Himself into five loaves meant to feed the multitude. Thank You, Jesus!

Philippians

"Notwithstanding ye have well done, that ye did communicate with my affliction." - Philippians 4:14

To the church at Philippi, Paul continues in much the same vein as before, pointing out his own weaknesses, and expressing his appreciation for the way these saints have ministered to his needs. At Galatia, Paul was saying "What changed in you that you so soon forget your teacher?" But at Philippi, he says, "You've really taken good care of me throughout all the trials and pressures I've endured." He goes on in the next verses to let these people know –"There were times when you were the only ones who supported me. You believed in what I was doing for the Kingdom and proved it by your giving."

Phi 4:15 Now ye Philippians know also, that in the beginning of the gospel, when I departed from Macedonia, no church communicated with me as concerning giving and receiving, but ye only.

Phi 4:16 For even in Thessalonica ye sent once and again unto my necessity.

The interesting part of Paul's expression of gratitude here is this: he clearly says the money doesn't matter to him; but their giving into the gospel will bring a reward to them, and that is what is important to him. Giving is counted as fruit. In other words, when you sow into a ministry that is advancing the Kingdom of God, spreading the good news, freeing the captives from the enemy and binding them to God, every person who is saved, every person who is set free, is a testimony of your bearing fruit in the Kingdom. You may not have been the one to pray the prayer of salvation with them, or the one to cast out the demon or to speak healing into their bodies, but the resulting fruit is being credited as much to you as to the one who plucked it.

1Sa 30:24 For who will hearken unto you in this matter? but as his part is that goeth down to the battle, so shall his part be that tarrieth by the stuff: they shall part alike.

1Sa 30:25 And it was so from that day forward, that he made it a statute and an ordinance for Israel unto this day.

    This scripture is the Old Testament confirmation in type and shadow of this New Testament truth. Every aspect of ministry involves warfare in the spirit, and the spoils of victory go equally to the front line soldiers and those who maintain the "stuff." In other words, the ones who watch over the welfare of the physical needs of the ministry share in the heavenly rewards of that ministry. The same thing is true about intercessory prayer. When you give prayer support to a ministry, you are undergirding the work the ministry is doing. Every ministry needs both physical and spiritual support to effectively accomplish the assignment of God.

    Here in Philippians, Paul says, "I don't need your money, because I've learned to be content no matter whether I have a little or a lot. But I'm appreciative of you and what you do for me – it makes my life easier. Still, I am happier for you that you've done it because you'll be better off for it. My ministry is a part of your fruit. Everything I am able to accomplish, you have a part in." Praise the Lord!

    We can gather from this verse, where Paul says "you're doing well for yourselves when you give into the gospel," that within our support of others in what they are doing for God lies another aspect of our deliverance.

Father God, thank You for the Bread of Life, our Lord Jesus Christ, sent down from heaven. Thank You for dividing that Bread so I may partake and distribute to others Your sustaining Word, the Word of Your power. Lord, I ask Your forgiveness for any time I've compromised Your truth by turning back to the ways of the world. I ask Your forgiveness for judging the weaknesses of Your appointed ministers, Lord, for discrediting them because I see faults. Forgive me for putting Your ministers above You, for looking to a man, and not to You as the authority over all things. I break all agreement, Lord, with spirits of compromise, spirits of judgment and criticism, and spirits of idolatry. I repent to You, Father, for expecting others to be perfect in their actions or attitudes, including myself, and for thinking others are perfect. Please forgive me. Help me show the same grace toward others that You have shown toward me. Thank You for helping me understand my place in this Body. Help me to be content wherever You have placed me, and in whatever situation I face. I want to be like Paul and rejoice in the fruit that abounds to others, not to concentrate on myself and what's in it for me. Get me out of the way, Lord. I break all agreement with spirits of "self" that would take my eyes off You – self-pity, self-centeredness, self-love, self-hatred – and every other unclean thing that turns my focus inward and backward. Free me, Lord, so that I can step fully into You. Make me a cheerful giver, Lord, not just of my money but also of my time as I commit to pray for those in ministry who are advancing Your Kingdom. Thank You, Father God, that it is in Your heart to credit the victories of those I pray for, and the victories of those I give to, into my account as well as theirs. I love You, Lord, and I declare I can do nothing without You, but all things with You. AMEN

GALATIANS
BIG BITE
BIRD ON A WIRE
RECALCULATING
TIME FOR MINISTRY
ROM 3:18
XII IX III VI
EPHESIANS
TRUTH -N-
CONTENTMENT
THORN IN THE FLESH
SLOW & STEADY
WHAT IS THE MOTIVATION OF MY HEART?
SELF
APOSTLE
PHILIPPIANS
WHO?
TEACHER
PROPHET
EVANGELIST
PASTOR
1
BREAD OF LIFE 2
3
4
5
JESUS... THE ESSENCE

Colossians

"Luke, the beloved physician, and Demas, greet you."
- *Colossians 4:14*

Here's an interesting verse. How do we see deliverance in this? Simply this – we need each other, and our freedom is inextricably connected to our relationship with others as well as with God. This Body of Christ, of which we are a part, is meant to recognize its parts and appreciate them. When you revile something about your own physical body, it opens the door for the enemy to physically affect you. The same is true in the spirit when it comes to the Body of Christ.

We need every part of the body, and should bless every part of the Body of Christ. There is no room in the Body for an "us four and no more" attitude. The Body is made up of more than my little church, or my denomination, or the Christians in my country. The Body of Christ consists of all colors, all races, all cultures. We don't all think alike, we don't all understand things the same way, we don't all have the same way of looking at things, we don't all have the same function or the same anything, really.

This is the last chapter in the book of Colossians, and Paul's closing statements are essentially an exhortation to the saints at Colosse to recognize and appreciate each other, and to do what they are appointed and anointed to do as individuals and as leaders and fellow-laborers in the Kingdom. Paul is naming a few of those who have stepped into their ministries and are advancing the Kingdom of God. The ones who are named in this 4:14 verse – Luke the physician and Demas - give us insight into two areas where freedom is manifested. It's easy to see why Luke is mentioned in this verse: the word physician means "cure" or to be made whole. Certainly healing and deliverance are connected, and there is deliverance in healing. So why understand why Luke is mentioned, but who is Demas and why is he named?

This person is also an apostle of God – a sent one. Because the focus of most Scripture is on certain apostles does not mean the ones we hear most about are the only ones there were! Jesus said in Matthew 24:14 that the gospel of the Kingdom would be preached in all the world for a witness to all nations and then the end would come. According to the Apostle Paul, Jesus' prophecy came to pass. The word "world" refers to <u>specifically the Roman empire</u>. "The end" means the end of the age, or <u>the old order of doing things</u>. The priesthood was changing. In the time span from the resurrection of Christ to the utter destruction of the temple and the city of Jerusalem, the Gospel was preached to the entire world, according to Paul.

Col 1:23 If ye continue in the faith grounded and settled, and be not moved away from the hope of the gospel, which ye have heard, and which was preached to every creature which is under heaven; whereof I Paul am made a minister;

A handful of men may have started this wave of information, but they cloned themselves many times over; and there were likely countless numbers of believers who propagated the truth throughout the entire known world. Demas is only one of this number, as is Luke the physician, and Demas is mentioned three times in the New Testament. Each mention most probably refers to the same person. There is also a Demetrius named in the New Testament, who could possibly be the same man, but not likely.

Let's look at the three times Demas' name is mentioned and get some great insight about him. The first mention of Demas is in our study verse – Luke and Demas greet you. The next time his name appears is in II Timothy.

2Ti 4:10 For Demas hath forsaken me, having loved this present world, and is departed unto Thessalonica; Crescens to Galatia, Titus unto Dalmatia.

The third time Demas is mentioned is in Philemon, where Paul is once again recognizing his "fellow laborers" in the advancement of the Kingdom of God.

Phm 1:24 Mark, Aristarchus, Demas, Luke, my fellow laborers.

Let's concentrate first on the verse in II Timothy. Demas has gotten a bad rap from the church because of the negative interpretation of Paul's words here; but in actuality, they are not negative at all. In this last letter of instruction to his "son in the faith" Timothy, Paul asks Timothy to "come see me – visit me in prison." He says he's finished his course and knows the end of his life is near, but he'd still like some company. I personally think Paul wanted to get in a little more one-on-one instruction with Timothy and with Mark, since he requested that Timothy bring Mark along. Paul saw potential in Mark, and wanted to teach him, as well, to be a good minister of the gospel. But let's get back to Demas.

When we read the word "forsaken" we automatically think of it in a negative sense, and that's where the most of the church may have missed it. Those words "having loved this present world" seem to enforce the negative connotation. It sounds like Paul is saying, "That n'er-do-well Demas has more love for the things of the world than for the word of the Lord, so he's deserted me." However, looking in context, we see this: Demas had great compassion on the people of the time, and wanted to continue spreading the good news of Jesus Christ, to save as many as he could.

Paul was actually commending him on his great love for people, knowing the perilous time and the persecutions happening in Thessalonica and other places. Paul said, "He's left me behind to go ahead and fulfill his calling to preach the gospel." He then names a couple of other apostles who did the same thing, Crescens and Titus. These two and several others also left Paul in his bonds. There was not much they could do to free him from prison, and even less to advance the Kingdom while keeping him company. We can safely conclude Demas was an evangelist apostle, one who was likely trained by Paul and sent out by direction of the Holy Spirit to spread the gospel.

So we find in our 4:14 verse in Colossians this message – healing and hearing are important to our deliverance. Luke the physician represents the laying on of hands for healing – the touch of God; and Demas the evangelist who had a passion to restore the world, represents the spoken word, the voice of God. Both Luke and Demas greet you. The word "greet" literally translates "as a particle of union, to enfold in the arms." Healing and hearing are available to wrap us in the embrace of God. Praise the Lord!

I Thessalonians

"For if we believe that Jesus died and rose again, even so them also which sleep in Jesus will God bring with him."
- 1 Thessalonians 4:14

Here is the hope of our bodily resurrection and the coming of the Lord. This message in I Thessalonians is the one in which Paul tries to correct the error of spiritual deception that was becoming prevalent in the church: that people missed the resurrection. It was thought, and taught, that the resurrection had already occurred – all those people who rose from the graves after Christ's crucifixion were it. Paul says, "No! There's more. When the Lord returns, He will bring with Him those saints who have died, and they will have their bodies restored to them, in glorified form. Those saints who have not died will meet Him and the returning saints as an envoy or escort that is sent out to greet a dignitary, and we'll all come into the Kingdom together."

It's important, I think, to take just a moment to say something about this chapter and how much of the ecumenical world has used it to substitute the rapture for the resurrection. The word tells us we are to look for the coming of the Lord and anticipate the resurrection, the renewal and restoration of our own bodies – our hope of Glory, Christ in us, the corruptible putting on incorruption. But nowhere does the Bible tell us to sit around and wait for Jesus to return and make everything in our lives and the world "right" again. It is our job, our responsibility as the Bride and the Body of Christ, to occupy – to keep the peace and maintain control, to advance the Kingdom – until the Lord comes, the One whose right it is.

There has been a dynasty of fear built around the rapture, and fear is not of God. If you believe that you will be snatched away from all the troubles and trials and challenges of the world, and that belief gives you comfort, that's okay. Or I should say, that's okay as long as you are still doing what you are called to do, whatever that is, to advance the Kingdom. As Isaiah rightly prophesied "of the increase of His government and peace there will be no end."

Increase comes incrementally, not BOOM, it happens! Increase comes at the hands of the disciples, the Lord working with us. Think of the feeding of the multitudes …the Lord blessed and broke the bread, but the increase occurred as the bread was distributed by the disciples. The principle is the same. The Lord is not coming back to straighten it all out. That's our job. When we ever get it right, then He will return to claim the Kingdom He died to establish. Jesus sits at the right hand of the Father <u>until</u> His enemies are made His footstool, and the last enemy to be put under his feet is death. Heaven received and retains Jesus until the restitution (reconstitution, the restoration of health, home and organization) of all things. We've got work to do! Look again at this verse…

1Th 4:14 For if we believe that Jesus died and rose again, even so them also which sleep in Jesus will God bring with him.

This is perhaps the most comforting verse for all who have lost loved ones to the enemy of death. This is the eye of eternal vision, that death cannot hold our loved ones, that the grave is not final, that we will be together with them beyond all time. Our lives in this earthly state are less than a breath in view of eternity, and whatever the circumstance, the challenge, the trial or test or pain of situational happenings, there is eternal peace ahead. That in itself should give us peace in the circumstance, whatever the circumstance.

There is a big word in this verse, though, and that word is "if." If we believe. This is a choice we must all make... to live with eternal vision or present reality, to walk in the truth of the Word of God or the facts of the world. The Word tells us that belief in the resurrection of Jesus Christ is essential to our salvation. If we don't believe the Lord rose from the dead, we aren't even saved, according to Paul.

Rom 10:9 That if thou shalt confess with thy mouth the Lord Jesus, and shalt believe in thine heart that God hath raised him from the dead, thou shalt be saved.

It's not enough to say the words – our words must be a covenant in which we agree with the Lord Jesus Christ. It's not enough to believe in Jesus and the works He did. We must believe the sacrifice Jesus made by giving up His life in our stead was acceptable to the Father, and He was raised from the dead by the power of God. If we believe that, if we enter that covenant, then we are saved. That revelation and belief makes us able to believe that the same resurrection power, the power that raised Christ from the grave, dwells in us by the same covenant. By this, we know our freedom is connected to the resurrection of Jesus Christ, and also corporately to the rest of the saints, those who have gone ahead of us, and those who live in our present time.

I Timothy

"Neglect not the gift that is in thee, which was given thee by prophecy, with the laying on of the hands of the presbytery."
- 1 Timothy 4:14

Here is a clear directive that we are to use what we have been given, that we are to work the works of God in the world, not sit around and wait to be raptured out of it. "Neglect not" – don't be careless about, don't take it lightly, don't disregard your place in the Body. You have a purpose and the Lord expects you to fulfill your purpose. The devil wants to prevent you from fulfilling your purpose, and so he lies to you and tells you you aren't valuable, you can't do anything, you have no gift or talent or ability.

We can liken God's plan to a jigsaw puzzle, and each of us is a piece. All the pieces have to come together for the picture to be complete. If you choose to believe the lie of the devil, you will neglect the gift God has given you, and there will be a missing piece in the puzzle that depicts the restoration of all things, the earth and mankind.

When we fall into the snare of the enemy, we give over our piece of the puzzle to him and he holds it in Limbo. There is no way we can use the gifts and talents and abilities God has put within each of us when we are held at the gates of hell. That's what Limbo is.

The dictionary definition of "limbo" reads: 1. A region on the edge of hell for the souls of the righteous who died before the coming of Christ, and those of infants who die before baptism. 2. A place or condition for the relegation of unwanted or forgotten persons, things, etc.

We're going to look at this briefly. A region on the edge of hell would indicate the physical place just outside the gates. Limbo could be considered to be the place that is "at the gates" of hell. When Jesus went into the lower parts of the earth, He revealed Himself to those righteous souls who had believed on His coming, and He took captivity captive. The graves were opened and many who had died were resurrected and walked the earth for a while before going on with Jesus. Reference is made in Scripture to "Abraham's bosom" which is this same holding place. The people are no longer in this place, but the place still exists. We now know that when a person dies in Christ, meaning he or she has accepted the finished work of Jesus and trusts He is the risen Son of God, that person goes immediately into the presence of the Lord. There is no longer a waiting period. We enter God's presence through the torn veil of His flesh.

While we're at it, let's settle the issue of infant death and whether or not these innocents go to heaven. First, the dictionary definition and primary theological understanding of baptism is being dunked in water. But baptism into the Body of Christ is the process of becoming fully immersed in the blood of Jesus – in other words, our first baptism – and the only one which determines where we spend eternity – is our born again experience. Loving, trusting and accepting Jesus Christ is being baptized into His Body. Getting back to infants – a child too young to make the conscious decision to accept the Lord, is no longer held in Limbo.

God is a just God, His very nature demands justice. That truth tells me He will not send the souls of those young ones, nor the souls of those who have never had the opportunity to hear the gospel message, to hell. That action would not be just. It would be directly opposed to the nature of our Loving Father and the truth of His Word. There are many scriptures that teach of God's mercy in judgment and His just nature. Here are just a few verses to confirm in your hearts the just nature of God.

Gen 18:25 That be far from thee to do after this manner, to slay the righteous with the wicked: and that the righteous should be as the wicked, that be far from thee: Shall not the Judge of all the earth do right?

Deu 32:4 He is the Rock, his work is perfect: for all his ways are judgment: a God of truth and without iniquity, just and right is he.

Job 8:3 Doth God pervert judgment? or doth the Almighty pervert justice?

Job 34:12 Yea, surely God will not do wickedly, neither will the Almighty pervert judgment.

Job 37:23 Touching the Almighty, we cannot find him out: he is excellent in power, and in judgment, and in plenty of justice: he will not afflict.

Isa 45:21 Tell ye, and bring them near; yea, let them take counsel together: who hath declared this from ancient time? who hath told it from that time? have not I the LORD? and there is no God else beside me; a just God and a Savior; there is none beside me.

Act 22:14 And he said, The God of our fathers hath chosen thee, that thou shouldest know his will, and see that Just One, and shouldest hear the voice of his mouth.

Rev 15:3 And they sing the song of Moses the servant of God, and the song of the Lamb, saying, Great and marvelous are thy works, Lord God Almighty; just and true are thy ways, thou King of saints.

What does Limbo have to do with I Timothy 4:14 where we are told "neglect not the gift that is in you?" When the gift is neglectedand not used or cultivated, the gift in each of us which is our special piece of the puzzle that helps complete the plan of God, becomes in the spirit realm an unwanted thing and is captured in Limbo.

Here's the good news:

Mat 16:16 And Simon Peter answered and said, Thou art the Christ, the Son of the living God.

Mat 16:17 And Jesus answered and said unto him, Blessed art thou, Simon Bar-jona: for flesh and blood hath not revealed it unto thee, but my Father which is in heaven.

Mat 16:18 And I say also unto thee, That thou art Peter, and upon this rock I will build my church; and the gates of hell shall not prevail against it.

Mat 16:19 And I will give unto thee the keys of the kingdom of heaven: and whatsoever thou shalt bind on earth shall be bound in heaven: and whatsoever thou shalt loose on earth shall be loosed in heaven.

The church of God is built on the Rock of revelation knowledge that Jesus is the Christ, the Son of the Living God, the truth and the Word of God. You and I are the church. We are on the Rock. We are steadily growing in revelation truth. The gates of hell cannot prevail against us! We have been given authority and a directive to storm the region of Limbo and take back those forgotten and neglected gifts God put within us. This is an area of responsibility we must recognize to come into full freedom in our lives.

Isn't it wonderful that our merciful God has given us a way to recover, even if we've neglected our gifts and allowed the enemy to steal them from us? God in His justice has made a way for us to take back the gifts we thought we'd lost forever. God is stirring His church even now. He is stirring up the gifts He put within us. He wants a response... are you willing? Are you available? Are you ready to move onto a higher level and into a deeper understanding?

Willing – Available – Ready. W-A-R. That's what we must be – willing to line ourselves up in agreement with God and His plan. To say "Yes! I am who You say I am and I will not be defined by the lie of the devil or the limitations of the world." We must make ourselves available to answer the call of God on our lives, and ready to respond to His ability.

Remember, God has put within the gift itself the ability to succeed. He hasn't given us something that isn't true or that won't work, unless we're trying to work it without Him! It's not up to us. It's His gift, He just allows us to be the vehicle to bring HIs gifts to full function. It's war – willing, available, ready. Take back from the enemy what he took from you!

Father, thank You for showing me things in Your Word I hadn't seen before. Thank You for showing me deliverance through Your healing anointing and Your awesome gospel. Thank You for the power of Your resurrection and the hope of glory – Christ in me, resurrected daily as I die to myself and say "Yes" to You. Thank You for the insight into my authority to storm the gates of hell and reclaim the forgotten gifts within me that are a part of Your great restoration puzzle. I declare this day I want to add my piece to Your puzzle. I repent to You for neglecting the gifts You gave me, and for giving up at times - on You and on myself - and for giving in to my enemy and allowing the devil to steal from me, to snatch away my purpose and to hold it and me in Limbo. I ask You to forgive me, Father, and I ask that the curse be broken. I forgive all my ancestors for any time they participated with spirits of hopelessness, despair, and loneliness, or any other unclean thing that would allow hell a legal right to steal my gifts and my purpose. I forgive all those in my life, from my childhood until this very day, who have hurt me or brought shame into my life through their words or their actions. I forgive them and I release them into Your hand. I ask for blessings on them every one, and I ask that You deal with them in Your mercy, Lord, and bring them, and me, into a deeper revelation of who You are, and who we are in You. I break all agreement with every unclean and ungodly spirit and spirit guide that caused me to overlook, not recognize, or

neglect the gifts You put within me. I ask that You stir up those gifts, Lord, as I join others in Your church to storm the gates of hell and restore gifts and purpose to each one of Your precious children. In the name of the Lord Jesus Christ and by the power of the Holy Spirit, I command Limbo to loose the godly gifts within me that have been stolen and bound from operating. I declare that the blood of the Lord Jesus Christ is all powerful and effective to restore those gifts in me, and to restore me in those gifts.
AMEN

II Timothy

"Alexander the coppersmith did me much evil: the Lord reward him according to his works:" - 2 Timothy 4:14

Paul continues giving Timothy instructions that are essentially his last. This chapter records the last of Paul's words to his "son in the faith" and in this verse, he names a man that Timothy is to watch out for, Alexander the coppersmith. The name Alexander means "man-defender," which would indicate his allegiance to the flesh and not the Spirit, to the law and not grace. This man is believed to be the same Alexander that the Jews put forward at Ephesus to speak, but was shouted down in the uproar of craftsmen defending the goddess Diana. According to Clarke's historical commentary, Alexander was a Jew who was sent out from place to place to speak against the gospel and to defend Jewish law and customs. He was a constant adversary of Christian doctrine.

Also, we need to note Alexander's occupation, his trade. He was a coppersmith, which is one who works with brass or money. In Biblical imagery, brass relates to judgment. Apparently, Alexander had an accusing manner, and he spoke out in judgment against Paul and the teaching of Christianity. He was the "front man" of the Pharisees. He must have been pretty persuasive, too, since Paul says Alexander caused him much evil.

The second part of our verse, when examined in tense and context in the original language gives us a declaratory statement rather than an pleading entreaty. Paul is not calling on the Lord to punish Alexander, he is declaring the Lord <u>will</u> judge rightly and reward him according to his works. This is true for all of us.

1Co 3:13 Every man's work shall be made manifest: for the day shall declare it, because it shall be revealed by fire; and the fire shall try every man's work of what sort it is.

1Co 3:14 If any man's work abide which he hath built thereupon, he shall receive a reward.

1Co 3:15 If any man's work shall be burned, he shall suffer loss: but he himself shall be saved; yet so as by fire.

Paul states it isn't his job or responsibility to judge Alexander, and he makes it clear the Lord is the Judge and the Lord will right all wrongs. At the same time, he wants Timothy to be aware of the man and his evil intentions, and to steer clear of him. In verse immediately following Paul's declaration of Alexander's evil opposition, Paul tells Timothy to "beware" of Alexander.

2Ti 4:15 Of whom be thou ware also; for he hath greatly withstood our words.

In other words, Timothy, stay out of the way because Alexander doesn't give up and go away, he zealously remains faithful to the agenda of the Jewish opposition. I think Paul is advising this young disciple to refrain from a passionate doctrinal debate, and not attempt to defend Jesus Christ and the truth. He is telling Timothy, "The Lord will straighten it out, you don't have to." We need to heed that advice as well.

Pro 22:3 A prudent man foreseeth the evil, and hideth himself: but the simple pass on, and are punished.

When we are prudent, using good judgment and discernment, we will avoid evil confrontations. We can – and should - be worldly wise, without slipping into the ways of the world. If we are foolishly ignorant of the world system and what's going on around us, we can expect to suffer for it, because we will waltz blindly into the trap of the devil. Satan wants us to be in judgment of others, to strive to defend God. If you think about it, isn't that stupid? Why do we think God needs us to defend Him?

We must leave it to the Lord to correct others, in order not to fall into judging them. When we judge others, whether we're right or whether we're wrong, we're wrong. Why? Because we've just put ourselves in the place of God. Judging others, and debating points of doctrine, does not advance the Kingdom of God. It can result in our becoming the very thing we say we hate. We become unteachable when we declare we have all the answers.

Our point of deliverance in this verse in II Timothy is simply this: there are those who will oppose us and the gospel. We should leave it to God to handle them, and just continue to do what we are called to do. A big part of gaining and maintaining our freedom is staying out of contention. We can easily lose ground if we fall for the wiles of the devil that lead us into the wilderness of doctrinal debate.

Hebrews

"Seeing then that we have a great high priest, that is passed into the heavens, Jesus the Son of God, let us hold fast our profession." - Hebrews 4:14

With the coming of Jesus Christ, the priesthood changed in the natural world. No longer was the rabbinical law the supreme authority in a believer's life. A higher law was written on the tables of our hearts – the law of love. God's mercy came down and dwelt among us.

Joh 1:14 And the Word was made flesh, and dwelt among us, (and we beheld his glory, the glory as of the only begotten of the Father,) full of grace and truth.

Jesus Christ, the true high priest. There are many scriptures revealing Jesus as the high priest. My favorite is the account of the 10 lepers in Luke.

Luk 17:11 And it came to pass, as he went to Jerusalem, that he passed through the midst of Samaria and Galilee.

Luk 17:12 And as he entered into a certain village, there met him ten men that were lepers, which stood afar off:

Luk 17:13 And they lifted up their voices, and said, Jesus, Master, have mercy on us.

Luk 17:14 And when he saw them, he said unto them, Go show yourselves unto the priests. And it came to pass, that, as they went, they were cleansed.

Luk 17:15 And one of them, when he saw that he was healed, turned back, and with a loud voice glorified God,

Luk 17:16 And fell down on his face at his feet, giving him thanks: and he was a Samaritan.

Luk 17:17 And Jesus answering said, Were there not ten cleansed? but where are the nine?

Luk 17:18 There are not found that returned to give glory to God, save this stranger.

Luk 17:19 And he said unto him, Arise, go thy way: thy faith hath made thee whole.

When Jesus said, "go show yourselves to the priests" the word "priests" means "high priest." He instructed them to fulfill the law, which stated that only the priests could declare a leper cleansed. There are several points to be made here, the first being that "as they went" they were cleansed – their act of obedience to the word of the Lord had a bearing on their cleansing.

Next, and this is the point of deeper revelation, while nine of the 10 continued to follow the religious order of the day, one recognized the true High Priest and turned away from religion to worship God. This is the one who was not simply cleansed, he was made whole. Receiving the revelation of who God is and worshipping the true God, is essential to our wholeness. It isn't enough to be cleansed; we need to be made whole. Putting our trust in a program, or a denomination or a doctrine of man or a certain pastor or leader and worshipping that thing might give us a pretty good earthly life, but it won't make us whole. It is our faith in the true High Priest that opens for us eternal, abundant life.

Our study verse tells us we have a "great" High Priest – He's BIG! It says He has "passed into the heavens." Let's first look at the phrase "passed into." The word is "traverse" and it means "come, depart, go about, go abroad, go everywhere, go over, go through, go throughout, pass by, pass over, pass through, pass throughout, pierce through, travel, walk through." This is a very active statement. It isn't simply "Jesus was here and now He's in heaven." It's a present, active and continuous movement. Our High Priest is not only the greatest and biggest, He's the most active.

Also, "the heavens" does not refer only to the abode of God or some nebulous location in or beyond the sky in another dimension, where the Father sits on a throne with the Son at His right hand. Implications of this phrase "the heavens" include: "Happiness, power, eternity and specifically the Gospel, or Christianity." Our High Priest, Jesus the Son of God, continually moves in happiness, power, and eternity, which should be the realm of Christendom in the earth. In us. The Kingdom of Heaven is at hand – at your hand and at my hand, and at the hand of every believer. The Kingdom of God is within us, and the Kingdom of Heaven moves at our hands. Happiness, power and eternity are ours because of our High Priest who moves in and out as we allow Him access.

The writer of Hebrews, and most scholars believe it was Paul, exhorts us to "hold fast our profession." We are to use strength – that's what "hold fast" means – to seize or to retain the truth we have been given. Our "profession" is the acknowledgment of our covenant with the Lord. We are to uphold the agreement that gives us dominion through Jesus Christ to work the works of God in the earth. This is a responsibility and a privilege the Lord has provided that once again reinforces our part in His plan for complete restoration of all creation. Hold fast the covenant – use strength to seize and retain it. The Kingdom of Heaven is at hand!

I Peter

"If ye be reproached for the name of Christ, happy are ye; for the Spirit of glory and of God resteth upon you: on their part he is evil spoken of, but on your part he is glorified." - 1 Peter 4:14

As we've been made aware, there will be opposition to the Gospel, and it is strong opposition. When we work the works of God, we can expect to be defamed, railed at, chided and taunted. But our response is to be happy, to maintain a heavenly attitude, knowing the Spirit of "very apparent glory, dignity, glorious honor, praise and worship" rests on and refreshes us. When we exhibit the joy of the Lord, which is our strength, no matter what we are going through in terms of persecution, Jesus is glorified. We have the great responsibility and privilege to glorify the Lord by our actions and attitudes in tough times; and when we do, we have a far-reaching impact in the world.

When fruit is squeezed, it gives up its essence. If you apply pressure and squeeze an orange, you get orange juice. When pressure is applied in the life of a Christian, what comes out should be Christ, the great High Priest who moves through happiness, power and eternity. Be happy, demonstrate power, walk in the vision of eternity. That's the message of deliverance. That's our freedom.

I John

"And we have seen and do testify that the Father sent the Son to be the Savior of the world." - 1 John 4:14

Finally, we wrap it all up with this summation of the Gospel. God's heart of deliverance, shown throughout the Bible in specifically numbered verses, culminates in this last 4:14 verse that gives us the bottom-line solution.

"We have seen" – we have looked closely at, perceived and visited... to visit is to be in the presence of. It's up to us to look closely into the Word of God, and into the face of Jesus. It's my choice as to whether or not I approach the cross to kneel at the feet of Jesus and allow His saving blood to drop on me, or whether I stand afar off and look "at" and not "into" my full salvation package.

When Peter and John were passing the lame man who sat at the gate Beautiful, Peter said, "Look on us." That literally translates "Look into us." See what we have that is available to you, partake of this covenant in which we walk; and you will walk, too. This is a powerful truth of deliverance. To be fully free we first must look into the Lord, get to know Him, come into covenant relationship with the Living God, our High Priest Jesus Christ. You can't truly love someone you don't know, and you can't truly know someone you don't spend time with.

"We have seen and do testify." Here is another powerful truth of deliverance. Our testimony is one of the legs that holds the three-legged step-stool of overcoming that allows us to elevate ourselves over the circumstance and reach into the throne room of heaven itself, to grab hold of that covenant promise and receive what we need for today.

Rev 12:10 And I heard a loud voice saying in heaven, Now is come salvation, and strength, and the kingdom of our God, and the power of his Christ: for the accuser of our brethren is cast down, which accused them before our God day and night.

Rev 12:11 And they overcame him by the blood of the Lamb, and by the word of their testimony; and they loved not their lives unto the death.

We have seen the blood of Jesus as our salvation, and we speak out His greatness and what He has done for us. Testify. Testify, saints! Worship Him, testify of Him. Your testimony is the power of God, the spirit of prophecy that works to bring to pass the Word of the Lord in your life!

Rev 19:10 And I fell at his feet to worship him. And he said unto me, See thou do it not: I am thy fellow servant, and of thy brethren that have the testimony of Jesus: worship God: for the testimony of Jesus is the spirit of prophecy.

"We have seen and do testify that the Father sent the Son." God Almighty set apart His Word, the Lord Jesus Christ, from before the foundation of the world, and then sent Him into the world as a Son of man. God Himself came in the flesh.

1Jo 1:1 That which was from the beginning, which we have heard, which we have seen with our eyes, which we have looked upon, and our hands have handled, of the Word of life;

1Jo 1:2 (For the life was manifested, and we have seen it, and bear witness, and show unto you that eternal life, which was with the Father, and was manifested unto us;)

He was sent forth with purpose, on a mission to redeem for a loving Father the spirits and souls of His wayward children. Jesus gave us the same mandate:

Joh 20:21 Then said Jesus to them again, Peace be unto you: as my Father hath sent me, even so send I you.

"Sent" in this verse is the same word as in "the Father sent the Son to be the Savior of the world." We are set apart for the purpose of God, sent out with a specific mission, and that mission is the fulfillment of the restoration of creation. It has to start within us – within each individual believer. Then the glory of God that rests upon us becomes very apparent and begins to spread His mercy and His love and His delivering power to those around us. Freedom in God is contagious! It spreads, replacing heaviness with joy, replacing torment with peace, replacing fear with love, replacing pain with comfort.

Religion tells us we're in the world to win the world. No! We're in the world to win Christ! When we win Christ, the world will follow. The goal is relationship, to know the Lord intimately. Religion is like an inoculation – when you get an inoculation they give you just a little bit of the virus or bacteria or whatever so that your body's immune system develops antibodies to fight off the illness if it comes along. With a religious inoculation, we get just enough Jesus to miss the real thing.

Speaking forth the glory and goodness of God and not putting Him in a box of denominational doctrine or man-made tradition can help us avoid an inoculation of religion. Our declarations, the word of our testimony is a "do it again, God!" for those who have ears to hear it.

1Jo 1:3 That which we have seen and heard declare we unto you, that ye also may have fellowship with us: and truly our fellowship is with the Father, and with his Son Jesus Christ.

1Jo 1:4 And these things write we unto you, that your joy may be full.

Praise be to God! The Father has sent the Son to be the Savior of the world. The word "savior" translates "deliverer" and is a derivative of the Greek word "sozo" which is often interpreted as "salvation." Sozo (our salvation) has more than one aspect. It encompasses a complete package of deliverance. The word means "Save, deliver or protect – heal, preserve, save, do well, be or make whole." Our deliverance, our salvation, includes:

<u>healing</u>… we can walk in health

<u>preservation</u>… we are forever sealed unto God and have eternal life

<u>deliverance</u> and protection from the enemy… we are saved from fear of evil

<u>prosperity</u>… the state of "doing well" is ours, and

<u>wholeness</u>… mental and emotional soundness.

As born-again children of God, we are meant to grow up into Him, and to bring the world into order under the full Lordship of Jesus Christ. He was sent by the Father to be the Savior of the world. He did His part as a man in the flesh, and now it's our turn to allow Him to transform us into His image and continue the work He began. He now wants to use our hands, our hearts, our minds, our emotions, our desires, our will to complete the prophecy spoken of Him in Isaiah.

We made note that there was not a 4:14 verse in the book of Isaiah, but the one in Matthew gave us insight into the fact that the message in the New Testament verses would give us a description and summation of the Deliverer prophesied in Isaiah.

Mat 4:14 That it might be fulfilled which was spoken by Isaiah the prophet, saying,

Isa 61:1 The Spirit of the Lord GOD is upon me; because the LORD hath anointed me to preach good tidings unto the meek; he hath sent me to bind up the brokenhearted, to proclaim liberty to the captives, and the opening of the prison to them that are bound;

Isa 61:2 To proclaim the acceptable year of the LORD, and the day of vengeance of our God; to comfort all that mourn;

Isa 61:3 To appoint unto them that mourn in Zion, to give unto them beauty for ashes, the oil of joy for mourning, the garment of praise for the spirit of heaviness; that they might be called trees of righteousness, the planting of the LORD, that he might be glorified.

Isa 61:4 And they shall build the old wastes, they shall raise up the former desolations, and they shall repair the waste cities, the desolations of many generations.

Jesus read from the book of Isaiah when He began His earthly ministry, but He stopped reading in the middle of the prophecy.

Luk 4:18 The Spirit of the Lord is upon me, because he hath anointed me to preach the gospel to the poor; he hath sent me to heal the brokenhearted, to preach deliverance to the captives, and recovering of sight to the blind, to set at liberty them that are bruised,

Luk 4:19 To preach the acceptable year of the Lord.

Jesus stopped reading at that point and closed the book and sat down. That was the extent of His ministry assignment as an individual on the earth. But the prophecy in Isaiah involved more, didn't it? Yes! Jesus is still the focus of this prophecy, but now we understand it is Jesus working in us – the corporate Body of Christ in the earth. Each of us, in concert with every other, has been set apart and sent out to fulfill the last of Isaiah's prophecy.

Isa 61:2 To proclaim ... the day of vengeance of our God; to comfort all that mourn;

We are anointed to bring the day of vengeance of our God, not against people, but against evil spirits. Remember the demoniac whose demons spoke to Jesus and said, "Have you come to torment us before the time?" Well, it's now time. Jesus has come in us so that we can now torment demons, cast them out and send them back to the pit of hell where they belong. It's time. The vengeance of our God is against evil, bringing justice to people by bringing judgment on evil spirits! That's where the comfort comes in… when the evil spirit can no longer operate in a person, that person is no longer in mourning. He or she is comforted by the peace and freedom that comes through deliverance from evil.

> Isa 61:3 To appoint unto them that mourn in Zion, to give unto them beauty for ashes, the oil of joy for mourning, the garment of praise for the spirit of heaviness; that they might be called trees of righteousness, the planting of the LORD, that he might be glorified.

Zion speaks of the church of Jesus Christ, the Body. Zion was the place outside Jerusalem where the wheat was brought to be threshed. It was tossed, cracked, crushed and ground into fine flour. That's pretty much the process in the refining of a believer. There is a preparation, a separation of wheat and chaff where everything unusable is sloughed off of us. There is a grinding, crushing process that leaves us suitable as an offering. Then, we still have to face the fire. We don't get the beauty until He gets the ashes. The fire of God comes to burn away the impurities of our lives, and He skims off the dross from our hearts. Oil is added – Isaiah calls it the oil of joy for mourning. There is an exchange.

As we yield to the process, a marvelous exchange takes place. In keeping with the comparison of wheat and flour, oil and leaven are added to the flour to make bread. The Bible speaks of three kinds of leaven. There is the leaven of malice, the leaven of the Pharisees and the leaven of the Kingdom, which is love.

It appears we have a choice as to which leaven is added to our lives. If we choose to take offense, we get the leaven of malice that will leave us embittered at what we've suffered. The leaven of malice will cause us to be burned and not worth much – no one wants to eat burned bread.

The leaven of the Pharisees is religion, the traditions and doctrine of man that will cause us to leave the process before we're fully processed. We end up like Ephraim, a cake not turned – half baked - and again not acceptable. But when we choose the leaven of the Kingdom, which is the love of God flowing in us and through us, we will stay in the fire until we're perfected. We then come out in the image of Jesus, the Bread of Life that will feed many.

Isaiah prophesies the Body of Christ as trees of righteousness, the planting of the Lord. It is His righteousness, and it is to His glory. When you are nothing but ashes, then you know the beauty others see in you, the very apparent glory that emanates from your inner being, is all Him and not you. Trees speak of leadership.

Isa 61:4 And they shall build the old wastes, they shall raise up the former desolations, and they shall repair the waste cities, the desolations of many generations.

Here in verse four is our final destination, the purpose for which we are called, set apart and sent out. Here is the restoration of creation, by the Lord Jesus Christ through His saints, you and me. We are to "build the old wastes." Build also means repair. We are to build and to repair the values and things that have been concealed – old in this verse means concealed, or "out of mind" as in eternity – the things that once were and were meant to be eternally enjoyed, but vanished from sight. These places, physically in the world (like the Garden of Eden) and spiritually in our lives and hearts, became desolate and dry, a wilderness.

We are to "raise up the former desolations." The word "former" here is actually "beginning." God has set us apart unto Him to rouse and renew the ancient ways, to return mankind and the earth to the way things were meant to be, and the way they were in the beginning. We are to "repair the waste cities and the desolations of many generations." That is, we rebuild the dry and useless encampments. Spiritually, "city" often refers to the heart. What's in our hearts? This phrase in Isaiah has the implication of waking something up, of opening our eyes. The "desolations of many generations" speaks to the hopelessness we experience when we see the same problems over and over again in our lives and in our families.

Our responsibility, our purpose, our destiny is to allow the Lord Jesus to work in us, to teach our fingers to fight and our hands to war. To allow Him to plant us by the river of life as trees of righteousness and put our roots down deep to drink of Him. To allow Him to rebuild, repair, restore, renew and return to an Edenic state of being our hearts and our lives so that we can rebuild, repair, restore, renew and return to an Edenic state of being this world and everything in it. Praise the Lord!

Isn't it good to know you have a part in what God is doing in the earth? You and I are vital to His plan. The Father sent Jesus, Jesus sent us. The question now is this: Are we willing to go? Am I willing to crawl up on the altar and allow the fire of God to come and burn away my rights and my very life as I know it – all I am, gone… so there is nothing left but ashes?

That is the third leg of that stool we talked about – we love not our lives unto the death. When we are willing to give up everything, even our lives, to follow on to know the Lord, we are overcomers.

Rev 12:11 And they overcame him by the blood of the Lamb, and by the word of their testimony; and they loved not their lives unto the death.

The end of the matter is this. My deliverance, the health of my body and mind, the freedom of my soul from bondage, lies in the choice I make to become bound – bound to the word and the truth of the Living God, bound to the purpose and destiny for which I was born, bound to the Lord Jesus Christ. Only then can I be free from the bondage of the world and the lie of the enemy. Only when I am yoked to the Lord Jesus Christ am I completely free!

Father God, You are an awesome God! Thank You for the insights You've given me in this book. Thank You for the courage and the resolve to commit my life to You in every aspect. To give over to Your care, custody and control all that I am. I declare to You now, I want to be bound to You, Jesus, to know the perfect will of our Father in every situation and circumstance. To allow You to use my hands, my heart, my mouth, my will, my emotions, my desires, my mind... to build the old wastes, to raise up the former desolations, to repair the waste cities and the desolations of many generations. Lord, as an act of my will, I choose to forgive my mother and father and all my ancestors, for any time they opened the door for hindering spirits to attach themselves to me. I forgive them and I release them from responsibility for any curse that has come down to me. I take those curses and I give them to You, Lord Jesus. I forgive every person in my life who has brought harm or shame into my life, Lord, and I release them into Your hand. I ask blessings and mercy on those people, Father, and I ask that You bring them into a saving knowledge of the Lord Jesus Christ. I break agreement with spiritual error, spiritual deception, spiritual deafness and spiritual blindness that would keep me from fulfilling my part in Your plan, Lord. I repent for participating with those spirits and I ask to be free of them. Lord, I forgive myself for all the times I've allowed others to define my identity and to guide my destiny. I now know that there is no person, other than the Lord Jesus Christ – not even me – there is no person that has the authority to define my identity or to guide my destiny. Now that I know my purpose, Lord, I pledge to listen and obey as You lead me into my purpose day by day. In the name of Jesus, I make this supplication and declaration.

AMEN

Prayer of Salvation...

Father God, I come to You today, just as I am, in the precious name of Your Son Jesus; and I ask You to forgive me of all my sins. I'm sorry, Lord, for not fully recognizing Your love for me, and for standing afar off from You. I want to draw near to You today, and I come to the cross so that the blood of Jesus may touch me.

I know in my heart that Jesus is come in the flesh, that He is the Son of God and my Redeemer, that He died on the cross and was resurrected by the power of the Holy Spirit. Wash me in the blood of Jesus as I declare today that I open my heart and invite Jesus to come in and reign as my Lord and my Savior.

Father, I receive Your forgiveness and Your love, and I forgive myself. I declare that from today, I am Your child, and You are my father. I dedicate my life to You, Lord. I open my mind and my heart to Your Word, and my spirit to the leading of Your Holy Spirit; and I thank You for my salvation, in the name of Jesus Christ of Nazareth who is come in the flesh.

Other books by Vicki Smith White:
  The Counterfeit Kingdom
... a false principality with a powerless king
Published 2005
  Who's Using Your Tongue?
...the language of the spirit realm
Release Date 2012

For more information about Freedom's Way Ministries, to obtain personal ministry, or to schedule a group freedom meeting or conference, please call 904-757-2501.